GREATER THAN BRADMAN

Celebrating Sachin - The Greatest Batsman in Cricket History

GREATER THAN BRADMAN

Celebrating Sachin - The Greatest Batsman in Cricket History

RUDOLPH LAMBERT FERNANDEZ

First published in India in 2014 by CinnamonTeal Publishing

Copyright © 2014 Rudolph Lambert Fernandez

ISBN 978–93–83175–64–2

Typesetting and Cover Design: CinnamonTeal Publishing

CinnamonTeal Publishing,
Plot No 16, Housing Board Colony
Gogol, Margao
Goa 403601 India
www.cinnamonteal.in

CONTENTS

CHAPTER I

Introduction

SACHIN TENDULKAR IS THE GREATEST batsman in *cricket* history. This book is a tribute to him. It corrects the injustice done to him by those who maintain with certitude that the crown belongs to Donald Bradman.

Critics are quick to dismiss such comparisons as futile and stupid, cunningly suggesting that they are an insult to the gentlemen being compared. But that is disingenuous. It is also lazy. Having brazenly declared Bradman the favourite, it is poor form to deride comparison. Having placed Bradman in cricket's Hall of Fame, high above batting greats of the late 20th century, it is odd to rubbish comparative analysis.

The word 'Bradman' appears in every article, every book, that has anything to do with the greatest batsmen. Branded indelibly into the world's cricket scrolls, it emerges as faithfully as a header-footer, on every sacred page. Bradman's rank, exalted. The arguments, unassailable. It matters little whether the discussion is about the 1960s and 70s or the 1980s and 90s.

An analyst writing about Garry Sobers, Sunil Gavaskar or Viv Richards always pays his 'taxes' – duly reminding them of Bradman, hovering like a monsoon cloud above their adolescent batting averages. A list that includes Brian Lara, Jacques Kallis or Ricky Ponting always has a disclaimer warning that they are but children frolicking in the shade of the near-infallible 'Apollo of batting'. When these batsmen take pride in their feats, they are rapped on the knuckles. They are told to stand in line not just *behind* Bradman but at a suitably venerable distance behind him.

Bradman was a phenomenon. His grit and single-minded application of skill had never been seen, in any sport. But he was a phenomenon unique to his time. While he was excruciatingly real in the era that he dominated, he is more myth than man in the modern era. Today, he appears so huge that he still dwarfs those placed next to him. He is the Man of Steel, The Incredible Hulk, the Amazing Spiderman all rolled into one. His 'super-powers' make everyone else seem so Clark Kent, so Bruce Banner, so Peter Parker.

What of the other batsmen? They are well worth defending.

Sunil Gavaskar, no more than 5'5" tall, once faced the most awesome bowlers: Garry Sobers, Lance Gibbs, Michael Holding, Malcolm Marshall, Andy Roberts, Joel Garner, Imran Khan, Richard Hadlee, Ian Botham, Bob Willis, Dennis Lillee and Jeff Thomson. Some were 6 to 12 inches taller than Gavaskar, the ball at release point, often flying in at terrifying pace from a height of about nine to ten feet. He stood up to them not with aggression but with a technique, timing and temperament that were uniquely his. He was the first to reach 10,000 Test runs. His debut series *away* score of 774 was against one of the most intimidating Test attacks ever – the West Indies in their prime. His 34 tons came from 125 Tests; Brian Lara's 34 tons came from 131 Tests.

Viv Richards, one of cricket's most magnificent warriors, treated even good bowlers with unprecedented contempt. A modern-day Samson, he swung his bat as he would the jaw-bone of an ass.

Like Sachin, these and other great batsmen have been wronged, with Bradman ranked above them, year after year, decade after decade. I have chosen Sachin because he *is* the greatest – by a long shot – and, in many ways, the most deserving. The insult has been shameful but he has taken it in the only way he knows – politely, with not even the slightest trace of hurt or defiance. Not even a murmur of protest, all these years.

This book is a salute to Sachin, the batsman. I have stayed clear of his achievements as a bowler, fielder and captain. What I have applied to my analysis is an insistence in getting beneath the surface. As a surgeon would, I have used a scalpel to lift the skin-flap. Instead of a simple magnifying glass I have used a microscope – with good reason.

Almost everyone refers to Sachin as 'one of the greatest.' A few writers place him behind Lara, Viv Richards and Bradman. The majority place him behind Bradman alone, even if at an appropriately respectful distance behind him.

SACH: Genius *Unplugged*, is a compilation of essays on Sachin. But in it, Ayaz Memon, who as the blurb suggests, has been 'writing on the game for three decades', rather magnanimously puts Sachin *amongst the top ten* batsmen in cricket history. Unlike others who wrestle with just two or three names, Memon wrestles with many. He wonders whether Sachin outshines Grace, Ranji, Trumper, Hobbs, Hammond, Hutton, the three Ws (Walcott, Weekes and Worrell), Kanhai, Gavaskar, Border, Miandad and Greg Chappell. Reassuringly, the majority do not share Memon's helplessness – he is more the bewildering exception than the rule.

The majority of authoritative comments on Sachin refer to him as the 'greatest batsman' but place him one notch below Bradman (and no other batsman), albeit with a suffix, 'since Bradman' or 'after Bradman' or granting him a rank 'lower only to that of Bradman'.[1][2][3][4]

Most commentators agree that, once you set Bradman aside, it is Sachin who is the greatest batsman – not just of his generation but of all generations in cricket history.

Bradman is the final frontier. Not Ponting, not Kallis, not Lara, but Bradman.

In his masterful biography Gulu Ezekiel provides a balanced, yet gripping account of Sachin's career, but is emphatic that Bradman's claim to the title is beyond censure.

Vaibhav Purandare's biography is a compelling tale of the boy, the man, the legend. While Purandare takes time to put comparisons with the good Inzamam firmly to bed and places Sachin above Lara, he does not examine Bradman's claim to enduring greatness. Tantalisingly, a whole chapter compares their batting styles.

---

[1] *Last Chance to Salute India's Bradman*; Mike Coward in *The Australian*, 24 November 2007.

[2] *Sachin: The Story of the World's Greatest Batsman* (*The God of Indian Cricket*; Prologue, Page 2); Gulu Ezekiel; Penguin Books, Revised Edition 2010 (published 2002).

[3] *If Cricket is a Religion, Sachin is God* (*The Case for Sachin Tendulkar*, Chapter 8, Page 104); Vijay Santhanam and Shyam Balasubramanian; HarperCollins Publishers (India), 2009.

[4] *Sachin Tendulkar: A definitive biography* (*The Golden Year*; Page 246); Vaibhav Purandare; Roli Books, Fourth Revised Edition 2011 (published 2005).

Everyone lauds Sachin. In that same breath they insist that it is impractical to compare Bradman with batsmen of the modern era. That's the point – Bradman's continuing claim to the title *automatically* compares him with (and places him above) batsmen who excelled decades after he did. Comparison is embedded in the very definition of Bradman's greatness. Some compare him with *all batsmen* and occasionally with *all cricketers*. Others go further...

Comments authoritatively refer to Bradman as the 'greatest batsman' but with incongruous prefixes and suffixes: 'unquestionably', 'greatest cricketer ever', 'one of the finest sportsmen of all time', 'without any question', 'greatest ever'. Some refer to him as the most awesome phenomenon not just in cricket but across **all ball games**.[5][6] That particular claim, if taken seriously, obviously overrules greats from baseball, snooker, volleyball, basketball, squash, golf, tennis, hockey, football and table tennis!

In 2006, *TIME* magazine commemorated **60 Years of Asian Heroes** by publishing a list of greats. Sachin appeared alongside Bruce Lee and other Asians. But even in this 'tribute' piece, *Sachin: the greatest living exponent of his craft*, the author Simon Robinson is anxious to begin with the usual header-footer about Bradman: 'Cricket's **greatest ever player**...'

Geoff Armstrong in his *Legends of Cricket: Profiles of the Game's 25 Greatest* is careful to ensure that Bradman leads the pack. The book explains the challenge of singling out one sportsman who towers above others, but settles into rhythm soon enough by agreeing that the majority of commentators vociferously endorsed the Australian as the 'greatest batsman who ever lived'. Almost all books on Bradman are unequivocal – no other batsman's name, living or dead, can be taken in the same breath.

Brett Hutchins in his *Don Bradman: Challenging the Myth* suggests that Bradman's larger than life image was partly cultivated by him and partly a result of his social and cultural milieu. He argues, credibly, that Bradman was made out to be a far greater icon than he actually was. But he does not compare Bradman's ability *as a batsman* with those who came after him.

So there you have it. Everyone denouncing the notion of comparison, yet gratuitously comparing all the time – and how! 'Unquestionably.... the greatest ever... the greatest of them all.'

---

5 ESPNcricinfo's profile of Sir Donald Bradman.

6 *Five Cricketers of the Century*: Sir Donald Bradman, Wisden Almanack, 2000.

This book is an attempt to clear the mist. It is not a biography of Sachin... or Bradman. It is an attempt to set the record straight. I have not dwelt on Sachin's enviable contracts, his early life, his training, his family, his hobbies, his tax obligations or his apparent lack of statesmanship in matters beyond the field. I do not share the mania of his fans, eager to write out his name in their blood. I have not studied his rise to fame or his apparently unimpressive stint as captain.

Bradman as writer, administrator and statesman was far ahead of Sachin who has yet to establish himself beyond the field. Both dealt with personal loss, cricket politics and career-threatening health crises. Both faced pressure on and off the field, although it is easy to argue that Sachin faced it on a scale that cannot be imagined by any sportsman, let alone any cricketer. Others have documented these aspects more eloquently.

But this is not a hagiography either. Sachin is the greatest batsman; he does not also have to be St. Dominic Savio. Like the rest of us, he is entitled to his character flaws. I have no intention of defending his every move. Long may he make mistakes that remind him that he is not the god his crazed fans say he is.

My focus has been on the field, where both men staked and won their claim to greatness. I ask readers to see anew. To look at the *same* reality differently and through that, perhaps, discover a *new* reality. A closer look, almost always, reveals more.

But we also need to cast aside a certain blindness; one that is dismissive of the idea of comparison. Or we may peer through the lens all year and still see nothing. Bradman's prowess has been extolled in full measure in the written and spoken word. Therefore, when comparing the two gentlemen, this book does not offer 'balance' by acclaiming them in turn – that would be redundant, particularly in Bradman's case; he has 80 years of adulation behind him.

Sachin too has been breathlessly glorified – with one solemn difference. All that has been said about him falls appallingly short of the tribute he deserves because he has repeatedly been ranked below Bradman. One would be hard pressed to find language about Sachin as intemperate as that used to describe Bradman. On the contrary, while the number of Sachin's critics has quadrupled in the last ten years – give or take a few – their attacks have grown more venomous with each passing year. Bradman never witnessed such anger directed at his professional contributions or his personal choices – from any nation, let alone his own.

While Bradman's virtues are referred to in passing, the celebratory spotlight in this book remains unabashedly on Sachin. I hasten to add that this has been applied only to the distinguished aspects of both batsmen. I have taken the opposite approach in analysing the 'flesh and blood' challenge they faced; the focus has been on Bradman.

Here's why.

21st century cricket readers **need** a closer look at Bradman. They appear all too familiar with Sachin, having seen his every shot dissected a hundred times on TV. He has been discussed in blogs and on billboards, in sermons and in snatches of conversation. They have seen his ducks, his run-outs, his many, many failures – in hundreds of matches. Yes, they have heard the pundits but they have made their *own* assessments as well. After all, what's to assess when you can see the man's iris in ultra slow-motion?!

The challenge that Bradman faced is somewhat hidden in the clouds. Yes, they have read the books, watched the film clips and pored over the statistics. Yes, they are familiar with his feats, but they have never seen him – in action, on the field. Having retired over 63 years ago, he remains as inscrutable as a faded photograph. Yes, they have heard the experts but having not *seen* Bradman – in even a single match – they have not made their *own* assessments. Their conclusions are not entirely theirs. They often tamely endorse the judgement of 'experts'. They rely on the gilt-edged accounts of the few who saw him in action; the haziness rendering him *more* sacred with every passing generation.

Theory is often best understood through practice, study often perfected through play. Sometimes, the best way to understand your subject is to look away.

I take a close look at Sachin... by taking a *closer* look at Bradman.

I take a new look at Sachin... by taking a *newer* look at Bradman.

Unlike Bradman, Sachin has no veil that hides him from our eyes. Unlike Bradman, he is not 'hidden in the clouds'. On the contrary, Sachin is part of our yesterdays, todays and tomorrows, whether we are historians, fans or budding batsmen. He is in many ways more 'here and now' than any other sportsman we know. Why, we can still hear the 'thwack' of his willow as he sends even dangerous deliveries to the ropes. We can still see the agony on his face as he edges one to the slips. No cricketer is as recognisable, no batsman as familiar.

We do not write or speak as easily about Donald, Garry, Sunil, Allan,

Steve, Brian, Jacques, Ricky, Rahul or Virender as we do about Bradman, Sobers, Gavaskar, Border, Waugh, Lara, Kallis, Ponting, Dravid or Sehwag. Somehow we seem to write and speak as easily about 'Sachin' as we do about 'Tendulkar'. This boy-man has become more intimate to us than all the others. He has endeared himself to our collective consciousness. Not through his stirring speeches or his insights on matters administrative, but through his game.

That is precisely why we need to see 'beyond' and 'beneath'. Familiarity should not hide fact. More importantly, it should not invent fiction. At least it should try hard not to.

Many of the statistics I present are new. I hope I am also offering a new way of looking at their achievements, a more persistently honest way of looking at them.

In applauding Sachin, I hope I am celebrating the same spirit of cricket that applauded Bradman for 80 years and W G Grace before him. Tomorrow, if someone takes Sachin's place as the greatest, I hope another writer will commend him (her?) in the same spirit that applauds Sachin in this book.

I am drawing a picture of the *world's* greatest batsman: my preoccupation is with international, not domestic cricket. First Class heroics are good fun but the stakes – for the lack of a better word – simply do not exist as they do in the international arena. There is a good distance between the best bat in Essex and the best in England. There is a good distance between the most dangerous bowling arm in Indore and the most dangerous in India. A County Championship is good practice all right but it can never be the real thing.

Bradman's international career was limited to Tests. So to a large extent, I look at Sachin's Test record but his ODI record is equally important. ODIs have been around for nearly half a century and are an indispensable part of international cricket – essential oils when painting a picture of the greatest batsman *in cricket history*.

A majority of the statistics in this book, where the two are being compared, are as of 6th January 2011. No doubt, Sachin has since been busy making a hatchet job of the statistics table, but for my purpose, it was essential to freeze the figures at some point. A 21-year career (Sachin's playing span as of 6th January 2011) is perhaps a better measure of enduring greatness than a 10-year career (Bradman's playing span)?

Besides, an absolutely up-to-date, real-time record of Sachin's career is not crucial to my theme. If indeed an absolutely up-to-date record (i.e., 'stats as of 2013') was considered, it would probably move conclusions up or down by a fraction because he has played only a handful of matches after January 2011. So, while real-time accuracy (a digit up here, a decimal down there) may be of academic interest, it will not alter the overall conclusions by much.

Today, he is a shadow of the batsman he once was. The maniacal pressure over two decades and the gut-wrenching ride he's had has caught up with his mind, his muscle, his mastery. And it shows on the field and off it. As far as I am concerned, the debate was settled *many years ago.*

Now, that Sachin has scored 100 tons in international cricket, it would be tragic if that were the reason he is eventually crowned the greatest. In recent years, he is being considered a *failure*, going by the manic-depressive commentary around this particular milestone. Critics hold his indifferent form against him like some misdemeanour that they have sniffed out in the locker room. Now that he has crossed the mark, some have eased up; if he had not, they would have mockingly torn his monument down, piece by wretched piece.

Critics so used to seeing Sachin now 'up', now 'down', have a romantic notion of Bradman firing on all cylinders each time he walked in to bat. This is pure fiction.

0, 0, 0, 0, 0, 0, 0, 1, 1, 2, 4, 7, 8: This is not a list of runs conceded by Michael Holding in his first thirteen overs. It is a list of Bradman's Test scores.

12, 13, 13, 13, 14, 16, 18: This is not a list of runs conceded by Geoff Boycott in his first bowling spell. It is another list of Bradman's Test scores.

...and Bradman played just 80 Test innings.

In spite of the astoundingly meek, sneakily brief challenge that he faced, Bradman too had the luxury of ups and downs. Some 35 of his 80 Test innings saw him score 40 or fewer runs – that's 44% of the time. Fans who are furious with Sachin for not reaching a 50 or not scoring a 100 should remember that for nearly half his exceedingly short career, Bradman had scores of less than 40.

As if that were not enough, Bradman had scores of 18 or fewer runs for about a fourth of his career – some 22 out of his 80 innings. Bradman had the leg-room to get away with May Day scores, yet Sachin has often been lip-lynched for it.

Rudolph Lambert Fernandez

For all that, no batsmen from the 1920s, 30s or 40s can challenge Bradman's claim to be the greatest batsman of that era; his scores of 1 in his second Test innings and 0 in his last make no difference. Let us not grudge Sachin his greatness either – because his twilight scores are not spectacular or because he has been 'bowled' with embarrassing frequency in recent times. We judge greatness by 'the complete works' not by the canvas finished last Christmas.

Sachin's critics have been right to advise him to loosen up, to play his natural game of calculated aggression and not sweat over statistics. They have been right to suggest that he attacks each ball on its merit, as he has been doing for most of his career. But no one on the planet has been *excelling* at international cricket for over two decades. No sportsman has been as cruelly nagged about statistics and milestones as he has. Even the greatest of climbers is known to fret about his finger-grip or to fidget with his oxygen mask when he is above the cloud line. It is no great thing if he fusses now and then about his next foothold. The energy with which he scrambled up the foothills is a thing of the past. We may quibble about his climb to the next ridge taking all morning and lacking that early elegance but we cannot – must not – grudge him his greatness.

This book is not about Sachin being 'the greatest batsman in 1998' or 'the greatest batsman in 2010'. It is about him as the greatest batsman *in cricket history.* So you will need to take your eyes off the TV screen playing last year's ODI or replaying last year's Test, to appreciate the arguments here.

I first wrote on the subject as 'R F Lambert'. It was as far back as 2003 and at the time, I wrote in frustration, even anger. Not at any personal affront but at what I saw as a great injustice.

In 1963, Neville Cardus named six *Giants of the Wisden Century*: Sydney Barnes, Bradman, W G Grace, Jack Hobbs, Tom Richardson and Victor Trumper. Nearly half a century later, Wisden's Millennium edition listed *Five Cricketers of the Century*: Bradman, Garry Sobers, Jack Hobbs, Shane Warne and Viv Richards. To the more observant it was obvious that two names from 1963 – Bradman and Hobbs – appeared *again* in 2000. Their re-appearance placed them on pedestals, high above greats who excelled in the 1950s and since.

The editor [Matthew Engel] of Wisden's 2000 edition wrote rather tellingly that he was reassured at the resounding endorsement of Bradman although he did fear that the odd fan or critic out there would turn out to be 'contrarian, but no one dared'. Some choice of phrase that. Rebuke in every word, and barely concealed. If any historian did dare, it would have been heresy. If any cricketer did dare, it would have been blasphemy.

But I write not to be contrarian. I write to correct a serious injustice. I write to honour Sachin the batsman in a way he has never been honoured before. In honouring him, I hope it will become evident that I am also honouring other batting greats who came before Sachin who were also superior to Bradman yet never considered to be in Bradman's league, let alone above it.

As I write, Sachin Ramesh Tendulkar has scored 34,347 runs (15,921 in Tests and 18,426 in ODIs), 100 centuries (51 in Tests and 49 in ODIs) and played 663 international matches (200 Tests and 463 ODIs) around the world.

An edited version of the article I first wrote was published in *The Hindu*. It was brief and had hardly any statistics to back the arguments. But the conviction was, as I remember it, all there. The years since then have only reinforced my conviction. Sachin has been *for many years* the greatest batsman, across cricket-playing generations of the 19th, 20th and 21st centuries. His recent exploits have merely secured his place *for the future*, making it that much more difficult for someone to take his place. Not impossible; just that much harder.

If that article grew out of disappointment at the way history was treating him in 2003, this book grew out of despair at the way history is still treating him in 2013. But I finish on a note of optimism.

Nasser Hussain, Simon Hughes and Dennis Lillee are among a small but growing minority who, when referring to Sachin as the greatest batsman, use more accurate prefixes and suffixes – '...of all time', '...better than Sir Don Bradman', '...best batsman who ever took guard', 'greatest... to have ever played'. Thankfully, none of these gentlemen suggest that he should elbow out sporting greats from beyond the realm of cricket.[7][8][9]

In 2011, Griffith University researcher Dr. Nicholas Rohde used economic theory to compare batsmen from across several decades in the 20th century. His conclusion: Sachin is the greatest, even greater than Bradman.

---

[7] *Mighty Sachin Tendulkar even tops Lara, Ponting, and The Don!*; Nasser Hussain, *The Daily Mail*, 25 February 2010.

[8] *Sachin Tendulkar is the best batsman ever to play cricket*; Simon Hughes, *The Telegraph*, 29 March 2011.

[9] *Tendulkar greatest batsman to have played cricket*; Dennis Lillee, *The New Indian Express*, 26 June 2012.

Rudolph Lambert Fernandez

So I write in hope.

I write in the hope that Sachin will eventually be given his rightful place in history. It will never undo the wrong done to him over so many years – **nothing** can repair that. But I hope it will go some way in making amends, even if justice – of a sort – comes several years late.

Why is it important? Why is it so necessary to demonstrate that Sachin is indeed the greatest ever? Sachin himself could not care less whether he is compared with someone – anyone. If anything, he feels deeply humbled when compared with Bradman, even unfavourably. He has never sought to prove his greatness. Why bother?

In Harper Lee's tale *To Kill a Mockingbird*, lawyer Atticus Finch went out of his way to defend Thomas Robinson because no one else cared. Why would they? It was the word of a 'negro' man against the word of a white woman and Alabama at the time knew only one justice – the white kind. But there was a reason why Atticus did what he did – it mattered. Robinson was innocent and *had* to be defended. So Atticus staked his reputation and his career by defending a black man in an overwhelmingly white neighbourhood. Of course Atticus 'lost', but isn't that beside the point? What counted was that he had spoken up for one who could not – would not – speak for himself.

Sadly, I am no Atticus, and fortunately, Sachin is no Robinson. Yet, Sachin's greatness – like Robinson's innocence – cries out to be defended. He must be defended because it matters.

Cricket is said to be a gentleman's game; at least, at its best it is believed to aspire to be just that. I hope that, having read this book, the gentlemen who play or have played the game, those who watch it, speak about it and write about it will review without passion the evidence and grant Sachin his rightful place in cricket history. They owe it to themselves and to cricket, not to Sachin. What we owe to Sachin is a debt of a different kind, a debt that cannot be repaid. A debt of gratitude for being the boy-wonder and man that he has been for over two decades – opener, No:4, warrior, idol, leader, teacher, student, sage.

Of course I may 'lose', but isn't that beside the point?

Rudolph Lambert Fernandez
Chennai, India, January 2014.

CHAPTER 2

The Mountain... and The Measure of Greatness

CHARLES LINDBERGH ONCE SAID THAT success is not to be measured by what a man achieves but by the resistance he faces and the fortitude he displays in the struggle against overwhelming odds.

What places the great above the good is the odds they have faced and *consistently* defeated. This isn't a notion that was invented last Wednesday. It is the prism through which we have recorded and rewarded greatness for centuries.

The prefix, 'greatest', must be used with care.

The suffix '...in history' must be used with the greatest care.

Mount Everest towers nine kilometres into the sky. The odds a climber faces on Everest far exceed those he faces on his neighbourhood hillock. Some are obvious – fierce winds, fading light, failing oxygen and frostbite. But there are others. Treacherous crevasses, hidden gorges, sheer drops, sudden landslides, blizzards and the mountain's almighty smirk, the avalanche. Gravity, a gentle tug at the foothills, becomes a sledgehammer near the summit. Every toe-hold becomes a conquest. Lower down, victory is measured in miles. Up among the clouds, it is measured more dearly – in inches.

If only one climber has ever scaled Everest, then he would be the greatest not only because he has blood frozen inside his nostrils but also because he has beaten back the mightiest of odds. He has battled longer and crawled longer and hung on longer than the others. He will stay the greatest until someone else scales an even more colossal peak, perhaps on another planet, making Everest look like a mound on a sunny beach.

The swimmer who crosses The English Channel is not in the same league as one who swims The Maelstrom. Agreed, The Channel can be rough, but The Maelstrom, off the Norwegian coast, is a whirlpool six *kilometres* across, with waters raging at speeds of up to 20 feet a second and currents flowing in *both* directions. We are talking about a different kind of swimming. We are also talking about a different kind of swimmer.

In cricket, the greatest batsman must be the one who has faced the most severe odds – in every sense. Frozen blood or not, he must be triumphant, utterly alone – on the *highest* mountain.

Bradman was the greatest of his era. When his contemporaries faced about the same odds, he surpassed everyone. He stood triumphant and alone – on *his* mountain. We must limit his greatness to that conquest, not stubbornly insist that he glow far beyond his station.

Bradman's greatness is founded on fact. His immortality is founded on error.

Why fact? He outdid his peers, on several counts. Why error? Bradman should never have been compared with greater batsmen who played since the 1950s, let alone the boy from Bandra.

But he *has* been compared to Sachin; only that comparison has, time and again, been crudely drawn and therefore produced the most unjust conclusions.

If comparisons must be made, let us draw them as fairly and as accurately as possible. Let us take a closer look at the mountain. Let us take a closer look at the wind and light. How deep were the gorges, how sudden the landslides, how sheer the drops? Was gravity a gentle tug? Or was it a sledgehammer?

In the context that he played, Bradman was champion – he scored fast, stayed at the crease for days at a stretch and defied fielders and bowlers to amass runs. His concentration and his will to dominate, transcend the record books. His technique, his sense of purpose and his application of both were exceptional, placing him head and shoulders above those who shared the field with him.

Notwithstanding the title of his book *The Art of Cricket*, Bradman was rarely, if ever, guilty of art. He never set out to be an artist in the first place. While he was no beauty to watch, *in his era*, he was second to none in the grim and lonely business of run accumulation.

But.

> The kind of cricket Bradman played and the depth and range of opposition he faced just did not test him enough and consistently enough for him to justifiably be called the greatest batsman *in cricket history.*

A certain Swiss gentleman is said to be the greatest tennis player because he has stayed on top of one of the most physically challenging games. He has done it when the game has been at its most competitive and the playing environment the most demanding. Roger Federer is considered greater than Rod Laver because the intensity of every parameter on the court had increased several-fold by the time tennis reached the 21st century.

Federer and his rivals serve the ball at speeds of around 200km an hour. The racquets of the 1960s and 70s would frankly not find purchase with the top-seeds of today, armed with their more deadly weapons – at *both* ends of the lawn. Weapons of stamina, agility, power and speed: awesome in themselves, even before these men pick up their turbo-charged racquets. The modern game is not being played at a different level. It is actually a different game.

In 1991, Bjorn Borg, who had won 62 tournaments in his prime in the 1970s, tried to make a comeback by taking on Jordi Arresse. Borg won only five games, out of seventeen. He was out-served, out-volleyed, out-matched, and outclassed. Arresse's reflexes, his ability to spot the ball and move toward it, were of an incomparably higher order. He had grown up in an era where everything – especially the ball – moved over 30% faster than it did in Borg's era. If the serves were faster, the returns were faster too. The words 'power', 'speed', 'agility' and 'stamina' in Arresse's era had a new meaning that the mighty Borg could not fathom. Exasperated, he may well have exclaimed: 'It's just not tennis!' Granted, Borg had aged and was not in his prime but at the time the good Arresse was ranked 52nd in the world.

The Borg of the 1990s apparently went on to lose to Andrei Medvedev,

Chris Pridham, Goran Prpić, Lionel Roux, Nicklas Kulti, Olivier Delaître, Thomas Hogstedt, Wayne Ferreira, Alexander Volkov, Jaime Oncins and Joao Cunha-Silva. Naturally, many of these names are unrecognisable to the modern tennis fan. They are like pebbles that sank soundlessly into the depths of tennis history, without so much as a ripple.

What separated Borg and Arresse? About two decades. *In that time*, the game had transformed so much that Borg was out of his depth. On courts he was accustomed to, Borg was in over his head. One shudders to imagine what the 21st century tennis 'serial killer' Federer, might have done to Borg, let alone what he might have done to Laver.

Laver was the greatest *of his time*, nothing less; more importantly, nothing more.

Federer is considered by many to be the greatest *ever*. He has faced and beaten far greater odds, at every level imaginable. He has done it convincingly, in every possible playing environment. His feat is not some fantasy, some 'what if' script in a virtual-reality game: What if he were tested on grass? What if he were tested on clay? What if he were tested on hard courts? What if he were tested another two years, another three? What if he were tested by more rivals? Federer has *fought for and won* every serve, volley, game, set, match and tournament against his name.

If Laver had Rosewall, Ashe and others to contend with, Federer has had Djokovic, Murray, Roddick, Nalbandian, Nadal and a host of others – all incredibly fast, powerful, aggressive and agile. If there is an imagined tussle for the crown, surely it must be whether it is Nadal-Federer or Djokovic-Federer, not whether it is Federer-Laver, or Nadal-Laver. Or it might be between Federer and a player who preceded him by a few *years* – Sampras, or someone else. Laver may be an obvious first choice for the 1960s. But his name would probably not show up in discussion about the greatest *in tennis history*. Particularly in a discussion about a game that has morphed into a new avatar with each passing decade. Nearly half a century separates Laver's era from the present moment.

Like Sachin, Federer is no longer the player he once was but we are looking at the history of the game, not the last season or the last year.

At first glance, Bradman's achievements appear *impressive when compared to* Sachin's – only at first glance. If Bradman had played in the 1990s and since, simple batting averages, strike-rates and tons would settle the matter. Sheer figures would decide everything.

A farewell leader in *The Times* concluded that if statistics were all that mattered, it would be simple to demonstrate that Bradman was the greatest but, it continued, 'happily, they are not'.[10] Why? What's wrong with statistics being the last word?

Over six decades separates Bradman's retirement from the current moment. We must look harder at the circumstances in which he scored, before blindly accepting his batting average and strike-rate as a sign of *enduring* greatness. We must look more diligently at his playing environment to understand the kind of odds he was up against before declaring that his greatness transcended his playing era.

Bradman's batting average has all along been accepted as proof of his 'matchless' greatness. It was so far above the exploits of others of his day that he *was* the greatest. The monumental error has been in embracing it like a tablet of stone and hauling it past the 1950s into an era where the 'volumes, velocities, voltages, heights, weights, temperatures and pressures' were simply not the same. More chemicals, more burners, more dials... bigger lab. The intensity of every parameter on the pitch had increased several-fold by the time cricket had reached the 1990s. The game was not being played at a different level; it was actually a different game.

It is not a matter of simply looking at what other batsmen have achieved over 50 Tests. It is not a question of asking other batsmen about their batting average or strike-rate over a span of 50 matches. Or whether they wore helmets or caps! Or if they played on uncovered pitches! Or if their bats weighed a kg or two! Those are too crude to be measures of enduring greatness, particularly when over half a century separates the two generations. *Note*: Of the 52 Tests against his name, Bradman was absent in the one against South Africa in February 1932 and in the one against England in August 1938; he played only 50 Tests.

When you are looking at well over 200 years of history, there are more important questions.

Writer Mukul Kesavan in his book *Men in White: A Book of Cricket*, unwittingly drives home this point about Bradman. He, quite rightly, laments the Barry Richards Syndrome. Talented and charismatic players such as C K Nayadu and Lawrence Rowe, while aggressive and dominant, could not really be ranked among the greatest because – like the inordinately celebrated Barry Richards – they just did not play enough Test cricket. Kesavan says that we have no way of knowing how good they

---

[10] *Bradman and the British*, Sir Donald Bradman, Richard Holt, Wisden Almanack, 2000.

might have been over a long Test career because they did not have 'long' careers.[11]Kesavan cites the example of Sanjay Manjrekar who is believed to have compared Sachin with Viv Richards, Graeme Pollock and Barry Richards. Kesavan, again justifiably, bristles at the inclusion of Barry Richards in that list because Sachin was being compared with a player who had been tried in just 4 Tests.[12]

Frankly, if you are looking at *cricket history*, what is a 'long Test career'? Does a playing span of 50 Tests justify greatness *across generations*? If a movement does not make a symphony, should we be discussing the complete works?

To put an image to it, consider the Zimbabwe brothers Paul Strang and Bryan Strang – between them, they have played all of 50 Tests. Bangladesh's top Test scorer, Habibul Bashar, ended his Test career after 50 Tests. India's Navjot Singh Sidhu finished with 51 Tests and Gautam Gambhir hovers about the 50 Test mark.

Now, consider the careers of *great* Test batsmen:

Chart 1: No: of Test matches played by great Test batsmen

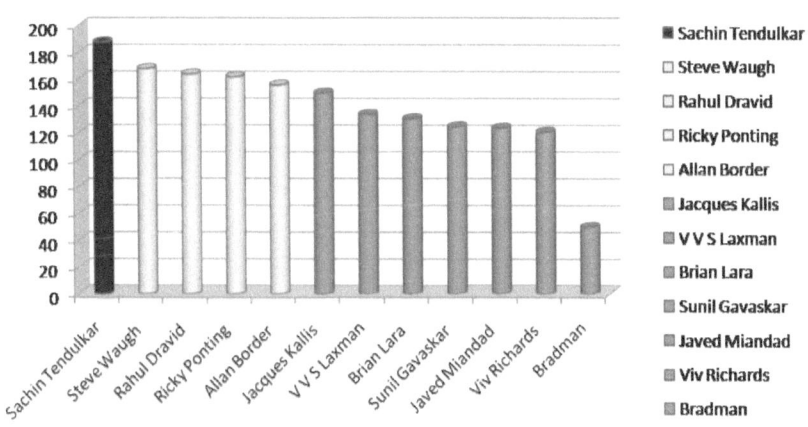

Note: Some gentlemen have since played more Tests (figures as of 2012); see Table 10 in the Appendix for detailed figures.

---

[11] *Men in White: A Book of Cricket* (*Local Heroes*; Pages 175-177); Mukul Kesavan; Penguin Books, 2010 (published 2007).

[12] *Men in White: A Book of Cricket* (*The Indian Game*; Pages 265-266); Mukul Kesavan; Penguin Books, 2010 (published in 2007).

Set aside Sachin's record for a moment.

Look at the chart. Richards, Miandad, Gavaskar, Lara and Laxman have played over twice the number of Tests that Bradman did: if the upright cylinders were stumps on a pitch, they speak of the frightening sobriety of their challenge. The stumps that loom large exposed their defenders to the most dangerous attacks: doubly so because these attacks were launched from different directions, in different places, at different times and demanded the widest range of skill and experience. Figuratively speaking, you have to be twice the batsman you claim to be, to defend a 'stump' that appears that large to bowlers.

Now look at the 'stumps' that Border, Waugh, Ponting, Kallis and Dravid have been defending – they have played over *three times* the number of Tests that Bradman did. That's not all. Many of these men have played ODIs at the same time.

Table A: ODIs played by great batsmen

Sachin Tendulkar	462 ODI matches
Ricky Ponting	375
Rahul Dravid	344
Steve Waugh	325
Jacques Kallis	320
Brian Lara	299
Allan Border	273
Javed Miandad	233
Viv Richards	187

Note: figures as of 2012.

Some gentlemen appear to have been busier than others.

Allowing for the absence of ODIs at the time, if Bradman had played at least 70 Tests then measures such as 'consistency' would matter. If he had played 100 Tests then measures such as 'percentage of team runs' would matter. If he had played 150 Tests then measures such as 'percentage of 50s and 100s' and 'strike-rate' and 'batting average' would count for something. But 50 Tests?! Honestly, would Pelé be accepted as one of the greatest footballers if he had succeeded in only one, instead of four World Cups?

The MCG is considered one of the greatest cricket grounds because it has 'seen a lot' - Tests since 1877, ODIs since 1971. Lord's too – having hosted

Tests since 1884, ODIs since 1972. They have hosted the most fiercely contested international matches for around 150 years. They are decidedly 'greater' than grounds that have been hosts for only a few years. One would not have Sophia Gardens in Cardiff or Cazaly's Stadium in Cairns be taken in the same breath as Lord's or the MCG! As far as cricket grounds go, a hundred years is a modest measure of league?

If we were naming great cricket umpires, perhaps Steve Bucknor (who officiated in 128 Tests over 20 years) would be considered greater than Mervyn Kitchen (who officiated in 20 Tests over 10 years)? Not that Kitchen was mediocre. He just wasn't challenged in as many Tests or in a variety of grounds. He has not had to decide on games involving a sufficiently wide range of teams or players. Bucknor has been called to umpire again and again – his skill and experience have been consistently valued, at the highest level. Of course, even veterans have been challenged over their inconsistency, their inaccuracy and been accused of bias. But as a rule, it is the more experienced ones like Bucknor, Shepherd and Bird who are among the greatest. Their greatness flowing from the odds they faced and the vast range of circumstances in which their judgement of field outcomes has been blessed as final. As far as umpires go, 100 Tests is considered a decent measure of rank?

Australia, having played cricket since the 19th century, is perhaps a greater cricketing nation than, say, Zimbabwe, who have been playing international cricket since the late 20th century... and so on. This is so much more than the mere ticking of the clock – Australia has weathered more change and challenge than Zimbabwe has. It is not just that more decades have come and gone in Australian cricket. The seasons in Australia have brought with them the births and deaths of so much that is cricket and so much that is about cricket, both good and bad. As far as cricket-playing nations go, 100 years is considered a measure of pedigree?

When measuring greatness in batsmen, there are more important questions. A long career implies proven skill because a batsman has been picked repeatedly to play at the highest level around the world. What is a worthy benchmark – 80 Tests, 100 Tests, 120 Tests or 150 Tests? Or should it be 80 Tests and 100 ODIs or 100 Tests and 150 ODIs?

There are other questions. What was the calibre of bowling, fielding and wicket-keeping? How established were rival Test nations? How many rivals worth the name did Bradman face and for how long? How accurate was decision-making in terms of judging a variety of dismissals? What was the level of on-pitch scrutiny at the time? What were a batsman's chances of getting to a 50? What were his chances of getting to a 100, 150, 200, 250, 300? Bradman's chances of reaching these scores were about the same as those who played alongside him. But were his chances better or worse than those who succeeded him?

There are still other questions. What have other batsmen achieved, against whom, for how long? Did Bradman have the luxury of playing at leisure or at a maddening pace? How easily did bowlers find his stumps? What was his command over the bowling – complete or conditional? How rich was his vocabulary as he 'spoke' to bowlers and fielders with his bat and his range of shots? Answers to these and other questions are crucial when painting a picture of Bradman's success and in placing it more honestly against Sachin's.

How do we get it right?

The military have an extensive procedure to test whether an officer merits a bravery award. No matter how seemingly immeasurable the landscape, no matter how distant and faded the images, they ask questions. They ask them harder and more persistently than they would if they were deciding on a prized piece of weaponry.

Those who approve canonisation or beatification in the Roman Catholic Church lead a protocol so steadfast that it is often seen as clinical, even inhuman. They peer in and pry open with a forensic fervour that often leads the uninformed to imagine that their motives are suspect. That is their mandate – to lift the veil, to heave up the floorboards, to peel back the plaster, to exhume.

But canonisation does not 'make' a saint any more than a military honour 'creates' a hero. It does not bestow on someone a quality that is not inherent. It merely recognises remarkable accomplishment. It merely announces the truth of a person's greatness that, for some reason has been 'hidden'.

What is being measured: What was he up against, for how long? How grim was the challenge? What were the obstacles? How daunting were they; overwhelming or relatively straightforward? How resilient was he? How consistently did he beat the odds? What skills were tested? How differently were they tested? Were they tested enough... long enough?

But effort in a vacuum ceases to be what it claims to be. For us earthlings, it is gravity that defines effort. So it takes effort to stand, walk, leap, run, swing and lift. The man on the moon does not labour. He faces virtually no resistance. His animation, no matter how frenetic, can hardly be called 'achievement'.

Rudolph Lambert Fernandez

Arnold Schwarzenegger in his book *The New Encyclopedia of Modern Bodybuilding* wrote that muscles grow only when tested. He should know! Of course muscles have to be tested within limits and with a calibrated increase in intensity. But the bottomline remains: no overload, no strength, no growth.

The compressive strength of a material is defined by the ability to withstand applied stress without buckling, deformation, collapse or 'failure'. The intensity of a telecommunications signal is defined by the ability to travel considerable distances without losing 'faithfulness'.

They are all defined as stronger or greater by the resistance or stress they overcome. They are, in a sense, defined by the odds they successfully 'defeat' in a range of conditions. The greatest, invariably, defeat the greatest odds in the widest range of conditions.

In sport, greatness is often loosely defined as superiority over fellow sportsmen. So the gold medallist is greater than the silver medallist and the silver greater than the bronze. The greatest are defined by much more; often by qualities with little difference in relative meaning – resolve, resilience, resourcefulness. It takes more than a couple of seasons and more than a couple of ordeals for this 'horsepower' to be tested – and therefore proven.

Booker T. Washington once said that success is to be defined by hurdles that one has faced and conquered and not so much by perceived achievement.

One who scales the village hillock is not greater than one who braves a 200mph avalanche on the shoulders of the Alps. *The Man of the Match* is not always *The Man of the Series*. *Cricketer of the Year* is not always *Leading Cricketer in the World* – one of them has climbed a more challenging mountain.

Bradman once said that footage of Sachin reminded him of his own compact and effective style. Asked by a TV interviewer to respond, Sachin said that he felt it was unfair to be compared to Bradman, especially since, at the time, he had himself played for only seven years whereas Bradman had played for twenty. Perhaps Sachin did not realise at the time that Bradman played for only 10 years. Sachin also did not predict that he himself would go on to excel for over two decades.

When Brian Lara broke the Garry Sobers record for the highest individual Test score and Sobers was asked for his views on 'greatness', he was explicit. John Woodcock introduced his *One Hundred Greatest Cricketers* with

Sobers' gentle but firm admonition that the term 'great' was deployed far too frequently. Sobers was convinced that only players who were consistent over a reasonably extended period of time could lay claim to greatness.[13]

It is a tribute to his greatness that Sobers – albeit mistakenly – saw himself lower down the pecking order and below Bradman. Like Sachin, Sobers was unmindful of the fact that he himself had played at the highest level for 19 years while Bradman had played for only 10 years.

---

[13] *One Hundred Greatest Cricketers* (Page IX, Introduction); John Woodcock, Macmillan, 1998.

Rudolph Lambert Fernandez

CHAPTER 3

Giant Among Dwarfs

PLAYING SPAN, RIVAL TEAMS, PACE OF CRICKET

'Great things are done when men and mountains meet. This is not done by jostling in the street.'

– William Blake

A KARATE MASTER STANDS IN SPLENDID solitude. Dozens of his students gaze in awe as he smashes ice blocks with his head, breaks hardboard with his fingers and bends steel with his bare hands. They are dumbstruck as he floors a volunteer with a single move. They go home in a daze, vowing to practise to the bone until they become like him – with the moves and attitude to match. That night just outside his studio, the master is confronted by a thief – a kid from the neighbourhood. The kid is barely 20 years old but towers above the teacher. The encounter lasts only a few seconds. The kid delivers the fatal blow. The master lies sprawled, as still as the ice block inside his studio.

The kid has grown up fighting – for food, for drink, for clothes, for shelter, for money, for 'stuff'. He has fought real people – other kids, other thieves, grown men, policemen. He has bloodied his fists not against hard-board but against other fists... and chins and jaws and noses. He has toughened his muscles against brute strength on the street. He has honed his moves against clubs and knives, not hanging limp from a wall but wielded viciously by other street-fighters. The blood in his mouth has on occasion been from victory, but on many nights it has been from defeat. His fighting skill is not make-believe. It does not help him excel. It keeps him alive.

The master met opposition too – stone, ice, wood, rope, steel... and starry-eyed volunteers, fresh from their 13th karate class. He met it daily – in the safety of his studio. He excelled because, as the saying goes, 'boards do not hit back'!

Coal and diamond are of the same essence – carbon. But they have hugely different atomic structures, immensely different molecular and chemical properties. They are made of the same 'stuff', but no two materials could be more distinct from each other or so incomparable in value. Under extreme heat and pressure, usually over thousands or millions of years, coal can become diamond. There's the rub – the heat *and* pressure must be both extreme *and* sustained.

The blacksmith fashions his metal not with a toothbrush and a strip of floss but with hammer and tongs. The suffix 'smith' is derived from the word 'smite', or 'to hit'. Unless it is twisted, bent and forged, metal remains a piece of scrap. It must be put through the most rigorous treatment before it can be of lasting use. The greatest arches stand tall because their metal has been through the worst.

In outdoor sport, skill becomes supreme only when *rigorously* tested for the *longest* possible time in the most diverse *and* trying conditions; until then, it remains practice. Good practice all right, but practice nonetheless.

Greatness results when skill is *tested*, under *extreme* **and** *sustained* pressure.

The martial artist may know the moves and execute them flawlessly. His skill may appear impressive but if he is not facing a rival worthy of that skill, if he is not tested, that skill is transient. He may flail about with all his might and arrest a punch a millimetre from its target but he will not qualify as a great fighter, not until he has defeated the fiercest rivals – in battle, consistently, against the odds.

A batsman, like a martial artist, struggles for physical and psychological dominance. His skill seeks to dominate everything and everyone on the green – ball, pitch, bowlers, fielders, keeper, spectators, dare we say it, even umpires.

From a point of view of *cricket history*, how real was Bradman's challenge?

Playing span

Over his career of 50 Tests Bradman played for only *ten* years.

- November 1928 to August 1934 (six years)
- December 1936 to July 1938 (two years)
- November 1946 to August 1948 (two years)

There were two 'breaks'. He played no Tests between September 1934 and November 1936. He obviously played none during the World War. Consider the span of *great* Test batsmen (chart below):

Chart 2: Playing span of great batsmen (years playing Test cricket)

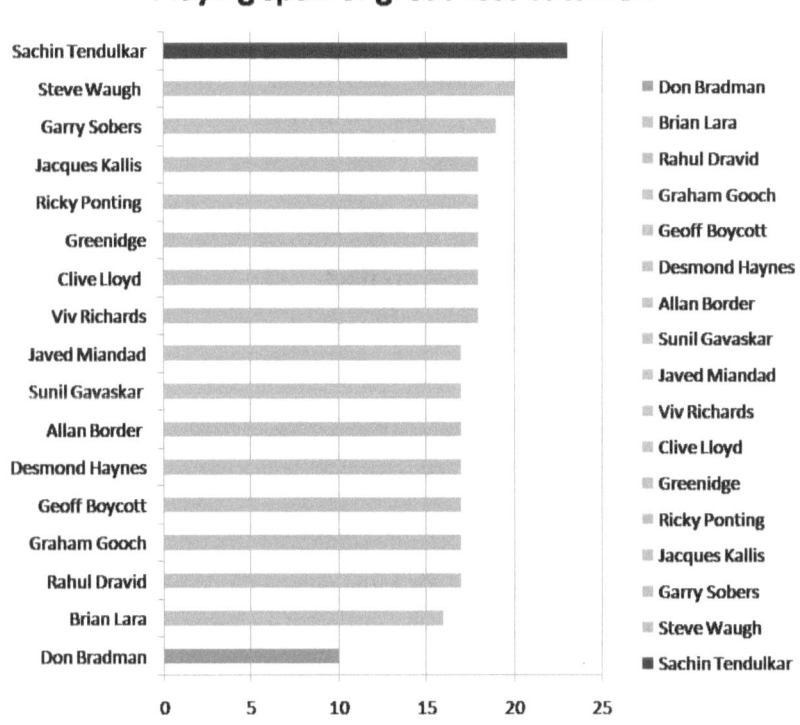

Note: See Table 10 in the Appendix for detailed figures.

Bradman is not to blame for the frugality with which nations played international cricket at the time. Nor is he to blame for the tragically lengthy break that the World War imposed on sport. The fact remains that there was too little Test cricket played by too few nations to allow *any man* – even the best – from that era to rightfully claim to be the greatest batsman ever.

The majority of *great* batsmen have had at least sixteen years playing international cricket - many playing both Tests **and** ODIs.

Bradman played for 10 years; Sachin, for over two decades.

Steven Lynch, Editor of the Wisden Guide to International Cricket 2012, confirmed that only 13.5% of the current total of 2,028 Tests had been completed by the end of 1939 (i.e., only 274 matches).[14]

By the end of 1939, Bradman was 15 Tests short of retirement; his career represents only about 2% of all Tests played. Sachin's 188-Test career represents about 9% of all Tests played. It is probably safe to say that about one in ten Tests played – at any time in history, by any nation, anywhere on the planet - involved Sachin Tendulkar.

Rival teams

What were Bradman's 10 playing years like?

- Some 72% of the time (36 out of 50 matches) his opponent was England.

- 66% (19 out of 29) of his Test centuries were against England.

- 70% (7 out of 10) of his unbeaten performances were against England.

- 72% (5,028 out of 6,996) of his Test runs were against England.

- 73% (some 498 out of 681) of his fours were against England.

- 77% (8,738 out of 11,391 minutes) of his time batting was against England.

- 76% (8,658 out of 11,391) of the balls were bowled by English bowlers [i.e., even assuming a-ball-a-minute throughout his career].

- 79% (63 out of 80) of his Test innings were against England.

---

14 *Ask Steven*; Steven Lynch in *ESPNcricinfo.com*, 17 January 2012.

- 92% (12 out of 13) of his half-centuries were against England.

- **Both** his triple centuries were against England.

- **All** his sixes were against England (barring the one against India) – he hit only six of them in his Test career anyway.

- His highest ever score (334) was against England.

Note: As it happened, 86% (6 out of 7) of his ducks were also against England.

It was the closest thing to monogamy in cricket. Out of every 100 balls, between 75 and 90 were being thrown at him by an Englishman. Out of every 100 runs he scored, over 70 were against England. He may have set out to conquer the world but for most of his career he found himself up against men from Kent, Middlesex, Sussex, Yorkshire, Nottinghamshire or Berkshire. As you can see from the chart below, England loomed so large in his little universe of 50 Tests that it shone like a giant sun dwarfing tiny planets. If he felt any heat at all it was from one source – a sun that rose nearly every morning, in pretty much the same place and set every evening, in pretty much the same place.

Look at the chart below.

Chart 3: Bradman's record against rival teams

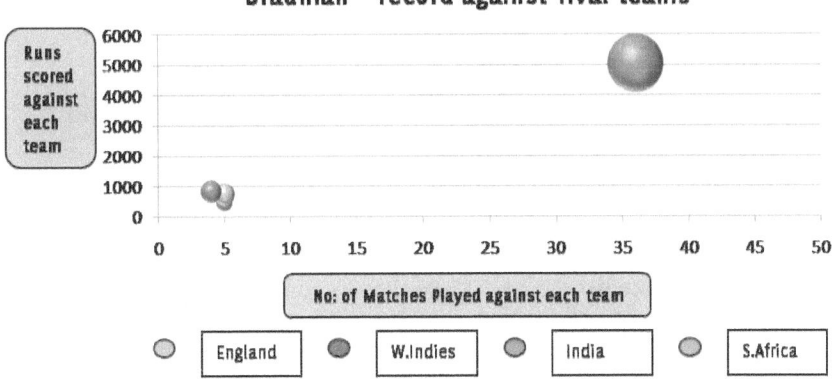

Bradman - record against rival teams

Note: for detailed figures see Table 12 in the Appendix.

There were four seasons all right but Bradman experienced predominantly one – summer. And it was for him, gloriously, almost endlessly, English.

Consider the opposition that most *great* Test batsmen faced (chart below):

 The *greatest* Test scorers faced between five and nine teams. But the majority of them faced *over twice* the number of teams that Bradman did. They also excelled in **both** forms of the international game.

Chart 4: Great Test batsmen and the range of opposition they faced

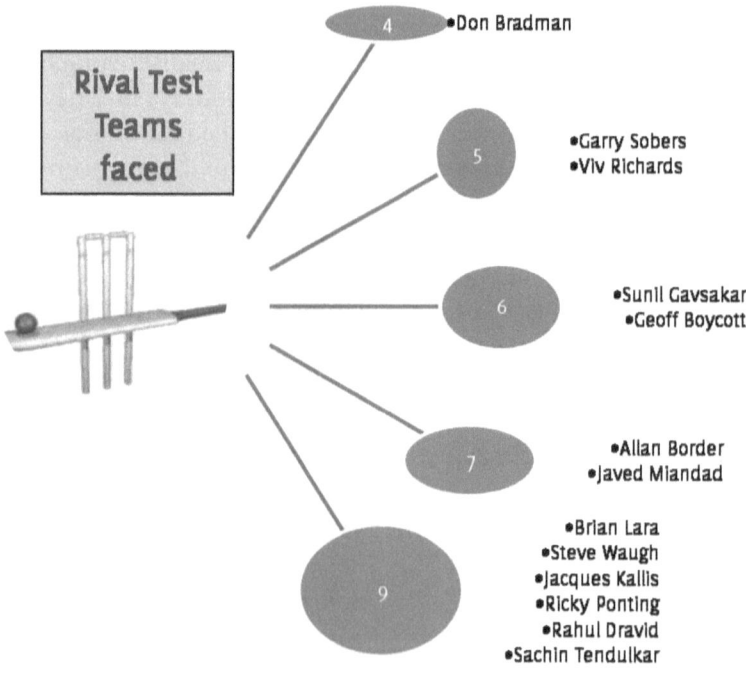

But wait... there is something beneath the floorboards.

Bradman's first nine matches (18% of his career) were successive matches against England (see list in Table 11 of the Appendix). By that time he had scored 21% (or 1,442 out of 6,996 runs) of his runs – *against anyone* and 29% (1,442 runs) out of all the 5,028 runs he scored against England.

Of these nine successive Tests against England, the first four were at 'home'; two of them on that single ground – Melbourne. We might call this Bradman's silver period and it lasted for a 'you-must-be-joking' period of two of his ten playing years.

It was to be followed by the 'golden' period which lasted for a 'you-must-be-out-of-your-mind' period of five of his ten playing years. That's right. From December 1932 up until February 1947 Bradman played a single team – England.

Hold that thought for a while.

In 22 successive Tests (see list in Table 11 of the Appendix), over a period of five of his ten playing years Bradman played a single team. 63% of these Tests (14 out of 22) played at 'home', four of them on a single ground – Melbourne. In that period he had scored 3,078 (or 44% of his career runs of 6,996).

In all, seven of his ten playing years were extended periods of successive matches against England. Together, these periods of nine, then 22 successive matches against a single team, turned out to be his most productive; from these 31 matches (62% of all Tests he played) he scored 65% (4,520 out of 6,996 runs) of his Test runs.

Nearly every season Bradman went out to bat, he saw pretty much the same level of bowling, fielding, wicket-keeping, pretty much the same tactics, the same level of cricketing knowledge and skills. And they were, for him, benevolently British.

We will soon look at the reality of the challenge that Sachin faced. At the moment it will suffice to say that by the time he was into his 33rd Test he had already played eight established nations. There was no 'match practice' against even a single nation.

Imagine, if you would, Sachin playing Australia – and no one else – in successive matches. If you considered 44% of Sachin's career, you would come up with one of these options. Sachin playing only Australia for:

- 78 Tests in a row (44% of his career of 177 matches) or

- 194 ODI matches in a row (44% of his career of 442 matches) or

- 272 matches in a row (44% of his career of 619 Test and ODI matches)

Note: as of January 2011.

Of all batsmen *from India*, it is Sachin who dominated Australia the most.

Of all batsmen *in the world*, it is Sachin who dominated Australia the most.

It is difficult to imagine what he might have done to the Australian attack over such a mercilessly protracted period, particularly if he had played 63% of those matches at 'home' in the reassuring settings of the Eden Gardens, the Feroz Shah Kotla or the Wankhede.

Think about it. Sachin playing *a single team* for 78 Tests in a row or 194 ODIs *in a row*. One thing is certain, his batting average, strike-rate and tally of runs would have troubled the scorers every season as he powered himself higher and higher, from one level to the next – tons, double tons, triple tons flowing from every match. His command over the bowling growing with each delivery as he drove, hooked, pulled and cut bowlers, in turn, all over the park. Mike Tyson in his prime, in the ring with a challenger, for 22 bouts *in a row* - a terrifying thought.

That's what happened in the 1930s. Bradman got the longest, closest possible look at everything that England could throw at him, *over a period of five years* – half his playing span. Imagine Sachin with the luxury of having the fiercest pace and spin bowlers in all of cricket history with him *in the nets*, bowling at middle and off, bowling at his pads, his upper body, bowling yorkers, bouncers and short-pitched ones, coming round the wicket and over just so that he could refine his square cut and straight drive. The impact on a team like Australia would have been several times more devastating than it has been in Sachin's career. The impact on his batting record would have been nothing short of miraculous.

Bradman, obviously an exceptional batsman of his time, took advantage of his extended 'session' with England and achieved a mastery of the bowling that was ahead of other batsmen of his era. Englishman Wally Hammond perhaps came closest and we will look at him later. As we shall see, Sachin had no such luxury, yet achieved a mastery that outclassed everyone who played before him.

England were not the greatest team of that era but they were an established team. That could hardly be said of Bradman's other rivals.

India

Before they got to Bradman in 1947, the Indians had played half a dozen matches against England. Of all the Tests that ended in a result, the Indians lost miserably – every time.

June 1932: India's first Test is at Lord's – they lose by 158 runs.

India's first Test was 'away'. More importantly, they were pitted against their colonial masters.

December 1933: India's second Test played at the Bombay Gymkhana; they lose again, this time by nine wickets.

January and February 1934 – India play two Tests; they manage to draw the one in Calcutta but lose the other in Madras - by 202 runs.

June 1936: India in a Test at Lord's; they lose again by nine wickets.

July 1936: India manage to draw the Test at Manchester.

August 1936: India lose, again by nine wickets, this time in London.

The millions affected by famine, disease, floods, earthquake or civil unrest in 1940s India were not the mere 'zones' that they might be in today's 'ocean' of 1.2 billion. At the time, they represented vast segments of the entire country. It is difficult to imagine the woeful psychological state of the Indian cricket team during these troubled years, but one can make a fair guess.

1946: India play three Tests – all in England. In June, India lose to England for the sixth time but not satisfied with having lost on three occasions, by nine wickets, this time they lose by ten wickets. They manage to draw the other two in July and August.

Around the time of these matches, communal riots erupt in Calcutta and rage for nearly a week; 5,000 Indians are killed and thousands injured. In 1947, India win freedom after centuries of colonial rule. This is the most tumultuous year for 20th century India. Weeks before the Test in Australia in November 1947, a number of things happen. British India is dissolved. Partition is announced. Hindus, Muslims and Sikhs flee to regions that they hope will welcome them, regions where they hope they will feel safe enough to build a future. A million are killed, injured, separated from their families or left homeless in the civil war that follows. A full-fledged war breaks out between the newly formed India and Pakistan.

Funnily, at this point (November 1947) India come face to face with Bradman. Fittingly, the man obliges in that Series of 1947-48 – scoring four of his 29 centuries, all of them on his home turf (185 in Brisbane, 132 and 127 in Melbourne and finally 201 in Adelaide).

Of the two Tests in 1947 against Australia in Australia, one is drawn but India lose the other by an innings and 226 runs.

Of the three Tests in 1948 against Australia in Australia, India lose all three:

- 1-5 January in Melbourne; India lose by 233 runs

- 23-28 January in Adelaide; India lose by an innings and 16 runs

- 6-10 February in Melbourne; India lose by an innings and 177 runs

Two of these Tests are played a few days before Gandhi is assassinated. Incredibly, the final match is played a few days after the assassination.

Bradman retires in 1948 after having one last go at his favourite team (England); he never faces India again.

The Indians linger on in the international cricket arena, limping from one defeat to another. In the 1930s and 40s they could only have been described as less than mediocre. Of all the matches that ended in a result, India lost every one, often by nine wickets and once by ten wickets.

At the time a report in The Mail described Australia's success against India, confirming that the Indian attack was 'brittle', not least because it lacked a dependable pacer and spinner.[15]

Embarrassingly for Bradman, 10% (715 out of 6,996) of his Test runs were against this team.

In 1952, India manage to win their first ever Test series – against Pakistan, bare infants in Test cricket at the time. India's next win comes in 1955 against New Zealand. It is only in 1962, *three decades* after they started out playing international cricket, that India win their first series against a world-class Test team, England.

The Indian bowlers, when they faced Bradman, were bowling 'away' – their first Test season in Australia and only their second Test series outside India. They simply could not have been a bowling attack worthy of Bradman's attentions.

Thanks to his age, debilitating illness and a harrowing period of war for Australia, Bradman, in 1947, was a shadow of the batsman he once was. The years he lost to the War are a loss to the cricketing world, not just to Australia. They were a loss not just to that era but to all cricketing generations. It is one of cricket's great tragedies that someone of his stature was one of its victims.

But by the time the Indians faced Bradman in 1947, he was no duckling; he was 10 matches short of retirement and had just about perfected his technique, from playing England in 22 successive matches over a period

---

[15] *Bradman triumphs in batting tactics*; W J O'Reilly, *The Mail*, 3 January 1948.

Rudolph Lambert Fernandez

of five years. The Indians, on the other hand, were struggling to overcome humiliation meted out to them by the English team, right through the pre-War years. At the time, the 'whites' were not just sporting peers from another country; to the Indians, they were 'lords and masters' – in every sense.

Against such an apology of a team, Bradman scored relatively little. Yes, he managed four centuries against India. Yes, Australia won a few of those matches *by an innings* (he did not have to come in and bat a second time) but his overall performance against a fledgling Indian team was prosaic. He faced 1,140 balls and scored, by his standards, a disconcertingly low 715 runs.

It was as if a group of novices from the local church choir had dropped in to a workshop on musical counter-point, where Mozart was the chief speaker. He spoke. They heard. That was that. Naturally, they were none the wiser for it but they went to town about how they rubbed shoulders with Mozart and how he taught them profound things. Mozart, for his part, quietly collected his speaker's fee and used that to fund his next operatic project.

West Indies

They had only just started international cricket in 1928 when Bradman began his Test career. Like the Indians, they were losers too but in their own right!

- In 1928, during their first international outing, they play three matches against England *in England*. They lose all – *by an innings* and then some.

- In early 1930, they play four matches against England. Two are drawn. They manage to win one but lose the other.

- December 1930: they face Australia... and Bradman on his home turf in Adelaide. They lose, by ten wickets.

- In early 1931, they face Australia in four matches. They manage to win one but lose all the others – by an innings and more. All are on Bradman's home turf – twice in Sydney and the other two matches in Brisbane and Melbourne.

- After a mere five matches, Bradman is done with the West Indies.

- In 1932, the West Indies do not play. When they get back to it in 1933 they face England in three matches. One is drawn. The West Indies stay firmly in 'form' and lose the other two – again by an innings and more.

All the matches that Bradman played against West Indies were on his home turf... and decidedly sombre engagements for him:

- December 1930 in Adelaide: Australia win by 10 wickets (Bradman scoring four runs in one innings and not batting in the other)

- 1-5 January 1931 in Sydney: Australia win by an innings and 172 runs (Bradman scoring 25 in one innings and not having to bat again)

- 16-20 January 1931 in Brisbane: Australia win by an innings and 217 runs (Bradman scored 223 in one innings and did not have to bat again)

- 13-14 February 1931 in Melbourne: Australia win by an innings and 122 runs (Bradman scored 152 in one innings and did not have to bat again)

- Feb/March 1931 in Sydney: West Indies win by 30 runs (but with Bradman scoring 43 and 0 respectively in that match)

Trinidad, Tobago, Barbados, Antigua and Jamaica were names associated with the American Civil War. The early 20th century saw the end of centuries of oppression, including the last vestiges of slavery. But as a people, the West Indies were only just stepping into their own shoes, let alone the notion of them as a team stepping on to the international cricket field. When you are preoccupied with surviving from day to day in an entirely new world, you are a little less likely to focus on perfecting that in-swinger!

If Bradman did not score as heavily against them (just 447 runs from five matches), it was probably because even then they were showing signs of greatness – winning and drawing matches against established teams of the day just weeks after having started international cricket. They would eventually dominate cricket but it would be years before that came to pass.

South Africa

Bradman played only four matches against South Africa (he was absent hurt in the other match); just as well... for the South Africans, that is. At the time they were nowhere near the team they were to become in the late 20th century.

In the late 19th century South Africa played four Test series; all four were against England – South Africa lost *every time*.

The South Africans in the late 19th century were a deadbeat team. In the early 20th century they were still a deadbeat team, even if they appeared to have lost a bit of their 'touch' – they actually started winning the occasional series!

Between the years 1888-89 and 1931-32 (just before facing Bradman), South Africa played 19 Test series; only one was drawn, the rest delivered a result. Of the 18 with a result, South Africa ended up losing 15 (or 83% of the time).

For four decades South Africa were habitual losers – this was **before** they faced Bradman. This was the afflicted crew he faced in 4 Tests – all on home turf:

- Nov/Dec 1931 in Brisbane: Australia win by an innings and 163 runs

- 18-21 Dec 1931 in Sydney: Australia win by an innings and 155 runs

- Dec 1931/Jan 1932 in Melbourne: Australia win by 169 runs

- Jan/Feb 1932 in Adelaide: Australia win by ten wickets

Note: Feb 1932 in Melbourne: Australia win by an innings and 72 runs [Bradman absent].

In February 1932 in Melbourne, the South Africans were so pathetic against Australia that they were all-out for 36 in the first innings. Then, just in case critics thought that was a fluke, they ended all-out for 45 in the second innings. Mercifully for them, Bradman was missing in action in that particular game. When he did face them in previous matches, he obviously made merry (226 runs in Brisbane, 112 in Sydney, 167 in Melbourne and 299 in Adelaide).

What happened? It was not that the best Australian bowlers of the 20th century had united in that one team to pulverize the South Africans. The Australian bowling was no better than it had been the previous year. South Africa's dismal record was not caused by a Bradman gone berserk. It was the portrait of a painfully floundering team, on its knees, whether Bradman played or not. If their batsmen were arthritic, their bowlers and fielders were worse.

In the history of Test cricket, of all *teams that have been dismissed for fewer than 50 runs*, South Africa holds top honours – four occasions in the 19th century and three occasions in the early 20th century.

The South Africa of Bradman's era held the world record – if we must call it that – for the **lowest** innings Test total; a record broken only in 1955 – a quarter of a century later – when New Zealand were bowled out for 26 runs against England in Auckland. Many of Bradman's achievements against South Africa, including his unbeaten 299 against them in January 1932 need to be seen in this light: It was great for Australia but was it ever a 'Test'? It was exhilarating for Bradman but was it ever a 'match'?

What do we make of Bradman's opposition, apart from the English team?

Around 28% (1,968 runs out of 6,996 runs) of all his runs and 35% (10 out of 29 tons) of all his tons were against these less than pedestrian teams. The West Indies, South Africa and India matches against Australia (and Bradman), were abysmally one-sided. They were essentially unexceptional cricketers. It would be several decades before they began to stride the cricketing world with any sort of confidence. **None** of their encounters with Bradman could be called battles. **All** of them were at 'home' – four in that single ground, Melbourne.

His seemingly staggering batting average and strike-rate should be seen in this sobering context. His challenge – for the lack of a better word – was all too meek and brief. Apart from his deathless conversation with England, in a space of about 14 Tests Bradman was done with 'the rest of the world'. Sachin has played 16 Tests against the West Indies alone.

The essence of Bradman's playing span is best captured in the silver and golden periods, when he saw only England. The platinum years – when he saw lame-duck teams such as South Africa, West Indies and India – were scattered rather than a series of successive matches.

Silver, gold, platinum: easy, easier... easiest.

The reality of the challenge was a bit like Michael Phelps sneaking into the Paralympics pool – only one man in the pool sees the funny side.

Every now and then great achievement shines forth, usually for the moment. *Enduring* greatness demands much more. Unless there is a crushing of grape, there is simply no wine.

Bradman's rivals did not test him. They did not test him enough. They did not test him consistently enough.

Bradman always chose his words carefully, so we would do well to pay attention to what he said about his batting. It is no small thing that on occasion he is believed to have referred to an innings as 'good practice'; more often than not that's just what it was.

Between 1886 and 1960, there were only two teams capable of whitewashing a rival – winning every match in a series (a minimum of three matches). For over seven decades, these two teams (England and Australia) successfully whitewashed not only each other but weaklings like West Indies, South Africa and India. No other team achieved that feat until 1961-62, when West Indies succeeded in the first non-English, non-Australian whitewash, hammering India on home turf.

Of 47 whitewashes in Test cricket history, South Africa pulled off only 2, to England's towering 13 and Australia's outrageous 19 whitewashes.

As far as England were concerned, for a good part of the late 19th and 20th century, there was only one rival – Australia. As far as Australia were concerned, there was only one rival – England.

Most importantly, Australia were by far the better team long *before* Bradman, and have remained by far, the best team in cricket history. We will soon examine this superiority. For now, it will suffice to say that the only rival that he faced – worthy of mention – was *also* inferior to his own team. The others were welcome amusement all right but amusement nonetheless.

The reality of Bradman's challenge was simple. His rival's face was as familiar as the grip on his bat and the gloves on his hands. On most occasions the battleground was his backyard – Australia. A fifth of his entire career was on that single ground, Melbourne.

The ancient Olympics had hardly any events to be called *world* championships. Only Greeks could compete and they had to be free men – not slaves. They were held only in Olympia and were meant to honour only Zeus. Imagine the gold medallist of a bygone era claiming to be the greatest *in history*. Even if he had won all the gold medals for several years in a row, would present-day historians give him a second look?

Regional tournaments celebrate *local* heroes. They also aim to create *global* ones. But, if that is the aim, one does not narrow down a tournament from global to regional. If anything the idea would be to expand upward, outward. After all, regional tournaments help build the confidence of lesser players so that they can compete one day against the best in the world. They offer opportunities of relative comfort – for victory and defeat - that full-fledged global tournaments do not. The Asian Games, for instance, produce an Asian champion, not a world champion. That Asian champion may go on to win the Olympics but not until he competes at a global level on a global stage. Olympians from decades gone by have been overthrown by newer winners who have won against many more rivals and have endured as winners.

Bradman's achievements were primarily against a single rival, not against the cricketing world; that world was yet to emerge. There were other teams all right but they were nowhere near world-class.

Regional crowns and medals and trophies sit well – on regional shelves.

Cricket until the middle of the 20th century was not too different from the early Olympics. It was played only in 'Olympia' – a handful of grounds. It was open only to the 'Greeks' (England and Australia) – the others (West Indies, South Africa and India) were, in terms of comparable ability or skill, not 'free men'.

Christopher Reeve is believed to have said, that a hero is someone ordinary who finds strength to persevere and endure in spite of overwhelming obstacles.

What raises a man above his fellow men is not that he has persevered but that he has endured in spite of often paralysing obstacles. Reeve ought to have known a thing or two about heroism. No struggle – no victory.

The boxer who lasts over 12 rounds is usually greater than the one who lasts only two. The rounds decide how tough he is, to withstand blows, to use his feet and neck and torso to dodge lethal punches, blink the blood out of his eyes and find an opponent's flaws before moving in for a kill. The greatest fights are not those where a knock-out is delivered in the first round, leaving no one in doubt that one of two fighters is way out of his league in weight or fighting skill, or both. A first round knock-out is impressive but can never be called great. The greatest fights test a boxer's stamina, his strength and will to win. The greatest fights 'reveal' a fighter's resilience, his ability to adapt – to injury, to new tactics, to foul-play, to fatigue. The greatest fighters endure from one round to the next, from one fighter to the next, from one ring to the next.

Rudolph Lambert Fernandez

Bradman did go a few rounds in the ring. Sachin has kept his outstretched gloved hands high, longer than any man before him. He has been through the most punishing fights, in and out of the ring. He is the super heavy-weight among super heavy-weights.

Pace of cricket

Batsmen face another challenge – the pace of cricket. But comparing the two epochs is a bit like trying to absorb the speed-antics of a 109-year old cyclist while following a blur of cars on a blistering F1 track.

The Bradman era was like a film clip of a groundsman in the 1930s taking a quiet 'rest day' stroll on the sprawling MCG – but with the clip played in slow motion. If there was a Test in March 1929, the next was over a year later in June 1930. If there was a Test in February 1933, the next was over a year later in June 1934. If there was a Test in August 1934, the next was over two years later in December 1936. If there was a Test in February 1937, the next was over a year later in June 1938. If there was a Test in February 1947, the next was eight months later in November that year.

The groundsman featured above is fictional but the Tests listed above are not. They are indeed from Bradman's career and demonstrate the space between Tests at the time. He had all the time in the world to invent a newer shot, correct that bit of footwork, perfect his stance and reflect on his approach. No matter how sports writers of that era portrayed the 'pressure' that Bradman faced, he at least had the time and space to steel himself – mentally and physically – before he walked out to bat.

Sachin's Test career has, in comparison, been a bit like trying to enjoy a Victor Hugo, while standing in a train leaving Mumbai's Victoria Terminus at peak hour. In 1990 alone, he played 7 Tests. He then played 16 Tests in 2002, 13 Tests in 2008 and 14 Tests in 2010. We can hold it right there. That is already 50 Tests over a period of just four years. This is before we even begin to describe his simultaneous boarding of the ODI train, futilely clutching his Hugo!

Sachin excelled at the highest level in both the dominant formats, in a gruelling schedule, under the most demanding conditions for another 19 years. Bradman's entire career, over ten playing years was complete in all of 50 Tests; Sachin has notched up more Test centuries.

Bradman did go through one or two rough Test series but his career against only one rival worthy of him over a leisurely playing span of just ten years can hardly be called a struggle, especially if the only rival worthy of mention was far inferior to his own team. His career can hardly be called a real *and* prolonged struggle, let alone real *or* prolonged.

Taking guard on a sunny morning in Melbourne, Bradman may have felt the way a lunar high-jumper feels before a jump on the moon, in a stadium packed with excited earthlings. Hop, skip and...! Bradman may have felt a bit like a Goliath in *Davidland*; *a* giant... among dwarfs.

As we shall see, Sachin on the other hand was, is and will remain a giant... among giants.

CHAPTER 4

Giant Among Giants

RIVAL TEAMS, CRICKET GROUNDS, BATTING POSITION

CARL JUNG ONCE SAID THAT resistance to the organised mass can be effected only by the man who is as organised in his individuality as the mass itself.

Resistance: it's what shapes and defines greatness.

In the 1958 football World Cup, Pelé beat the best Swedish defenders, to help Brazil win; he was a 17-year-old at the time. In the 1962 World Cup, he once beat four defenders to score. In the 1966 World Cup he was brutally attacked on the field. Then in the 1970 World Cup, he dribbled, he passed, he headed and he lobbed Brazil to victory.

The fence, the stairs, the trench, the bend, the cliff, the crest and trough, the gorge and canyon – these are what define greatness. The bruises and the bronzes are what define greatness. These are what set giants apart from dwarfs. They are also what set a giant apart from giants.

Here's why the boy from Bandra was a giant among giants.

Rival teams

Sachin has played *nine* Test rivals – over twice the number that Bradman faced. By the time he was into his 33rd Test, Bradman had played England alone in as many as 23 Tests. By the time he was into his 33rd Test, Sachin had already played eight Test nations; Bangladesh would have to wait until his 77th Test.

- In the 12 months of 2002 alone, Sachin played 16 Tests against 4 teams: West Indies, England, New Zealand and Zimbabwe – as many as Bradman faced in his career. A third of all the Tests Bradman played.

- In 2008 alone, Sachin played 13 Tests against 4 teams (South Africa, Sri Lanka, Australia and England) – as many teams as Bradman faced in his career.

- In 2010 alone, Sachin played 14 Tests against 5 teams: South Africa, Australia, Sri Lanka, New Zealand and Bangladesh. One more than the teams Bradman faced in his career. Apart from his seemingly interminable face-off with England, Bradman's career against the 'rest of the world' was all of 14 Tests.

Around 72% of all Bradman's runs were against a single team – England. Sachin's 14, 692 Test runs were against the cricketing world (chart below):

Chart 5: Sachin's Test record against 'the world'

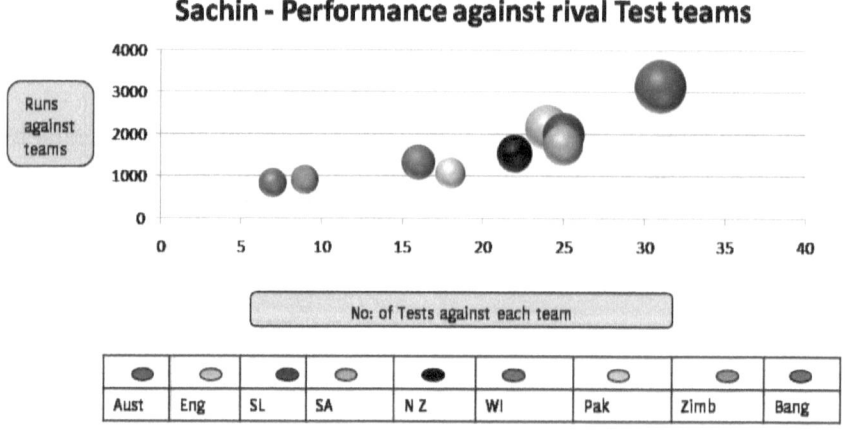

Note: see detailed figures in Table 13 of the Appendix.

It was as if Sachin were on some strange and unsettling planet, where a giant new sun rose from a different horizon every season, bringing on different climates with each rising and each setting. Every season he walked out to bat he faced a new rival team, a new set of bowlers, a fresh strategy aimed at sending him back to the pavilion. All his rivals, barring Bangladesh, were established in Test cricket. A few, having straddled a century of cricket, were dominant teams by the time he came on to the pitch.

England and Australia, for instance, having played since the 1870s were titans for much of the 20th century. They had claimed victory regularly, across continents, against all Test nations and we have only just looked at their record of 'whitewashing' rivals.

Of the three most prolific Test fielders, two are Australian – Ricky Ponting and Mark Waugh. Of the four highest Test wicket takers, two bowlers are Australian – Shane Warne and Glenn McGrath. Of the three highest Test scorers, one is Australian – Ricky Ponting. Of the three highest ODI scorers, one is Australian – Ricky Ponting. Adam Gilchrist is the most prolific ODI wicket-keeper. Of the three most prolific ODI fielders, one is Australian – Ricky Ponting. McGrath is the world's most prolific fast-bowler in Tests.

It is against Australia, the most feared team of his era, that Sachin has shown audacity – highest number of sixes and fours and highest number of Test centuries. In ODIs too he has reserved his most punishing treatment for Australia.

Sri Lanka's Muttiah Muralitharan is the highest Test wicket-taker, the most prolific *Player of the Test Series* winner and the 2nd most prolific *Player of the Test Match* winner. Kumar Sangakkara and Mahela Jayawardene have scored the highest Test run partnership (for any wicket); the pair below them is also Sri Lankan (Sanath Jayasuriya and Roshan Mahanama). Mahela Jayawardene is the 4th most prolific Test fielder and the most prolific ODI fielder. Yes, Sri Lanka were a weak international team in the 1980s, but since 1990 (when Sachin began building his career), have been defeating the best including England, West Indies, Pakistan, India, South Africa, New Zealand and the mighty Australians.

When Bradman started out, New Zealand had been playing Test cricket for only a few months. He never got to face them anyway. But by the time they faced Sachin, New Zealand had played against the world's best Test teams for six decades. Although they never defeated Australia, they had overpowered many proven rivals including England, the West Indies, India and Sri Lanka. Between 1999 and 2006, New Zealand won three Test Series against the West Indies and one against England. Sachin has pitted his wits against some of their most determined practitioners including John Wright, Nathan Astle, Daniel Vettori, Martin Crowe and Chris Cairns. New Zealand's Stephen Fleming is the 5th most prolific Test fielder.

Pakistan has had some of the most feared pace, swing and spin bowlers.

In the history of whitewashes (winning all matches in a Test series of 3 or more matches) Pakistan leads the second-rung pack with 5 whitewashes, a good sight better than the West Indies (3), Sri Lanka (3), South Africa (2) and India (2). In terms of dominating Test cricket, Pakistan are only a couple of notches below England and Australia. Wasim Akram is the 3rd most prolific *Player of the Test Match* winner. Of course Pakistan were a weak team in the 1950s but by the time Sachin had started playing, they were menacing indeed and they were the first to test him. Over four decades they had defeated the world's best (including Australia –in four Test Series). Akram and Younis are the world's most prolific fast-bowlers in ODIs.

These teams were not invertebrates.

What of South Africa, who started playing in 1889 (a hundred years before Sachin's debut)?

In Bradman's era South Africa were losers – 83% of the time. Ahead of Sachin's arrival they had transformed – they were winners. Between 1965 and 2001 (including exile in the 1970s and 80s) out of 33 Test series that South Africa played, 28 ended with a result (5 were drawn). Of the 28 series with a result, South Africa won 23 (or 82% of the time) – their pitiable state during the Bradman years had become a thing of the past.

Since the late 20th century, South Africa have been an incredibly powerful Test and ODI nation. They brought to the game some of the craftiest bowlers in Allan Donald, Shaun Pollock, Cronje and Ntini. Pollock is the 5th highest ODI wicket-taker. They brought the most expert fielders including Jonty Rhodes and Herschelle Gibbs. They also brought ruthlessly effective batsmen in Lance Klusener, Jacques Kallis and Gary Kirsten. Kallis is the 4th highest Test scorer, the most prolific *Player of the Test Match* winner and the 2nd most prolific *Player of the Test Series* winner. Boucher is the most prolific wicket-keeper (highest dismissals in Tests and second-highest in ODIs).

And the West Indies, who started playing in 1928? Infantile against Bradman, they were mighty in the 1960s and 1970s and were to become near-invincible soon after. Between 1980 and 1995, they played 29 Test Series against every powerful Test nation in the world; 20 ended in a result (9 were drawn). Of the 20 that ended in a result, they won every time. By the time they faced Sachin in 1994, they had been playing Test cricket for 66 years.

For fifteen years, every team worth its salt had a crack at the West Indies;

they stayed on top – arrogant, defiant and undefeated. Their bowlers at one end galloping like thoroughbreds, bowling with a speed and accuracy that made even good batsmen tremble within the deceptive comfort of their pads; their batsmen at the other end, showing rival bowlers scant respect. They looked like they'd been hewn out of some mighty rock in the Caribbean, making them almost indestructible. A rival batting pair could not be chided if they imagined they were in the middle of some barbaric Stonehenge, where the giant stones came alive and kept closing in on them.

Sachin caught only a glimpse of Greenidge, Haynes, Viv Richards and Malcolm Marshall. No doubt, he cherishes the matches he played against them. In hindsight, they probably cherish the time they shared the field with the greatest batsman in history. But Sachin did see a good deal of Patrick Patterson, Ian Bishop, Curtly Ambrose, Carl Hooper, Courtney Walsh, Winston Benjamin, Phil Simmons, Andy Cummins, Kenny Benjamin, Roger Harper and Merv Dillon.

These men were hardly cream puffs. Like the giants that Gavaskar faced in the 1970s and 80s, they towered 10 to 12 inches above the tiny Sachin, the ball often flying in from a height of around ten feet. Their confidence in the 1990s and beyond was built, every brick of it, on the edifice of that dream team of the 1980s. They were not quite the sabre-toothed tigers that walked the field before them. They were no lambs either. The West Indies of Sachin's era were among the most effective competitors ever. Among fast bowlers (setting aside the outrageously effective McGrath) it is Walsh who has the world's highest tally of Test wickets – ahead of Kapil, Akram, Hadlee, Younis, Imran, Lillee, Vaas and dozens of others.

Sachin has had to prove his mettle against these established cricket rivals – batsmen, bowlers, fielders, wicket-keepers, Players of the Match, Players of the Test Series. He has forged his tons and double tons in this cauldron of cricketing excellence. His batting average and strike-rate in Tests and ODIs need to be seen in this context.

Around 65% of Bradman's 29 Test tons were against a single team – England. Sachin's 51 Test tons, on the other hand, have come against them all.

Chart 6: Test tons (Bradman vs. Sachin)

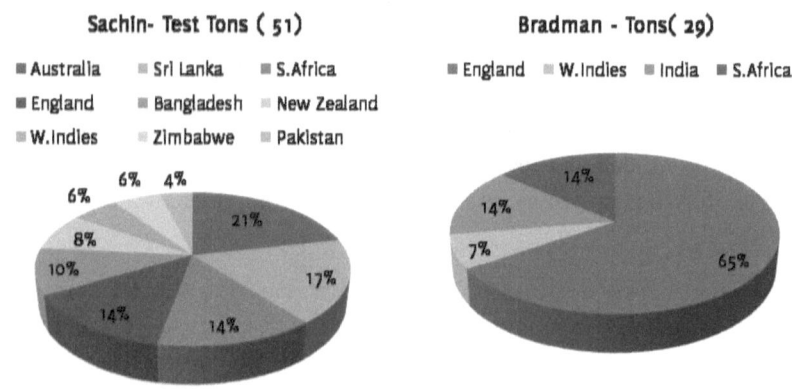

Sachin- Test Tons (51)

- Australia   ≡ Sri Lanka   ≡ S.Africa
- England   ≡ Bangladesh   New Zealand
- W.Indies   ≡ Zimbabwe   ≡ Pakistan

Bradman - Tons(29)

≡ England   ≡ W.Indies   ≡ India   ≡ S.Africa

Note: 2011; see Tables 7, 8 and 9 in the Appendix for Sachin's tons (% rounded off).

In ODIs too Sachin's 46 tons have come against them all; 9 against Australia, the strongest team of his era.

Chart 7: Sachin's ODI tons against 'the world'

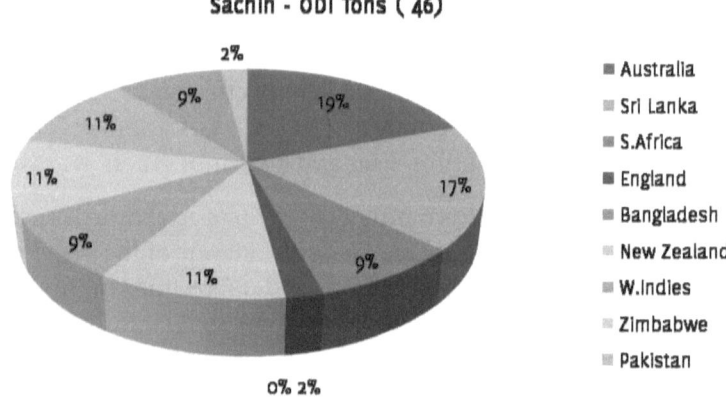

Sachin - ODI Tons (46)

- Australia
- Sri Lanka
- S.Africa
- England
- Bangladesh
- New Zealand
- W.Indies
- Zimbabwe
- Pakistan

Note: 2011 (% rounded off); see Table 7 in the Appendix for detailed figures.

International cricket grounds

One of the surest signs of batting greatness is to have excelled in grounds across the world, against the most hostile crowds and in the most alien playing environments, judged by umpires from an assortment of nationalities.

Awkwardly for Bradman, outside Australia, he played in just five grounds (Nottingham, Leeds, Lord's, Manchester and The Oval) – all in England. The others were in Australia (Melbourne, Brisbane, Adelaide and Sydney). Everyone seems to know this already. So let us look beneath the plaster.

- 24% (1,671 out of 6,996) of all his runs were scored in Melbourne.

- 31% (9 out of 29) of all his tons were scored in Melbourne.

- 64% (32 out of 50 matches) of his Test career was on pitches in Australia. He was absent in the one other match in Melbourne – against South Africa in February 1932.

- In Australia, 31% (10 out of 32 matches in Australia) of his Test career was from that single ground in Melbourne. He was absent in the one other match in Melbourne in February 1932.

- 62% (18 out of 29 tons) of his Test centuries were scored in Australia.

- 62% (4,322 out of 6,996 runs) of his Test runs were scored in Australia.

- 77% (10 out of 13) of all his half-centuries were scored in Australia; out of the ten fifties in Australia, three were in Melbourne.

- Bradman's first four matches were in Australia; two in Melbourne.

- In the first 20 matches of his career, Bradman had already played in Melbourne five times; a fifth of his entire Test career (and a third of his Test career in Australia) was in Melbourne.

Bradman was more than used to the teams, the pitches, the crowds. It was as if he were going to the same job – same tube station, same side-walk, same elevator and same cabin.

 Sachin played his first 32 Test matches *on 32 different grounds.*

Go ahead and read that sentence again – it helps to absorb the stark reality of Sachin's challenge.

If Bradman jostled in the street, Sachin climbed the highest and most dangerous mountain:

- Sachin's first four matches were on arguably the most hostile territory for an Indian 16-year-old: Karachi, Faisalabad, Lahore and Sialkot.

- Sachin has played in at least 56 Test grounds (around the world); Bradman in nine grounds (only in England and Australia).

- Of Sachin's Test grounds, only 14 were at 'home'; as many as 42 grounds were 'away' (see Appendix for full list). Some 75% of *the grounds* that Sachin has played on, were rival territory.

- Sachin has scored 57% (29 out of 51) of his Test centuries outside India. Whether it was his 241 in Sydney, 177 in Nottingham, 193 in Leeds, 194 in Multan, 203 in Colombo or 248 in Dhaka, each season Sachin

 Bradman scored 29 Test tons in his entire career (the majority at 'home'). Sachin has notched up that same number of Test tons in hostile grounds alone.

saw a new team, another crowd, a different ground.

- Setting aside the lone Test in Chandigarh in 1990 (against Sri Lanka), Sachin's first 20 Test matches were 'away' - in Pakistan, New Zealand, England, Australia, Zimbabwe and South Africa. It was not until his 22nd Test that he started playing more regularly at 'home' (after the Test against England in Kolkata in 1993).

- Sachin has played in **95 ODI grounds** across continents; only 32 of them in India. In ODIs, 66% (63 grounds) were rival or neutral grounds.

Put differently, when Sachin went out to bat it was as if each season was a new job – different address, new side-walk, no elevator (he had to take the stairs), and strange cabin. Some 56 different Test grounds and 95 different ODI grounds – he not only survived them, he thrived in them.

In ODI cricket Sachin has excelled outside India in diverse playing conditions:

- 65% (286 out of 442 matches) of all his matches have been outside India, including in places like Sharjah, Belfast, Kuala Lumpur, Dambulla (in the UAE), Pietermaritzburg (in Namibia), Bristol, Toronto and Singapore.

- 61% (28 out of 46) of all his tons have been scored outside India.

- 61% (57 out of 93)of all his half-centuries have been outside India.

- 60% (1,164 out of 1,927) of all his fours have been outside India.

- 66% (122 out of 185) of all his sixes have been outside India.

Chart 8: Sachin's ODI performance – against the odds ('Home' vs. 'Away')

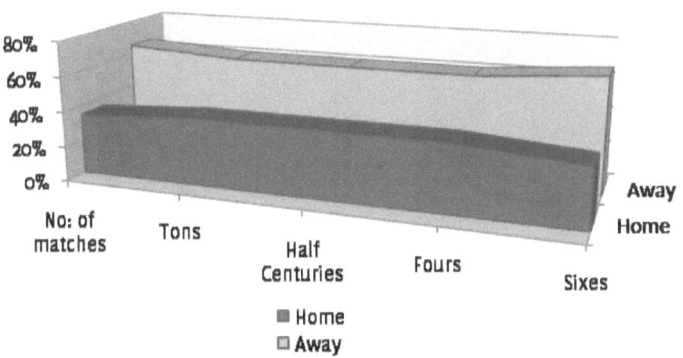

Look above at Sachin's 'away' wall; how it dwarfs the one at 'home'. He has carved his magnificent ODI career on the fastest, strangest, most hostile pitches around the world. He has fought everywhere and prevailed.

Chart 9: Away vs. Home –Test Runs, Test matches (Bradman vs. Sachin)

(See details in Tables 3 and 4 in Appendix)

Bradman
No: of Matches

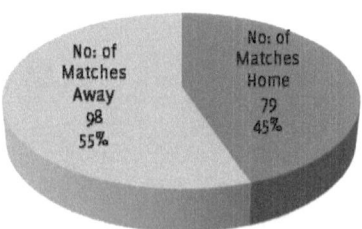

Sachin
No: of Test Matches

Bradman
No: of Runs

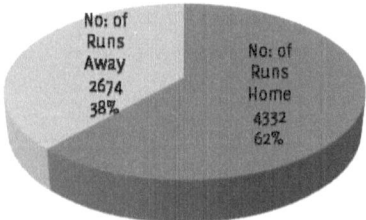

Sachin
No: of Test Runs

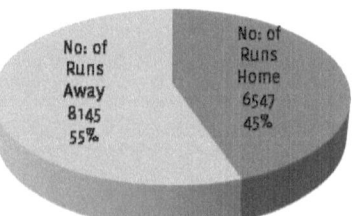

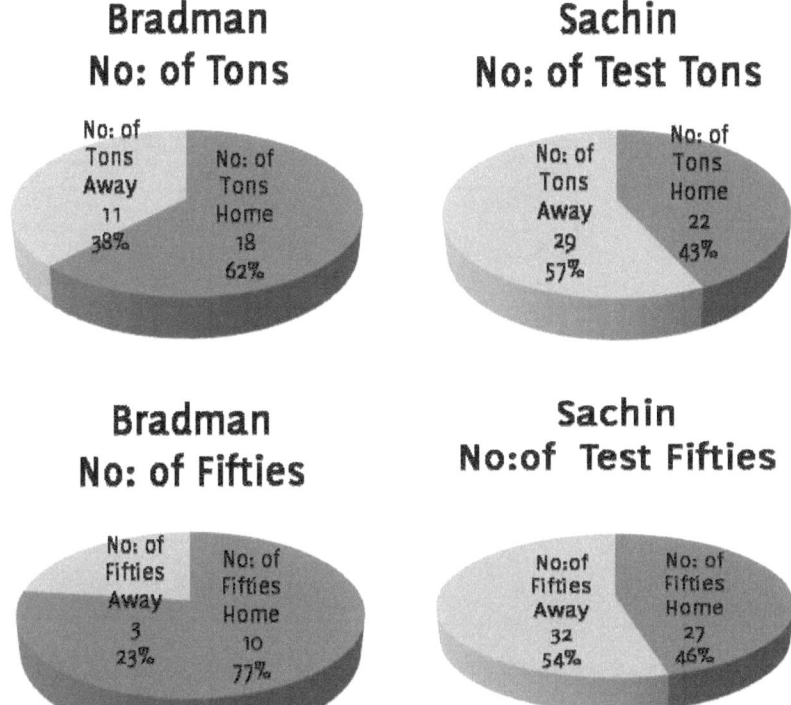

Bradman No: of Tons

No: of Tons Away 11 38%

No: of Tons Home 18 62%

Sachin No: of Test Tons

No: of Tons Away 29 57%

No: of Tons Home 22 43%

Bradman No: of Fifties

No: of Fifties Away 3 23%

No: of Fifties Home 10 77%

Sachin No:of Test Fifties

No:of Fifties Away 32 54%

No: of Fifties Home 27 46%

Millions of hardened Sachin fans are convinced that he has had it easy, that he has scored the majority of his fifties and hundreds on 'comfortable' Indian pitches in front of home crowds. Well, actually Sachin's reality has been a little different.

Table B: 'Away/Neutral ground' Test performance

Batsman	Tests	"Away or neutral" Tests as % of all Tests played	100s	"Away/neutral" Tons as % of all Tons scored	50s	"Away/neutral" fifties as % of all fifties scored
Sachin	177	98 (55%)	51	29 (57%)	59	32 (54%)
Ponting	152	69 (45%)	39	18 (46%)	56	22 (39%)
Steve Waugh	168	79 (47%)	32	17 (53%)	50	20 (40%)
Kallis	145	68 (47%)	40	19 (48%)	54	23 (43%)
Lara	131	66 (50%)	34	17 (50%)	48	22 (46%)

Note: as of 6 January 2011.

Sachin's fans, forget about his critics, would do well to look at the table above. On every count of batting excellence – particularly against hostile odds, Sachin towers above the rest.

- His 'away' Test exposure is 5-10% higher than the others.

- His 'away' Test ton performance is 4-11% higher than the others.

- His 'away' Test fifties performance is 8-15% higher than the others.

Batting position

When you are tying on your pads in the pavilion you are in a slightly awkward position to shape the outcome of your team's Test innings. The longer you take to get on to the field, the more awkward that position.

Bradman built his records by batting in 3rd position 70% of the time (56 innings in 3rd position out of 80 innings). Sachin batted in 4th position 82% of the time (237 innings in 4th position out of 290 Test innings). Bradman had the greater comfort of compiling his records by coming earlier on in the innings, almost right through his career.

Bradman had more batsmen coming after him, more time to settle in, greater scope to shape the team's innings and with the team being only 'one down' was under less pressure. Sachin had fewer batsmen after him, less time to settle in and less scope to shape the team's innings and with the team being 'two down' was under more pressure.

Rudolph Lambert Fernandez

In ODI cricket Sachin has faced a great challenge. Coming earlier on in the innings for most of his career (1st or 2nd position in 319 matches out of 442 matches), he has managed the new ball and scorching pitches. He has dealt with fresh-faced bowlers spitting balls like shotguns at one end while coping with a frequently crumbling Indian middle-order at the other. That said, in at least 97 matches he has come lower down - at 4th or 5th position. It is no small miracle that he has managed to carve out such an incredible ODI record while carrying the team on his shoulders for most of the way.

Sachin is the one who has been tested the most and excelled in the most trying circumstances. Sadly, the fury with which he is often denounced grows with each passing year:

Writer Mukul Kesavan once wrote that the only cricketer who could be called the 'God' of cricket was 'the aforementioned Bradman'. He appeared convinced that Sachin was not foremost, even in the **second** rung of batting greats below Bradman.[16]

With that sobering reminder about 'the aforementioned', let us press on.

---

[16] *Why the 100th does not matter*; Mukul Kesavan, *ESPNcricinfo, 3* December 2011.

CHAPTER 5

Welter To Super Heavy-Weight – The Other Corner – Part 1

BODYLINE, BOWLING GREATNESS IN TEST CRICKET

SIMON BRIGGS, IN HIS ARTICLE in the Wisden Almanack 2003, titled *The 21st Century Coaching book, different strokes for different times,* pointed out how the modern era demanded much more than artistry. He said that new age players needed to be sharp and flexible and could not afford to be predictable. He singled out Sachin because he, more than any other player, had proved his greatness by coming up with innovative tactics every few years.

The *Bodyline* series of 1932-33 is seen as one of the most wretched in cricket history. Tragically, those tactics targeted the most prolific batsman of that era. Bradman stood up to the attack with the steel he was known to possess – without excessive protective gear. He overcame the brief storm but thanks to the public outcry, the storm was indeed brief; more flash-flood than deluge.

Sachin fans habitually refer to an incident at Sialkot in December 1989. The ball struck the 16-year old Sachin. Bleeding from the nose, he fought on. It was his first encounter with world-class pace and hostile bowling tactics. It wasn't his last. Over the first two years of his career he faced the fiercest teams in Pakistan, England and Australia, away from the comfort of crowds and cheers in India. From time to time, there is noise about the 2001 India-England matches with critics labelling the infamous Nasser Hussain tactics against Sachin, *Bodyline II*.

But the fuss over Bodyline, especially from historians who see the 1930s through a gilt-edged frame, suggests an inexcusable naiveté. Men like Larwood stood spectacularly accused precisely because such tactics were unheard of at that time – their deployment was exceptional not routine.

Duncan Hamilton, Larwood's biographer wondered whether Bodyline was really 'unscrupulous' or just 'lateral thinking that stretched the rules'. He wrote of how Archie Jackson denounced the whining of the Australians; Jackson seemed certain that they could easily have dealt with Larwood by improvising – hooking, pulling or simply using intelligent footwork.[17]

In the late 20th century, bowling through clenched teeth – short pitched or otherwise – was commonplace. Such practitioners were rewarded not reviled.

In December 1974, England were facing Australia in a Test. Storms had flooded the grounds just two days before the match. The pitch was uneven but the English still fancied their chances. Until a typhoon of a different kind broke – Jeff Thomson, bowling like a man possessed, cracked Dennis Amiss's thumb in England's first innings and took three vital wickets. Thomson at the start of his run-up may have looked a bit like a rogue bomber in the Brisbane sky, settling into a position before a sortie. When he returned for another innings, Thomson grimly proceeded to strip England man by man, 'bowling' four men out; he finished with 6 wickets for 46 runs. No one seemed stunned that Australia won.

Pain, pride, punishment (or the prospect of it) are just a few of the sparks needed to light a pacer's fire. Batsmen struck by venomous deliveries are not always able to pick the reason for a bowler's fury but they are left in no doubt as to the result. India's Anshuman Gaekwad will testify to that, having taken several hits in Jamaica against the West Indies in April 1976. Under Michael Holding's savage assault, Brijesh Patel hit on the mouth and Gaekwad on his temple were forced to retire hurt. Gundappa Viswanath had his finger fractured and dislocated. India declared their first innings closed not because they felt that 306 on the board was challenge enough for the West Indian batsmen: they wanted to protect their bowlers Bedi and Chandrasekhar from injury!

---

[17] *Harold Larwood* (*It Wasn't Your Fault*, Harold; Page 177, Chapter 7); Duncan Hamilton, Quercus, Paperback Edition 2010 (published 2009).

A year later it was Lillee. Hamilton in his book on Larwood wrote of how astonished Larwood was, watching the Centenary Test in 1977. Derek Randall was hit by Lillee and Rick McCosker by Willis. Larwood turned and told his mate Bill Bowes, seated next to him, that the new age bowlers were bowling more bouncers in a single Test than he had ever bowled in an entire season.

In July 1981, Bob Willis's supersonic spell at Headingley ripped through the Australian attack. It handed him a career-best 8 wickets for 43... and England, sweet victory.

A few years later it was Malcolm Marshall. In the 1984 Test series against the West Indies, England's Andy Lloyd was the victim. He had been England's top scorer in two of the three ODIs that season but in the very first Test was struck by a Marshall delivery. Andy was hospitalised for over a week. He had scored over 17,000 first class runs, but he never played for England again.

At Perth in Jan/Feb 1993, the 6' 8" inch Curtly Ambrose tore through the Australians like a twister, wrapping up their first innings with seven wickets for 25 runs in 18 overs; nine were maidens. A horrifyingly fast 32-ball spell from Ambrose conceded just one run. One!

Ian Bishop then fired alongside Ambrose and managed two wickets for 17 runs in 11 overs; 6 were maidens. Australian veterans Border and Boon were sent back in the same over; Boon's off-stump wrenched from the pitch by the sheer force of a Bishop bullet. In the second innings, the mirthless Ambrose twister passed over Perth again; he bowled 21 overs of which 8 were maidens. By then the damage had been done. The West Indies won by more than an innings. Ambrose, for his sins, was declared *Player of the Match* and *Player of the Series*.

Devon Malcolm's spell against South Africa at The Oval in August 1994 is recalled more for its ferocity than its figures. Having been struck on the helmet by a Fanie de Villiers delivery while holding the bat earlier on, Malcolm seized the ball with a vengeance and unleashed a volley that will stay in South African memory for a long, long time. As they trooped in to bat out their second innings against England, Malcolm ploughed through the South Africans like a farm-harvester gone berserk. Brian McMillan was hit hard. Jonty Rhodes, hit on the helmet, had to retire hurt and be taken to hospital. Daryl Cullinan was the only South African not to be dismissed by Malcolm. Eventually, Malcolm ended his violent run with nine wickets for 57 off 16.3 overs and the *Man of the Match* award.

Rudolph Lambert Fernandez

In October 2002, Shoaib Akhtar's scorchers decimated the Australian attack in the Test at Colombo. Once, in a space of 15 balls he had taken five wickets. In another innings he had three wickets in four balls. Pakistan lost the match but Shoaib's atheistic cameo brought them within licking distance of a victory.

A year later, in October 2003, Shoaib was at it again in a Test against South Africa in Lahore. His deliveries were flying in at their usual scary pace when Gary Kirsten tried to hook one and missed. The ball smacked Gary's visor with such force that blood gushed out; his broken nose and damaged eye socket needed ten stitches.

In March 2009, South Africa were up against Australia in a Test at Durban. Australia put up a spirited 352 in the first innings. Then some barbarous bowling from Mitchell Johnson choked the South Africans. They never quite recovered. One delivery broke Graeme Smith's knuckle, throwing him out of both match and series (Johnson had done something similar to him only a few matches ago). Jacques Kallis had to have three stitches on a bloody chin. Others barely got by with their elbows, hips, ribs and jaws intact. Their batsmen may have laid the foundation but Johnson's pillage had a lot to do with the Australian victory.

What's the point of this flashback?

The 1930s Larwood was a loner – and duly cursed. These men from the 1970s (and since) were a crowd – and duly celebrated. Larwood's 'unbecoming' behaviour stood out in peaceful Eden; its law-abiding citizens, appropriately aghast, hung him out to dry. But new-age gladiators unleashed a fusillade so terrifying it was unmatched by anything seen before – in intensity or intent. They performed in an arena where violence was the norm. If a gladiator was brutally struck, the crazed spectators stepped out merely to fill their cups. They always returned in haste to applaud the anarchy below.

Purists point to the 'comfort' of excessive protection and the alleged impact on scoring.

But the greatest fast, fast-medium and medium-paced seam bowlers emerged *after* Bradman. No wonder 'protection' came into its own in the latter half of the 20th century. There simply wasn't a strong enough or consistently enough 'felt need' in the first half of the century. Yes, Bradman sorely needed it (and did not have the benefit) during the Bodyline series. He showed courage in tackling the threat, however brief, without it. His brief encounter with intimidatory bowling was a dampener but it remained just that – a brief encounter. For most of his career, excessive protection was redundant, because of the leisurely pace at which cricket was played and the relatively indulgent nature of cricket competitiveness at the time.

Ask the victims of Lee, Walsh, Akram, Akhtar, Vaas, McGrath, Younis, Ambrose, Bishop, Devon Malcolm and Mitchell Johnson and they will shake their heads – protection is no guarantee. Of course Sachin was 'protected' but it did little to quieten fears about getting hit – he was hit in his debut Test series as a 16-year old. On the field he has seen peers get hit in nearly every series around the world for over 20 years. In the drawing room he may have watched footage of predecessors being hit in the 1970s and 80s. Small consolation when he padded up.

Others see excessive protection as a liability that limits the freedom and speed with which a batsman can play a wide enough range of shots. They also suggest that it restricts movement when running between the wickets. Either way, it is perhaps far-fetched to suggest that Bradman would have scored twice as many runs if he was 'protected' or that Sachin would have scored half as many if he wasn't.

Thankfully, there is a growing, if grudging, recognition that far too much was made of England's tactics against Bradman. Besides, many of the injuries during that 1932-33 Ashes were sustained when bowlers were not bowling Bodyline.

Gideon Haigh wondered about modern era batsmen who had been 'skewered by pace from four prongs'. If they could tackle such hostile bowling, could Bodyline have been as catastrophic as it was made out to be?

In a 2007 article, Haigh wrote that the belligerence displayed by modern players was more 'calculated and cruel' than the worst possible 'attack' in the early or mid 20th century.[18]

In hindsight, *Bodyline* offered Bradman and his peers a chance to become finer batsmen, compelling them to get out of their comfort zone, demanding from them a wider, more imaginative range of stroke-play. Apart from that pocket of turbulence, Bradman's short flight from 0 to 50 Tests was, largely, pleasant. Sachin, on the other hand, has faced unconcealed aggression from the time he put on his pads and he has, almost always, come out the better for it.

---

[18] *A tactic of its time: why Jardine's leg theory was almost uniquely a product of its age;* Gideon Haigh, *ESPNcricinfo Magazine*, 22 October 2007.

Rudolph Lambert Fernandez

Bowling greatness

Wally Hammond, Hedley Verity and Bill Edrich were bowling foes for most of Bradman's career – all Englishmen. Their faces, manner, body-language, strategy and skill were rarely new and he sorted them out soon enough – unsurprisingly, given that he saw English bowlers most of the time.

Sachin's bowling environment has, in comparison, been more Rainforest than Raccoon Park. Here is a list of the better bowlers he has faced since he started playing international cricket as a 16-year-old boy: Curtly Ambrose, Wasim Akram, Abdul Qadir, Ian Bishop, Brett Lee, Bruce Reid, Dale Steyn, Hanse Cronje, Chris Cairns, Chris Harris, Allan Donald, Andrew Flintoff, Jason Gillespie, Darren Gough, Richard Hadlee, Roger Harper, Carl Hooper, Imran Khan, Sanath Jayasuriya, Danish Kaneria, Jacques Kallis, Craig McDermott, Glenn McGrath, Muttiah Muralitharan, Malcolm Marshall, Merv Hughes, Makhaya Ntini, Heath Streak, Saqlain Mushtaq, Shaun Pollock, Shoaib Akhtar, Chaminda Vaas, Daniel Vettori, Courtney Walsh, Shane Warne, Waqar Younis, Shane Bond.

The mention of some of these names conjures up troubling images for even the most accomplished batsmen. Whether fast or slow bowlers, they were among the best practitioners who focused on the basics – line, length, accuracy, movement in the air, economy, effectiveness.

Given the range and pace of cricket that Sachin has played and the profusion of quality bowling in his era, one can easily imagine him standing at one end and facing a succession of the most dangerous bowlers in *a single over*.

Table C: Bowling greatness in Test cricket

Non-Australian bowlers in Bradman's era, when competition was, to put it mildly, limited.	Measure of bowling greatness	Non-Indian bowlers in Sachin's era; when competition was at its fiercest ever.
None *No bowler* from that era had over 155 wickets (Tate ended with only 155, Verity with only 144, Voce with only 98 and Larwood with just 78). Even Bedser ended with only 236.	**Experience and consistency: career haul of over 300 Test wickets**	Sixteen non-Indian bowlers have over 300 wickets, some well over 500: Muralitharan (800 wickets), Warne (708), McGrath (563), Walsh (519), Hadlee (431), Pollock (421), Akram (414), Ambrose (405), Ntini (390), Marshall (376), Younis (373), Imran (362), Vaas (355), Vettori (345), Donald (330), Brett Lee (310). Note: In ODIs too, Sachin's bowling rivals have been 'experience and consistency' personified: Muralitharan has bagged 534 wickets, Akram 502, Younis 416, Vaas 400, Pollock 393, McGrath 381, Brett Lee 357, Jayasuriya 322.
None No such rival bowlers in the Bradman years. The few (Mailey, Trumble and Noble) who did it were – thankfully for Bradman – all Australian.	**Experience and consistency: 50 or more Test wickets in a single year**	**Around two dozen** of the world's most consistent non-Indian Test bowlers, many of whom boast of a huge single-year wicket haul: Warne (96 wickets in a year), Muralitharan (90), Donald (80), Steyn (74).

Rudolph Lambert Fernandez

S F Barnes did it for England but retired 14 years before Bradman arrived.		Sachin has hammered the lot of them including Pollock (69 wickets in a year), McGrath (68), Flintoff (68), Walsh (66), Mitchell Johnson (63), Imran (62), Ntini (59), Vaas (58), Merv Hughes (57), MacGill (57), Brett Lee (57), McDermott (56), Younis (55), Gillespie (55), Swann (54), Vettori (54), Mushtaq (51).
One But this is misleading. Over his brief Test career of 8 matches, TWJ Goddard bowled to Bradman in only one match (25 July 1930); the rest of his career was against New Zealand, South Africa and West Indies. Note: *MJC Allom, who also had a hat-trick never played Test cricket against Australia and ended his 'career' after 5 Tests.*	**Effectiveness: Hat-tricks in a Test career**	Close to twenty The list includes bowling legends such as Walsh, Warne, Akram (two hat-tricks in a single year) and McGrath. It also includes others such as Merv Hughes, Damien Fleming, Dominic Cork, Darren Gough, Nuwan Zoysa, Abdul Razzaq, Stuart Broad, James Franklin, Matthew Hoggard, Andy Blignaut, Alok Kapali, Jermaine Lawson, Mohammad Sami, Peter Petherick and Ryan Sidebottom. Note: *Before Bradman started playing, seven bowlers had won hat-tricks from 1878 right up until 1912, just before the First World War, but only two bowlers from his era ever recorded a hat-trick, only one of them bowled to him - in only one match. Sachin has had no such luck, his era has been populated with hat-trickers.*

Bedser got his 236 wickets from 51 matches and Bill Voce got his 98 wickets from 27 matches. Both Englishmen bowled in an era when there was only one rival worth the name – Australia.	**Prolific and effective bowling**	Playing in cricket's most explosive era, Dale Steyn got his 238 wickets from 46 Tests and Kenny Benjamin got his 92 wickets from 26 Tests. Both bowled at a time when the 'world' was playing cricket and they bowled to an army of great batsmen.
One Bedser All the others bowled before Bradman arrived or, were Australian.	**Prolific: who have recorded the maximum "ten wickets in a Test match" in a bowling career.**	At least fourteen – Qadir, Muralitharan, Warne, Younis, Akram, Steyn, Ntini, Saqlain Mushtaq, Mushtaq Ahmed, Donald, Ambrose, Vettori, McGrath and Walsh. Sachin has been consistently tested by the most prolific and most effective bowlers in the world, right through his career.
None Apparently no record exists of this ever having happened in Tests before 1950.	**Prolific: Dismissed an entire team of 11 batsmen (across both innings of a Test match).**	**Three.** In the history of Test bowling only six bowlers have done this: One was Indian. (Venkataraghavan) Two played before Sachin. (England's Laker and Australia's Dymock) Sachin has hammered the other three – Qadir, Younis and Muralitharan.

Sachin – Bowlers he has had to face with over 300 Test career wickets

Bradman – Bowlers with over 300 Test career wickets

NONE.

Only one rival bowler from Bradman's era had a haul of over 155 wickets – Alec Bedser (he ended with 236 wickets).The others, who were far more successful, were all Australian.

Sachin – Bowlers who have taken the maximum 10 wickets in a Test

Bradman – Bowlers who have taken the maximum 10 wickets in a Test

One! Only one rival bowler from Bradman's era had ever taken ten wickets in a match – Alec Bedser.

The late 20th century bowlers were not just better than their predecessors, they represented an entirely new breed, a new calibre of bowling that had never been seen before.

There is a difference between the power of a 600bhp diesel locomotive from the 1930s and that of the late 20th century 44,000,000bhp Space Shuttle Endeavour. One faces – and overpowers – far greater resistance.

Still, let us take a closer look at the vast difference in the bowling challenge.

Rudolph Lambert Fernandez

CHAPTER 6

Welter To Super Heavy-Weight – The Other Corner – Part 2

C & B, EFFECTIVENESS, EXPERIENCE, BOWLING AVERAGE, BOWLED

Caught-and-bowled

RETURN CATCHES ARE A SIGN of a bowler's athleticism. They are also a sign of his skill, an admission by the batsman of his inability to drive, pull, cut, edge, hook, loft or effectively pad the ball away from the carpet. They reflect a helplessness that forces the batsman to meekly lob the ball into the hands of a cunning bowler.

Many great bowlers are among those who have been most successful at 'caught-and-bowled', having taken *ten or more* Test wickets this way.

- Harbhajan Singh and Anil Kumble are both Indian; naturally, Sachin never faced them in Tests.

- Two played in the 19th century, Giffen and Trumble – both Australian anyway; naturally, Bradman never faced them in Tests.

- Six came after Bradman and before Sachin – Derek Underwood, Richie

Benaud, Lance Gibbs, Hedley Howarth, Hugh Tayfield and Tony Greig. All effective bowlers and a testament to the vastly superior bowling in the mid or late 20th century, when compared to the relatively docile bowling in Bradman's era.

- But Sachin has faced all the others – Muralitharan (35 such return-catch Test dismissals), Warne (21), Vettori (20), Danish Kaneria (11), Paul Adams (10), Richard Hadlee (10). Muralitharan was perhaps the best of all; apart from his record in Tests, he has 34 such "return catch" dismissals in ODIs.

- Only one played during the Bradman years. Luckily for Bradman, that was fellow-Australian, Clarrie Grimmett.

Sachin has had his innings cut short by a mixture of devilishly effective bowling and athleticism. In spite of this vast difference in bowler competitiveness, his caught-and-bowled record is amazing, in comparison: Bradman – 4 times (from 70 dismissals), Sachin – 5 times (from 258 dismissals).

Effectiveness

Shane Warne is widely recognised one of the greatest bowlers – if not the greatest – in cricket history. While crowning him one of the *Five Cricketers of the Century*, the essay in Wisden drew attention to the Warne mystique – skill, novelty and drama – noting that John Woodcock (and others) would later record that few – if any – bowlers had the ability to 'aim the ball as precisely and turn it as far as Warne'.[19]

The most effective, most experienced, most consistent, most prolific rival bowler from Bradman's era was Alec Bedser and he took 15,918 deliveries to get his 236 wickets; most of them long after Bradman had moved on. A brief comparison with some modern-era bowlers shows they had about as many or more wickets than Bedser but with far fewer deliveries:

- Darren Gough: 229 wickets from only 11, 821 deliveries. Bradman-era bowler Hedley Verity used 11,173 deliveries (about as many as Gough did) but managed only 144 wickets – 85 wickets short of Gough's tally.

- Michael Holding: 249 wickets from 12, 680 deliveries. Bradman-era bowler Maurice Tate used 12, 523 deliveries (about as many as Holding did) but managed only 155 wickets – 94 wickets short of Holding's tally.

---

[19] *Five Cricketers of the Century* - Shane Warne, *Wisden Cricketers' Almanack 2000.*

Rudolph Lambert Fernandez

- Joel Garner: 259 wickets from 13,169 deliveries.

- Matthew Hoggard: 248 wickets from 13,909 deliveries.

- James Anderson: 240 wickets from 13,545 deliveries.

- Andrew Caddick: 234 wickets from 13,558 deliveries.

- Jason Gillespie: 259 wickets from 14,234 deliveries.

Note: figures as of 2011.

Those who bowled since the 1990s benefited from high-tech pitch scrutiny, vastly improved fielding and tighter lbw laws – happily for Bradman and his mates and unhappily for successor batting generations... and Sachin. Still, the picture above points more to an improvement in calibre of bowling than anything else. It had gone up several-fold. It had simultaneously *proliferated*. Bill Voce, for instance, bowled only 6,360 deliveries – *less than half* that bowled by most modern-era bowlers. Voce managed only 98 wickets. Even if he had bowled twice as much and secured twice as many wickets, it would still be only 196 wickets – by no means a career 'haul' in modern terms.

Experience

The more experienced you are as a bowler, the better your instincts, your judgement, your skill, your effectiveness. The more experienced you are as a bowler the more 'dangerous' you are likely to be. From the table below, McGrath and Muralitharan, Warne and Walsh were among the most dangerous Test bowlers ever.

Table D: A comparison of 'experienced and proven' Test bowlers

Non-Australian bowlers from Bradman's era; only one dominant rival	Measure of Test bowling experience	Non-Indian bowlers from Sachin's era; several established rivals
All (except two – see below).	Career of fewer than 50 matches	Well over fifteen bowlers: Steyn (46 matches), Ian Bishop (43), Shane Bond (18), Stuart MacGill (44), Paul Reiffel (35), Michael Kasprowicz (38), Phil deFreitas (44), Devon Malcolm (40), Monty Panesar (39), Shoaib Akhtar (46), Paul Adams (45), Brian McMillan (38), Pat Symcox (20), Merv Dillon (38), Kenny Benjamin (26) and many others.
Only two Bedser (51 matches) and Hammond (85 matches).	Career of 50-100 matches	Over fifteen bowlers: Ambrose (98 matches), Younis (87), Allan Donald (72), Brett Lee (76), McDermott (71), Kaneria (61), Gillespie (71), Hoggard (67), Caddick (62), Gough (58), Flintoff (79), Cairns (62), Streak (65), Merv Hughes (53)
None	Career of 100-120 matches	At least five bowlers: Shaun Pollock (108 matches), Akram (104), Ntini (101), Vaas (111), Vettori (105)
None	Career of over 120 matches	At least four bowlers: Muralitharan (133 matches), Warne (145), McGrath (124), Walsh (132).

If Test cricket history was being considered, none of the Bradman bowlers were 'experienced'. Yes, some had been around a long time, but even Bedser, was only just starting out two years before Bradman retired – he gained his experience a good seven years after Bradman had moved on.

Larwood bowled 4,969 balls; McGrath bowled 29,248 balls (in Tests alone).

Seven Bradman bowlers (Hammond, Bedser, Voce, Verity, Larwood, Leyland, Tate) had a combined experience of 304 Tests. Three Sachin bowlers (Muralitharan, Warne, Walsh) have a combined experience of 410 Tests.

Rudolph Lambert Fernandez

Ten Bradman bowlers (Allen, Edrich, Hammond, Bedser, Voce, Verity, Larwood, Leyland, Tate, White) had a combined Test haul of 971 wickets. Three Sachin bowlers (Muralitharan, McGrath and Warne) have a combined Test haul of 2,071 wickets.

Career bowling average

Career bowling average demonstrates the calibre of a bowler, in inverse proportion: the lower your career bowling average, the higher your calibre as a bowler. It reflects how you have performed (runs conceded per wicket taken), over time and against a range of great batsmen on diverse pitches.

The Bradman bowlers operated in a relatively reticent batting environment, against only one dominant rival and in just a few grounds. A study of career bowling averages demonstrates the inconceivably vast difference in quality of bowling between the two epochs.

Table E: Test bowling average (min of 2,000 balls)

Non-Australian bowlers who bowled to Bradman	Bowling average (career of at least 20 Tests)	Non-Indian bowlers who bowled to Sachin
None A sign of how easy it was for a batsman to score.	20-21	**Two** Malcolm Marshall (average 20.94) and Curtly Ambrose (average 20.99).
None	21-22	**One** Glenn McGrath (21.64)
None Yes, Bill Bowes had an average of 22.33 but his entire career was all of 15 Tests..	22-23	**Five** Allan Donald (22.25) Richard Hadlee (22.29) Imran Khan (22.81) Muttiah Muralitharan (22.65) Shane Bond (22.09)
Note: Muralitharan's average of 22.65 was over 133 matches.		

None	23-24	Four
		Shaun Pollock (23.11)
		Dale Steyn (23.70)
		Wasim Akram (23.62)
		Waqar Younis (23.56)
Two Alec Bedser (24.89) but over 51 matches. Hedley Verity (24.37) over a career of 40 matches. *Note: Walsh had an average of 24.44 over 132 matches.*	24-25	Four Courtney Walsh (24.44) Ian Bishop (24.27) Bruce Reid (24.63) Fanie de Villiers (24.27)
None A P Freeman had an average of 25.86 but his entire career was all of 12 matches. *Note: Warne had a lower average of 25.41 over 145 matches.*	25-26	At least two bowlers Shane Warne (25.41) Shoaib Akhtar (25.69)

Other Bradman bowlers are, frankly, off the chart – with bowling averages unforgivably above 26: conceding far more runs per wicket taken.

- Larwood and Allen had averages of over 28

- White and Hammond had averages of over 30; Hammond, as we will see later on, was more of a batsman anyway.

- Bill Edrich's average was 41.29; he bowled to Bradman in 14 matches.

- Compton's average was 56.40; Bradman faced him in as many as 9 matches.

Rudolph Lambert Fernandez

- Maurice Leyland's average was an inexcusable 97.50 (runs conceded per wicket taken) from 41 matches. Yet Bradman faced him in 11 matches.

> Now look at the table above in perspective. The Sachin bowlers built their low bowling averages in the fiercest environment possible, against the largest number of world-class attacking batsmen, in grounds around the world. Muralitharan, Shaun Pollock, Warne, Akram, Ambrose and Walsh built and sustained their incredibly low averages over *100 or more* Tests, compared to Bradman's bowling rivals who built their averages over far fewer matches – Bedser (only 51 Tests), Verity (only 40 Tests), Voce (27 Tests) and Larwood (21 Tests). McGrath had a mind-numbingly low average of 21.64 over a career *of 124 Tests!*

Importantly, the bowling prowess of the English team at the time was dwarfed by that of Bradman's Australian mates. The most dangerous, the most effective, the most prolific bowlers of that era were *on his team.*

See Table 14 in the Appendix, for an understanding of why Bradman was in the best bowling side of his era.

Happily for Bradman, he saw relatively meek Englishmen running toward him – not his far more lethal fellow-Australians, who were the best in the world at the time. Small wonder that Bradman ranked Australians Clarrie Grimmett and Bill O'Reilly as the toughest, most testing bowlers he faced. Sachin has had no such luxury: among the 25 highest wicket-takers in Test history, only three are Indian and among the 10 highest wicket-takers in ODI history, only one is Indian.

> Sachin has been compelled to face the best Test bowlers: they were, almost always, *in rival teams.*

Given his record against relatively celibate spin, it is perhaps just as well that Bradman did not face the likes of rapacious spinners such as Muralitharan and Warne. He did face accurate line and length but his encounter with intimidatory bowling was all too brief. If he did face 'swing' it was relatively modest as it was a good many decades before swing bowling came into its own.

Sachin and his peers have had to contend with blistering pace and devilish spin – the kind which had never been seen. They have also had to deal with lethal swing, reverse swing, the deceptive slow-ball, ball-tampering and seam-wetting, commonly used to make the ball take on a life of its own in the air. Modern tampering techniques have varied from the use of fingernails and bottlecaps to spikes, soil and Vaseline. Why, if it weren't for the wretched cameras, fielders would have merrily put a monkey wrench on the job.

Sledging that, until the 1950s and 60s, was down to sharp exchanges in the heat of the moment, had become orchestrated team tactics in the 1970s, 80s and 90s, designed to mentally destroy an attacking batsman. Wordy duels were meant not to 'let off steam' but to induce forced errors, to slow run-rates, to stimulate a quick tumble of wickets and take the pith out of a rival team. In the 1930s, competitiveness on the field was fierce, but its expression as it reached the willow was positively meek compared to what it had become in the 1970s and since.

The moving ball that Sachin thrashes into the stands comes at him at speeds, often close to 160kmph. The modern cricket ball has been honed to glide across the fastest and hardest pitches in the world, giving the batsman milliseconds between release and impact. The shorter that lead time, the better you have got to be.

In Wisden Cricketer's Almanack 2010, in a compelling article entitled *Cricket and the brain: KP and the case for neural plasticity*, Michael Armstrong-James argued that better batsmen assess a range of clues that indicate ball velocity, line and bounce. He said that the best batsmen can gauge length as well, giving them the time they need to pick between playing straight or across.

In August 1998, Sachin met Bradman at his home in Adelaide. Among other things, they reportedly discussed technique. Bradman is believed to have asked Sachin if he moved before a delivery. Sachin was unable to tackle the question. Bradman, however, appeared convinced that Sachin did move before the ball left the bowler's hand or it would have been impossible to score as he did.

Bowler dominance – 'bowling' a batsman out

Perhaps the truest sign of a bowler's dominance is to get a batsman dismissed by *bowling him out*. It beats getting him lbw, caught-at-slips, caught-behind, caught mid-field or in the deep, run-out, stumped or hit-wicket. A sign of the batsman's inability in spotting the ball out of the bowler's fingers, picking it while it is in the air and dealing with it as it hurtles toward the crease. Bowling a batsman out has nothing to do with lbw legislation, quality of fielding or intrusive umpiring. Bowlers who have a high record of bowling batsmen out are among the best ever. Now, dozens of great Test bowlers claim the top spot for having bowled out batsmen the most (50 or more wickets taken this way)

- Only two bowled to Bradman. Bedser, who bagged 70 wickets, and Tate, who bagged 59 wickets by castling batsmen.

- Sachin has faced many including Muttiah Muralitharan, Shane Warne, Waqar Younis, Wasim Akram, Courtney Walsh, Curtly Ambrose, Glenn McGrath, Makhaya Ntini, Brett Lee, Shoaib Akhtar, Allan Donald, Richard Hadlee, Imran Khan, Malcolm Marshall, Dale Steyn, Shaun Pollock, James Anderson. That's already seventeen quality bowlers... to Bradman's two.

- The rest of the bowlers happen to be Indian or played before Sachin debuted in 1989. None of the main Bradman bowlers figure in this elite list – not Hammond, not Voce, not Larwood, not Verity.

- Muralitharan and Warne have been frighteningly effective in this respect; 167 and 116 wickets respectively, by bowling batsmen out.

Note: figures as of 2011.

In ODIs, three bowlers tower above the rest in the number of times they have had a batsman bowled – Akram (176 wickets), Younis (151) and Muralitharan (120). Sachin has played all three of them.

Out of every 100 balls Bradman faced, nearly 80 were being thrown at him by an Englishman. Out of every 100 runs he scored, over 70 were against England. Of all bowlers who bowled to Bradman in six or over six matches of his career all were Englishmen. No bowler from South Africa, India or the West Indies bowled to him in over five matches. Therefore, let us look at the Englishmen who bowled to Bradman.

Table F: The 'Bradman bowlers':

'Bradman' Bowler	Matches as a Test bowler	Balls bowled in Test matches	Test wickets taken	Career bowling Average (runs conceded between dismissals)	Matches (bowled against Bradman's Australia)
Hammond	85	7,969	83	37.80	24
Verity	40	11,173	144	24.37	17
Edrich	39	3,234	41	41.29	14
Larwood	21	4,969	78	28.35	11
Leyland	41	1,103	6	97.50	11
Allen	25	4,386	81	29.37	11
Bedser	51	15,918	236	24.89	10
Voce	27	6,360	98	27.88	10
Yardley	20	1,662	21	33.66	10
Wright	34	8,135	108	39.11	9
Tate	39	12,523	155	26.16	9
Compton	78	2,710	25	56.40	9
Farnes	15	3,932	60	28.65	8
Bowes	15	3,655	68	22.33	6
Geary	14	3,810	46	29.41	6
Robins	19	3,318	64	27.46	6
White	15	4,801	49	32.26	5

- Only six bowlers came at Bradman in over ten matches.

- Only three (Hammond, Compton and Bedser) ended up bowling in 50 or more Tests (which in Sachin's language would be 'experience of at least 3-4 years in Test cricket').

- Only three (Verity, Bedser, Bowes) had a career bowling average of 26 or lower. At least eighteen bowlers who have bowled to Sachin have a career bowling average of 26 or lower.

- Only one bowler (Bedser) ended with over 155 wickets – to be called experienced or prolific or both. And he would pick up most of his wickets after Bradman had moved on.

For all the fuss about Larwood, he saw Bradman in only 11 matches and had stopped playing in 1933; Bradman played for another seven years

Rudolph Lambert Fernandez

(excluding his non-playing years) without Larwood around. Hammond and Verity were still bowling to Bradman seven years after Larwood had moved into quiet notoriety. Larwood had a gorgeous action from run-up to follow-through but he was nowhere near as effective as the Australian bowlers of his era or the Englishmen who would follow him.

Bedser arrived in the twilight of Bradman's career and therefore benefited the most from tighter lbw laws: he secured the highest number (among Bradman bowlers) of lbw decisions – as many as 27. He also benefited from improved fielding; well over half his dismissals involved getting batsmen 'caught'. The majority of Bradman bowlers, including Tate, Larwood, Verity, Hammond and Leyland had more of a struggle than Bedser and Voce: they bowled to Bradman before tight lbw legislation came into force.

Table G: Was Bradman ever severely and consistently tested by bowlers?

Phases	Why Bradman's bowling challenge was never a severe or consistent test
Vs England Phase I Nov 1928 – Aug 1930: Bradman's first extended session with England – his first nine matches were successive matches against a single team.	■ Bowlers included Hammond, White, Leyland and Geary but only two quality specialists – Larwood and Tate. Hammond was more of a batsman; his career bowling average was 37.80. White's career was all of 15 matches and he faced Bradman in just 5. Leyland managed just 6 wickets after a career of 41 matches and ended with an inexcusable career bowling average of 97.50. Geary's career was all of 14 matches and he faced Bradman in just 6. ■ Two years is a long time to be playing a single team. Bradman was more than familiar with Larwood and Tate; he scored 21% of his runs and played 18% of his matches in this phase. ■ Liberal lbw laws meant Bradman (and fellow-batsmen of that era) could enjoy themselves.
Vs others: Dec 1930 – Jan 1932	■ Bradman's brief sabbatical from world-class bowling involved him hammering weaklings like the West Indies and South Africa. ■ Liberal lbw laws remained

Vs England Phase II: Dec 1932 – Aug 1938: 17 successive matches over five years, against a single team. Bradman's bowling pack fell away, in turn.	■ Larwood disappeared in 1933; Tate had already stopped bowling at Bradman in 1930. ■ Only two quality bowlers stayed with Bradman – Verity and Voce. Verity dismissed Bradman eight times. ■ The rest were good but not great; fortunately for Bradman, they included Hammond and Leyland, whom he had mastered already. Voce played only 27 matches but ended with an unflattering bowling average of about 28. ■ Playing a single team over five years, Bradman could comfortably get on top of Verity and Voce. Barring the lone Bodyline series, Larwood did not trouble Bradman in this phase, as he had sorted him out from playing England – and no one else – for two years in Phase I. ■ Liberal lbw laws meant he simply tired out bowlers. Things began to change, but only as late as 1937-38, and slowly. But Bradman was a few matches away from retirement.
Vs England Phase III: After the War, Bradman played England in ten matches – in 1946, 1947 and 1948.	■ Voce and Hammond kept bowling for what it was worth. ■ The only world-class bowler to consistently take on Bradman in this period was Bedser. He dismissed him six times in ten matches but came on a little too late to have an impact on Bradman's figures. ■ The other bowlers were relatively mediocre and included Compton, Wright and Yardley. ■ Bradman's brief sabbatical from experienced bowling involved the Indians... and he thoroughly enjoyed himself.

At any given phase of Bradman's career – and this is vital – he faced only one or two quality bowlers; the rest were a mix of good to relatively mediocre bowlers. In all there were only a few genuinely high-calibre specialists to take him on consistently over his brief 50-match career, and they were all

Rudolph Lambert Fernandez

Englishmen (the best were Australian anyway). Bradman, who was without doubt in a class of his own, dealt effectively with this select group and cannot be faulted for enjoying himself with the relatively untested bowling that came at him for the bulk of his career.

Sachin has faced the craftiest, most experienced, most effective, most prolific, most consistent bowlers in cricket history. The same cannot honestly be said of Bradman. Sachin has performed against the most successful bowlers from all Test and ODI playing nations, having had to deal with a *band* of them in nearly every match. If he ever prayed to see off a high quality left-arm spinner, his prayer was quickly answered with a deadly right-arm pacer running toward him. If he ever prayed to see off a talented team, his prayer was quickly answered with another high-calibre bunch attacking his every move.

Muralitharan holds the record for the most consecutive 10-wicket hauls in a Test. He did this across four matches in 2001; against India, Bangladesh and the West Indies. Then, just in case critics imagined it was a fluke, the man went ahead and repeated the feat across another four matches in 2006, against England and South Africa.

Glenn McGrath holds the ODI record for the highest number of wickets in a Series – 27 wickets in the 1998-99 Series (against England and Sri Lanka). Then, just in case critics thought that was a fluke he went ahead and did something similar in the 2006/07 ICC World Cup, bagging 26 wickets. McGrath has the highest ever Test wicket tally among the world's fast bowlers.

Table H: Sachin was tested by bowlers – severely and consistently

Phase	Why Sachin's bowling challenge has been one serious test after another
1989-1990	As a boy, over an eventful span of international cricket away from India, he faced some of the most dangerous bowlers: Imran Khan, Richard Hadlee, Abdul Qadir, Waqar Younis, Wasim Akram, Sanath Jayasuriya. Others he faced included Phil DeFreitas, Devon Malcolm and Danny Morrison. Remember his first 32 Tests were on 32 different grounds and his first 20 Tests (barring the lone Test in Chandigarh in 1990 (against Sri Lanka) were "away".

1991-1992	Over two years, he continued to see Younis, Akram, Jayasuriya and others but he also began to see a new set of dangerous bowlers: Malcolm Marshall, Allan Donald, Shane Warne, Ian Botham, Craig McDermott, Bruce Reid, Curtly Ambrose, Ian Bishop, Winston Benjamin, Patrick Patterson, Merv Hughes. Others he faced included Hanse Cronje, Mike Whitney, Craig Matthews, Brian McMillan, Carl Hooper, Phil Simmons, Tom Moody, Eddo Brandes, Kepler Wessels, Derek Pringle, Chris Harris, Fanie de Villiers, Chris Cairns.
1993-1998	Over the next five years he continued to see many from the earlier phases but he also began to see a newer set of world-class bowling: Muttiah Muralitharan, Courtney Walsh, Kenny Benjamin, Roger Harper, Glenn McGrath, Chaminda Vaas, Shaun Pollock, Daniel Vettori, Heath Streak, Nuwan Zoysa, Damien Fleming, Lance Klusener, Paul Adams, Jacques Kallis, Saqlain Mushtaq, Jason Gillespie, Darren Gough, Paul Strang, Merv Dillon, Mike Kasprowicz.
1999 onwards and into the 21st century	After over a decade of playing against the best bowlers in the world, he kept seeing many bowlers from the 1990s but he also began to see a newer set: Brett Lee, Shoaib Akhtar, Dale Steyn, Andrew Flintoff, Makhaya Ntini, Shane Bond, Danish Kaneria, Matthew Hoggard, James Anderson, Steve Harmison.

Seventeen of the Bradman bowlers together bowled 99,658 balls. Three of the Sachin bowlers (Muralitharan, Warne and McGrath) have together bowled 113,992 balls in Test cricket alone (forget about their ODI deliveries).

Australian bowler Stuart Clark once wrote of Sachin's ability to drive bowlers and captains nuts, his wristy style giving him power to play the same shot three times but sending the ball to three different spots on each occasion.

In 2012, Clark wrote that if the ball was straight Sachin would shoot it to square. If a fielder was then shifted to square, Sachin would drive to mid-wicket. If a further fielder was brought up Sachin would simply tap the ball elsewhere.[20]

---

[20] *Tendulkar, a fine combination of willpower and willow magic*; Stuart Clark, *Sydney Morning Herald*, 3 January 2012.

Rudolph Lambert Fernandez

Purists point to the weight and size of bats and their alleged impact on scoring. Bradman's bat was said to weigh about 1kg; Sachin's about 2.5kg. But in the larger scheme of things, the significance – of a bat – is probably exaggerated. 'Light', 'heavy', 'lighter', 'heavier' – a great batsman's intent and ingenuity ultimately decide whether his bat is an asset or a liability.

Others did use heavier bats in Bradman's era. Many used lighter bats in Sachin's era. A lighter bat was Bradman's choice; a heavier bat was Sachin's. Neither of them felt it was a 'playing condition' imposed on them or they would have changed tactics after their debut Test series. If anything, a heavier bat may have restricted Sachin's ability to consistently hit alpine scores – a double or triple hundred, for instance. A heavier bat is also a liability if you have to play delicate strokes, a wide enough range of strokes and worse, carry the wretched thing through 650 international matches.

Bradman's peers and predecessors happily hit huge sixes, with the relatively light bats of that era. Sachin and his club-carrying peers weren't gifted 12 runs just because their 'six' flew higher than the non-striker's. They weren't granted 8 runs just because their 'four' flew to the fence faster than the non-striker's.

Bradman and his batting peers faced some challenges little known to the modern era. Bowlers of that era frequently over-stepped the crease and could send down bouncers as they pleased. Uncovered pitches made 'reading' the ball more unpredictable, even dangerous. However, on balance, the tables in this chapter and the previous one suggest that Bradman and his batting mates had it far, far easier. In summary, not a single bowler, among those who bowled consistently at Bradman had:

- A haul of 155+ wickets (except Bedser); 17 Sachin bowlers had 300+
- A haul of 50+ wickets in a year; some 24 Sachin bowlers qualify
- A hat-trick (except T W J Goddard); at least 19 Sachin bowlers qualify
- Dismissed an entire team; at least 3 Sachin bowlers qualify
- A haul of 10+ 'caught-and-bowled' dismissals; 7 Sachin bowlers qualify
- A haul of 50+ 'bowled' dismissals in a year; at least 17 Sachin bowlers qualify
- A career of 100+ Tests; at least 9 Sachin bowlers qualify
- A career bowling average below 24 (except Bill Bowes); at least 12 Sachin bowlers qualify

If little or no protection, lighter bats, bouncer fests and tailor-made 'bowler' pitches were so in favour of the Bradman bowlers, how come they seemed so ineffective in comparison? Bowlers from the 1980s, 1990s and 2000s faced tighter bouncer laws, bowled on 'truer' pitches to batsmen with heavier bats and excessive protection. Still, they were far more effective.

Sachin has mastered an incomparably wider, deadlier range of bowling. He has faced the greatest pace, spin, right-arm and left-arm bowlers in cricket history. He has faced those with the highest career wicket-hauls, the best career bowling averages, the best record in 'bowling out' batsmen, the best 'caught and bowled' record, the best innings figures, the best Test match figures, the highest number of wickets in a single year, the highest number of wickets in an ODI Series, the most consecutive '10-wickets in a Test match'. He has faced the most prolific Test and ODIs bowlers ever.

If Bradman was a bit like a welter-weight who had wandered into the bantam or fly-weight arena, Sachin was a bit like a welter-weight who put on heavy-weight gloves and strode right into the arena where he felt he belonged – the super heavy-weight ring.

Edgar Rice Burroughs had a sense of perspective. Rarely was the Lord of the Jungle caught mud-wrestling with a man; the 6'2" species from across the great oceans that hugged the dark continent. Comic-book character all right, but when Tarzan was ever in battle, it was against an enormous lion, a muscular python, an angry crocodile or a great bull-ape. If he did face a man, it was usually a brute – a cruelly strong leader of a tribe or a magician with superhuman powers. Somehow there was no beauty in those great sinews struggling against an ordinary man; it was either brute or beast. If it was neither, there was usually no battle. Somehow there seemed to be no 'truth' in those thews of steel breaking into a sweat because a city-dweller had dropped in for a taste of jungle adventure. If Tarzan struggled, it had to be real. When the city-boy did drop in, he would have to quickly forget his toy-house and look for a trench; things were about to get ugly.

Rudolph Lambert Fernandez

CHAPTER 7

Field Combat – Fielders, Keepers

THE EARLY 20TH CENTURY IMAGE of gentlemen in spotless white strolling on the green, had transformed in the late 20th century to become a wave of attacking white and coloured soldiers. The game's greatest fielders have stopped near-certain runs, dismissed batsmen with stunning catches in the slips or the outfield and pulled off 'impossible' run-outs: Rhodes, Herschelle Gibbs, Cairns, Hooper, Harper, Lara, Jayasuriya, Gary Kirsten, Botham, Desmond Haynes, Kallis, Gower, De Villiers, Richie Richardson, Stephen Fleming, Mahela Jayawardene, Azharuddin, Muralitharan.

Some have stopped rivals by reputation alone – batsmen, often staying rooted to the crease, not daring to test their speed, throwing power or accuracy. Through sheer body-language, they converted an intended 'three' to a 'two', an intended 'two' to a 'single' and an intended single to 'no run'. Others have stood shoulder to shoulder with bowlers and wicket-keeper choking the run-rate, inducing a sudden fall in wickets and manufacturing maiden overs just when rival batsmen were aiming to attack. Still others have been faithful to cupping the ball at the right second – over and over again.

Not one of them was on the field when Bradman went out to play after breakfast. Not one of them came on after lunch. Not one of them remained after tea. Sachin has had these and many others prowling near pitch and boundary all day, including the best Australian 'hands' Mark Waugh, Mark Taylor, Steve Waugh, Border, Ponting, Dean Jones.

A 'fielding attack' as it is understood today, was unheard of during Bradman's era. Of course, men crowded the stumps a lot but quality fielding was only just evolving at the time. Wisden's Match Report of the First Test Match between Australia and South Africa in 1931-32 confirmed that Bradman was fortunate 'being missed off Quinn when 11 and again at 15'. The report confirmed that 'after those escapes he completely mastered the bowling'.

Captains in the 1970s and 80s were not as easily pleased with their fielders as captains before them. They sought prowess, not presence. They wanted accomplishment, not attitude. They wanted craft, not cunning. They demanded competence, not cleverness. They occasionally applauded effort over effectiveness but left no one in doubt about where the prize lay.

Captains in the 1990s were more demanding, unimpressed when their fielders skidded and swerved this way and that. All they wanted to know was: Was the job done? Was the boundary stopped? Was the 'six' picked up? Were the bails knocked down in time? The captain would often watch from the distance as his fielder scrambled off boundary boards, after valiantly failing to stop a four. He would clap in encouragement as his fielder dusted himself down. The captain would even smile, as if in solidarity, but the smile would seldom reach his eyes.

In the 1930s, diving was not standard for the men in their immaculate flannels. The most athletic fielders emerged long after Bradman had quit. The legendary Colin Bland, for instance, was a 10-year old child when Bradman retired. Return throws from the boundary that shattered the wickets were rare (if they happened at all) in the 1930s and 40s. But to today's fielder it does not matter whether the ball is flying at him near the pitch or hurtling toward the boundary. Balls, otherwise destined to reach streets outside the ground are often returned to the bowler, a second after they've left the bat. Balls that seem set to crash into the stands are frequently met an inch from the boundary and contemptuously kicked back to the outfield.

Sunil Gavaskar recalled watching a Test at Lord's with Len Hutton. Seeing David Gower at cover diving and cutting off what would have been a certain boundary, Hutton told Gavaskar that modern era cricket made it much harder for batsmen to find the gaps. Hutton confessed that he and his peers would not have been able to score the runs they did in the face of such athletic fielding.[21]

Test legends include fielders who have pulled off memorable catches, saves and run-outs. If there were good fielders from Bradman's era they were in a minority and therefore relatively helpless in checking a batsman on the rampage. The most incandescent fielding performances in cricket history have been during Sachin's era. These fielders stopped the world's best in their tracks, pulling off the most stunning catches and the most stupendous run-outs or direct-hits. Sachin has, as fielder, been part of this class action.

Table I: Field-combat - a study of Test fielders

Non-Australian fielders on Bradman's field; fielding at its meekest: One dominant rival – England	Fielding greatness	Non-Indian fielders on Sachin's field, when fielding was at its fiercest with at least 7-8 established world Test teams
None Happily for Bradman, the only fielder from this list, VY Richardson, was Australian.	Top five fielders with the most catches in a Test innings (5 catches in an innings)	One Sachin has faced **one** of them (Stephen Fleming) The others are Indian (Azharuddin and Srikanth) or played before Sachin anyway (Yajurvindra Singh and V Y Richardson)
None	Top five fielders with the most catches in a Test match (7 catches in a match)	Three Sachin has faced **three** of them (Stephen Fleming, Hayden and Tillakaratne). Of the other two, one is an Indian (Yajurvindra Singh) and the other an Australian (Greg Chappell) who played before Sachin's time.

---

[21] *Straight Drive (Why does anyone have to be a Bradman?* Page 73); Sunil Gavaskar; Rupa & Co; Paperback 2011 (published 2009).

None	The world's most prolific fielders (125 or more Test catches)	Ten Barring Dravid (who is Indian), Sachin has seen **all the others** on his field – they include Mark Waugh, Stephen Fleming, Brian Lara, Ponting, Mark Taylor, Border, Jayawardene, Kallis, Hayden and Warne.
One England's Wally Hammond	**Many have taken 70 or more Test catches.**	Almost all They include Astle, Crowe, Shaun Pollock, Atherton, Kirsten, A B de Villiers, Hick, Miandad, H Gibbs and Trescothick, Richie Richardson, Greenidge, Muralitharan, Younis Khan, David Boon, Tillakaratne, Chris Gayle and Jayasuriya, Gooch, Steve Waugh, Carl Hooper. Sachin has seen all of them on his field.

At the time, a report in The Mail described Bradman's success against the powerless Indians, agreeing that Bradman may well have held his breath on the 'several occasions' when 'simple catches' were dropped.[22]

Of course there are butter-fingered fielders in the modern era but when you have played only 50 Tests, as Bradman did, the 'life' you get because of a dropped catch or missed run-out is crucial to your batting average.

Several great Test fielders have taken 70 or more catches in Tests:

- Only one (Hammond) had started fielding in the 1920s but **none** in the 1930s or 40s. Bradman was in his prime.

- 4 in the 1950s: Tom Graveney, Colin Cowdrey, Bob Simpson, Garry Sobers. Bradman was long gone.

- 3 in the 1960s: Clive Lloyd, Ian Redpath and Ian Chappell.

- By the 1970s, it was a royal crowd: Dilip Vengsarkar, David Gower, Allan Border, Greg Chappell, Viv Richards, Ian Botham, Sunil Gavaskar, Graham Gooch, Gordon Greenidge, Javed Miandad and Tony Greig.

---

[22] *Bradman triumphs in batting tactics*; W J O'Reilly, *The Mail*; 3 January 1948.

Rudolph Lambert Fernandez

- In the 1980s, it was a population: Carl Hooper, Steve Waugh, Azharuddin, Boon, Richie Richardson, Tillakaratne, Atherton, Lamb, Martin Crowe and Mark Taylor.

Of all fielders in Test history only 18 have 120 or more catches. Only two played before Sachin's era – Greg Chappell and Colin Cowdrey. Two are Indian – Dravid and Laxman (even if neither of these names jumps out at you when you close your eyes and think 'world-class fielder'). The remaining 14 fielders played in the 1990s, when Sachin was in his prime –- Ricky Ponting, Jacques Kallis, Mahela Jayawardene, Mark Waugh, Stephen Fleming, Brian Lara, Mark Taylor, Allan Border, Graeme Smith, Matthew Hayden, Shane Warne, Viv Richards, Andrew Strauss and Ian Botham. They were all in rival teams.

South African legend Colin Bland was the best sign of quality fielding that was to become standard in the post-War era. Unfortunately, for the cricketing world, his career was limited to the 1960s but he turned matches, saved runs and ran out or caught batsmen so brilliantly in that brief period, that he was held in regard decades after his retirement. The 'Golden Eagle' would consistently pull off direct-hits while on the move.

 Bland would not have loomed as large as he did on the cricket horizon of the 1960s and beyond, if his brand of fielding was the norm before him.

After Bland faded from the field, things got worse... for batsmen.

The fielders got better... and there were so many of them, each wave fiercer than the last, making the 'impossible' more 'possible' with every passing innings.

In June/July 1984, England were up against the West Indies at a Test at Lord's and sailing along. Geoffrey Miller, wandering to the non-striker's saw Eldine Baptiste fling the ball from long leg – it flew over 100 yards and knocked the middle stump over. 'Dusty', short of his crease may have had his jaw wide open; he still had to walk, run-out for a duck. This is not to say that fielder Baptiste won the match but it is not out of place to say that England lost, by nine wickets.

In December 1999, India were playing Australia in the Border-Gavaskar Test at Adelaide. Australia had put up a daunting 441 in their first innings. During India's fight-back, the first wicket fell at 7. What went wrong? Devang Gandhi and Sadagopan Ramesh who had opened for India watched as the ball headed for the massive Adelaide outfield. After 'running' for three, they were audaciously attempting to 'run' for four, when Ramesh was caught short of his crease by a direct throw from the long boundary – a good *115 yards away*. Greg Blewett's throw had an alarming effect on India's performance. Australia's fielding beast then bared its fangs. Following that spectacular dismissal, the next five Indian batsmen were out caught; the sixth was out stumped. This isn't to say that fielders won the match but it isn't out of place to say that Australia won, by 285 runs.

Jonty Rhodes may have had a brief ODI career and an even shorter Test career but he took 105 catches in ODIs, holds the record for the highest number of catches in an ODI (five catches against the West Indies in 1993) and is among record holders for the highest number of catches in an ODI Series (nine catches in the 1997-98 Carlton & United Series).

- In November 1996, in the Ahmedabad Test against India, Rhodes caught Sachin off a Symcox delivery in his first innings. He then caught Sachin again, off a McMillan delivery in his second innings. India won by 64 runs but South Africa's defeat may have been crushing had Rhodes not sent Sachin back soon on both occasions.

- In February 1997, in the Durban day-night ODI match [Standard Chartered International final], India had come in to bat. Sachin had hit 6 fours, had put on 32 runs on the board off just 27 deliveries and was in ominous form with a strike rate of 118.51. Then Rhodes picked him off a Klusener delivery. Thanks to rain, the match was abandoned, but the South Africans heaved a sigh of relief at getting rid of Sachin early on.

When Rhodes went after the ball his feet, neck, head and arms simply moved as one – left, right, up or down – at lightning speed – until his fingers closed over the ball. It did not matter that the ball was metres away from where he had been standing or that it was zipping by too fast to spot mid-flight. He flew like an arrow – often almost parallel to the ground. Once his fingers touched the ball, options were limited – the batsman was caught or run-out or had been denied runs.

Exclamations such as 'Four!', 'Six!' and 'Shot!' from the early 20th century now had challengers in the late 20th century and early 21st century, who prowled the ground like cheetah, shouting with equal certainty: 'Out!' and 'Gotcha!' and 'Back!'

Rhodes personified this breed of fielders who bodily brought the scoring rate down and bullied batsmen into making forced errors. They re-defined

Rudolph Lambert Fernandez

the word 'reflex' – it was no longer a sheer fluke. It was now commonplace. Of course the millisecond micro-processes in say, a stunning catch, make it seem like a miracle. Increasingly, it is nothing of the sort. The reflex is no longer a quirk in the muscular, nervous or skeletal system. It flows from hours of practice, giving a fielder a skill that walks with him on to the field, almost like the T-shirt or cap he wears. Captains often regulate a rival's run-rate by moving a classy fielder this way and that, as they would a piece on a chessboard.

Remember TV footage of the legendary Azharuddin? A rival batsman lets rip and the crowd is on its feet for what is certainly a four or a six. The camera moves to where it *thinks* the ball is, then swivels back to 'frame' Azhar; he is grinning that grin of his, but his hands dangling limp at his sides are empty. He has already leaped, picked the speeding comet and flung it back – at bowler, wicket-keeper or stumps. Replays can barely pick him at slip or cover; he has darted clean out of the frame. His fielding hand, which once held the ball, no longer does. It is over in a fraction of a second. The shoulder has barely moved; it is all in the wrist. And what a marvellous wrist! One that has saved so many runs, pulled off so many dismissals and put on so many memorable innings with the bat. But it has never been more marvellous than when it flicked the ball back to the pitch. To the non-striker it was a gentle rebuke, a warning of sorts. To the striker it was more to the point – the difference between a long innings and a short one.

In February 1999, India were playing Pakistan in a Test at the sprawling Eden Gardens. Pakistan had put up a feeble 185 in the first innings and India had replied with a tentative 223, but already quality fielding was taking its toll – Mongia was run-out. Pakistan then came back strongly with 316 in the second innings and it was now up to India to settle things, either way. The first three Indian batsmen put up only 120 runs. Sachin walked in and things looked set for India; everyone wanted him to stay on and pummel the Pakistani bowlers.

What went wrong? As luck would have it, as Sachin was running between wickets, he ran into... well, he ran into Shoaib Akhtar. Substitute fielder Nadeem Khan's throw, from the Eden Gardens boundary, knocked down the stumps. Not a bad throw if you've stood in the middle of Eden Gardens and tried to spell a sponsor's name on a boundary board. Amidst allegations of 'obstruction', Sachin was declared out. True to form, after his shock departure, the rest of the Indian line-up simply caved in. Pakistan won.

Spectators in the 1960s were stunned when they saw a new breed of fielding from the likes of Sobers and Bland. They were shocked when they saw Viv Richards in the 1970s, Azhar in the 1980s and Rhodes in the 1990s. Every few years, the fielding kept getting better. Catches kept getting more spectacular. Return throws kept getting more outlandish whether from near the pitch or further afield. The oasis of fielding excellence had become an ocean. Today, when a writer declares that a match has been won almost single-handedly by agile fielding, he is probably not exaggerating.

Some 41 Test bowlers have the most wickets taken (100 or more wickets) 'caught by a fielder'. Bowlers who enjoyed the harvest from top-class fielding are:

- In the 1920s and 30s: Not a single bowler. Bradman was in his prime.

- In the 1940s: only one bowler – Bedser (reflecting the relatively low, but gradually increasing impact of fielding on batting and bowling fortunes). Bradman played just 15 of his 50 matches in this period and would soon retire.

- In the 1950s: three (Benaud, Trueman, and Lance Gibbs); fielding across the world was improving... slowly. Bradman had retired in 1948.

- In the 1960s: four bowlers (Derek Underwood and India's spin trio of Bedi, B K Chandrasekhar and Prasanna); fielding across the world was... er, it was *still* improving.

- In the 1970s, eight bowlers (Bob Willis, Ian Botham, Kapil Dev, Malcolm Marshall, Dennis Lillee, Imran Khan, Abdul Qadir and Richard Hadlee) and in the 1980s, five bowlers (McDermott, Akram, Merv Hughes, Walsh and Ambrose). Quality fielding was now commonplace.

- In the 1990s: fourteen bowlers (Warne, Muralitharan, Saqlain Mushtaq, Brett Lee, MacGill, Caddick, Flintoff, McGrath, Ntini, Vettori, Shaun Pollock, Kallis, Vaas and Donald). Quality fielding had become part of the attack. Sachin was in his prime.

But even if you consider bowlers with 200 or more wickets 'caught by a fielder', Sachin has faced five of the top seven bowlers (Muralitharan, Warne, Walsh, McGrath and Ntini); the other two happen to be Indian (Kumble and Harbhajan Singh).

Now, look carefully at the snapshot above. Which was the 'safest' era for a hungry batsman?

Rudolph Lambert Fernandez

What of wicket-keepers?

Wicket-keepers of the 1930s and 40s weren't mannequins but they weren't the glove-machines behind Sachin's stumps either.

- In Test history where teams notched up the highest match aggregates without a bye, the *only* recorded instance before 1970 was in 1959. Pakistan and Australia going head to head in Karachi and giving away no byes (although 2141 balls were bowled and 821 runs flowed from bats). A sign of superior wicket-keeping in the late 20th century?

- Three wicket-keepers have accounted for the maximum Test career dismissals – Mark Boucher (521 career dismissals), Adam Gilchrist (416) and Ian Healy (395). Sachin has had all of them behind his stumps and they are way ahead of legends such as Rodney Marsh (355), Wasim Bari (228), Jeff Dujon (270) and Syed Kirmani (198).

- Bradman had to contend primarily with England's L E G Ames, T G Evans and G Duckworth. Evans, the most successful of the three, came on only in 1946, when Bradman was about to retire. Their combined Test career dismissal record of 374 dismissals from a combined 162 Tests is more modest than Healy's individual Test career record of 395 dismissals from only 119 Tests.

- Duckworth and Ames had 155 dismissals from 71 matches. India's Dhoni has 198 dismissals from a mere 61 Tests.

- Duckworth, Ames and Evans had 290 catches from a combined 162 matches. Boucher alone has 499 catches from just 139 matches.

- The modern wicket-keepers have a high dismissals-per-innings rate: Boucher (1.97), Gilchrist (2.19), Healy (1.76), Alec Stewart (1.71). Those in the 1930s and 40s had a much lower rate: Ames (1.17), Evans (1.25) and Duckworth (1.39).

- Around two dozen wicket-keepers appear in the list of those with the highest dismissals in a Test innings (6 or more dismissals). All of them played after the 1940s; not one during the Bradman years. Sachin has seen at least seven of them behind his stumps – Healy, Stewart, Boucher, Rashid Latif, Matt Prior, Robert Charles Russell and Ridley Jacobs.

- Some two dozen wicket-keepers figure in the list of those with the highest dismissals in a Test series (20 or more dismissals). Only one of them played during the Bradman years – England's T G Evans had 20 dismissals from five matches in the 1956-57 series against South Africa. But this was nearly a decade after Bradman had retired and when wicket-keeping standards around the world had begun to gradually climb. Sachin has seen many of the others on this list and they all have a far better record than Evans – Charles Russell (27 dismissals from five matches), Healy appears five times in the list (including one performance of 27 dismissals from six matches in 1997), Boucher (26 dismissals from five matches), Gilchrist also appears five times in the list (including one performance of 26 dismissals from five matches).

Note: figures as of 2011.

What happened in the 1930s? A report dated 28 November 1931 in *The Canberra Times* tells us. The report titled *Bradman Shines, Costly Misses for South Africa* tells of how Bradman had several 'lives' thanks to shoddy fielding. He got away once when 'he skied Quinn'. He then nearly got out to Vincent – 'The fieldsman touched the ball, but could not hold it'. He later edged Quinn 'to Mitchell at first slip, but the fieldsman dropped the ball'. Finally at a score of 74 'he survived an lbw appeal by Bell.'

Put simply, Bradman escaped the most tested fielders and wicket-keepers in the world. Sachin has faced and most often got the better of both: he emerged in an era where fielding and wicket-keeping conspired to hold even the best batsmen in a pincer-like grip – it is from within that grip that he built his records. Bradman, on the other hand, scored on the back of relatively feeble field combat.

What should have been a single became a two, what should have stayed a two became a three, what should have been a maiden-over ended up peppered with boundaries. A ball that should have been nestling comfortably in the hands of a fielder or in the gloves of the wicket-keeper, kept bouncing deferentially until it reached the boundary.

Rudolph Lambert Fernandez

CHAPTER 8

The Devil is in the Detail – Part 1

TV REPLAYS, RUN-OUT, LBW, CAUGHT, APPEALS

MICROSCOPES IN THE LAB AND microphones in the studio have an astonishing quality – they 'reveal' the truth. The truth isn't missing; only our perception of it. We see and hear things we haven't seen or heard before. We shamefacedly admit to realities we've missed. We sheepishly confess to facts that have escaped us.

Like telescopes, these tools bestow on us a *fresh* honesty, a *new* truth. Radiology, forensics, astronomy and microbiology help us revise our Commandments. They encourage us to re-write our histories, reconstruct our myths and re-tell our fables.

The stubborn among us cling to our tablets of stone. The more humble among us sit up and are willing to say: Yes, the earth is *round*. Yes, the *earth* revolves around the sun. So on and so forth. Technology has been to cricket what astronomy was to the New Age. Astronomy transformed the way we saw the world and its place in the universe. Technology has transformed the way we capture, compare and celebrate achievement on the cricket field. In many ways, the high-tech era 'disciplined' cricket, made it more truthful, more accurate, more honest than it had ever been. For the first time folk in the stands were able to see achievement in 'high-def'. It was awfully exciting for spectators but for players and historians it transformed the meaning of greatness. Well... at least it should have.

TV replays

Ivo Tennant once wrote that it took a while for this truth to dawn on the cricket fraternity – the umpire's decision was not necessarily final or correct.[23]

TV replays do not whisper the 'truth' to a few thousands in the stadium. They shout it to millions around the world. Millions who in one moment dismiss a piece of real-time action: 'That's Sachin batting, read my lips – he... is... not... out!' are the same millions who, the next moment, after watching a replay, mutter: 'I know that's Sachin batting but that's... definitely.... out. What a pity!'

Tests were first televised only as late as 1938; ten years into Bradman's career and less than three playing years before he retired. By then he had already amassed nearly 70% of all his runs (4,854 out of 6,996). The replay, if it existed at the time, was nothing more than a grainy grab from a Charlie Chaplin film. If you were looking to make a decision on the strength of a replay you'd be 'stumped' even if you weren't!

It made little difference to the umpire's verdict, the views of commentators, spectators and cricket writers. They all simply 'knew', for instance, that Bradman would go on playing, delivery after delivery, over after over, session after session, day after day, innings after innings, match after match, series after series. There may have been the odd mid-pitch commotion among those closer to the 'truth' but in the pavilion it would have been a simple: 'Don't worry, that's Bradman playing, now would you pass the biscuits, please?'

No third umpire to challenge the (in)decision of the field umpire. No 'knowing' eye that played it all out – agonisingly slowly and from uncomfortably different angles.

Sachin, rather poignantly, is the first cricketer in the world to have been a victim of technology. Just three years into his career, playing South Africa in 1992, he was the first batsman to be declared out using a TV replay. Strange that Cricket, when asked in the New Age to spill blood on the pitch, picked its noblest prince.

The New Age for Bradman, came too late, and for Sachin, too early.

---

[23] *The umpire is not always right* (Innovation Series); Ivo Tennant, *ESPNcricinfo*, 22 February 2011.

Let's look in turn at the devastating impact (in Bradman's case – the lack of it!) of new-age TV cricket on a variety of dismissals.

Run-out

Of Bradman's 70 Test dismissals, he was run-out just once. Once!

The Bandra-boy has been declared run-out 39 times (7 in Tests and 32 in ODIs).

Bradman depended more on singles, twos (and threes?) than anything else.

 Bradman was a runner – in spirit and in truth.

He depended more on footwork between the wickets than on powerful forearms or supple wrists. He was an accumulator, not an artist. He 'ran' for as many as 61% (or 4,236 out of 6,996 runs) of all his runs, seeking boundaries from a far lower percentage of deliveries. He wanted to dominate the opposition but remained intent, right through, on preserving his wicket, piling on the scores and records. Yet with all that running, Bradman was declared run-out just once (1% of his 70 dismissals) – a testimony as much to evolving fielding as to the absence of TV pitch scrutiny.

Rob Steen wrote that Bradman was so hungry for runs that he once ran a 'four' and then hinted at scampering for a 'fifth' run, before his batting partner Alan Fairfax turned him down.[24]

It is unclear what it takes to be able to run a 'five' in cricket – a corrugated outfield, crippled fielders or both. But Bradman remains an example to batsmen, of all generations: he ran his first run like it was the last ball in an over with his team one or two runs short of victory. Such was his desire to put pressure on fielders.

What about Sachin? A lot is made of his incredible running between the wickets but for the better part of his career, he has simply dominated the bowling through aggressive and artistic stroke-play. He 'ran' for only 46% (6,740 out of 14,692 runs) of all his Test runs and for only 50% (8,780 out of 17,598 runs) of all his ODI runs. Yet with relatively little running as a percentage of overall runs – when compared to Bradman – Sachin has been run-out 32 times in ODIs (8% of his 390 dismissals) and 7 times in Tests (nearly 3% of his 258 dismissals).

---

[24] *The coming of our Don;* Rob Steen, *The Age;* 4 June 2005.

Run-out record in Tests: Bradman 1%, Sachin 3%

In the absence of TV replays and the third umpire, imagine the number of times Bradman was actually run-out, but carried on playing. The flip-side is terrifying; imagine Sachin without TV replays, escaping all the run-out decisions and continuing to hammer hapless bowlers all over the park.

...lbw

Pad-play was in full flow during the Bradman years; the pad on a clever batsman's leg was like another bat. Perhaps there were days when batsmen played with three 'bats'! The anguish of bowlers from Bradman's era has to be heard to be felt.

Larwood once moaned to his biographer, Duncan Hamilton, that cricket at the time favoured batsmen as there was 'no pressure on them at all'. Hamilton wrote that to secure an lbw, the bowler had to pitch wicket-to-wicket while batsmen could happily pad balls that strayed.

It took several years for people to realise that the 'sport' was inexorably leaking from the game. Cricket was in danger of being ridiculously one-sided... in favour of batsmen. It was only in the late 1930s that people started exploring ways to do something about it. They started tightening lbw decisions.

The new lbw law brought down scoring, livened up the game, threw up more wins and losses (as opposed to draws) and levelled the fight between bat and ball. An article in the Wisden Almanack in 1936 highlighted how the new law influenced the game 'in all respects'.

The article confirmed that County Championship victories went up by 27 over the previous summer – of 234 matches, those with a definite result went up from 134 in the year 1934 to 161 in the year 1935. The article also confirmed that Wally Hammond, one of the most prolific batsmen of the early 20th century saw his batting average fall that year, from 76.32 to 49.35. New lbw legislation had arrived and its impact, to put it mildly, was telling.[25]

And to think that Bradman's batting average still holds him aloft titans of the late 20th century!

The reform started off in England's county scene and took a while to find its way to the cricketing world. The 'experiment' went on for a good two

---

[25] *Success of the lbw experiment;* Wisden Cricketers' Almanack, 1936.

years before the new law came into full effect across international cricket as late as 1937.

Those who welcomed the tighter lbw law agreed that it made batsmen play at more balls outside the off stump, removed a significant amount of pad play, quickened the game and ensured that more matches ended in a result. They also agreed that it, quite rightly, helped bowlers – after all, they were the ones who needed help against batsmen so used to padding balls that their bats couldn't pick.

Not everyone was happy, though. Howls of protest mingled with heaps of praise, but broadly there emerged agreement that a game marked by its love of fair-play was now fairer than before. 'The fight between bat and ball became more equal than it had been for many seasons...'

The 'many seasons' happen to include an embarrassingly sizeable part of Bradman's career. But by December 1936, the damage had been done – Bradman had amassed 3,969 runs or around 57% of all his Test runs. He was a few matches short of retirement and five of those matches would be against a luckless India. One can only speculate on the many occasions that he benefited from a crucially liberal lbw regime. As it happened, of all his dismissals only 8.5% were lbw decisions (6 out of 70 dismissals).

Sachin, on the other hand, has been declared lbw 20% of the time (52 lbw decisions out of 258 dismissals) in Test cricket alone. In ODIs, Sachin has been declared lbw 9% of the time (37 lbw decisions out of 390 dismissals).

A brief illustration: About two dozen of the world's Test bowlers have secured the highest number of lbw decisions (52 or more wickets): Kumble, Muralitharan, Warne, Akram, McGrath, Kapil, Younis, Vaas, Pollock, Hadlee, Botham, Imran, Walsh, Marshall, Vettori, Hoggard, Harbhajan, Lillee, Gillespie, Alderman, Garner, Zaheer Khan, Swann, Qadir and Ambrose. Four are Indians and some played before 1989, but Sachin has faced the majority of them.

Can you spot even one bowler from the 1960s? No? Or a bowler from the 1950s? No? There's a good reason for that: all started in the 1970s and since. But look closer. Among the top five in the list, if you leave out the Indian (Kumble – who leads the pack with 156 lbw dismissals) the other four are 'Sachin' or '1990s' bowlers – Muralitharan, Warne, Akram and McGrath – each with well over 100 lbw dismissals.

The tighter lbw law came into its own in tandem with the technology era. It bit deep after Bradman retired but kept biting deeper with each passing decade – with most devastating effect in the 1990s. Sachin was in his prime.

ESPNcricinfo's statistics editor S Rajesh, in his article on 13 January 2006, *A lowdown on lbws* said that lbw dismissals as a percentage of total dismissals have kept crawling skywards. In the period 1877-1899, for instance, lbws were a mere 4.71% (101 lbws out of a total of 2,143 dismissals). But, Rajesh confirmed, that over the latter half of the 20th century that percentage had shot up by an incredible 50%.

- In the period 1900-09, lbws were 7.85% (109 lbws out of a total of 1388 dismissals). Nearly a century later, Waqar Younis alone secured 110 lbw dismissals.

- In the period 1910-19, lbws were 8.01% (76 lbws out of a total of 949 dismissals). Nearly a century later, Malcolm Marshall alone secured 76 lbw dismissals.

- In the period 1920-29, lbws were 11.80% (180 lbws out of a total of 1525 dismissals). Jack Hobbs was still making merry; Bradman started playing Tests only in 1928.

- In the period 1930-39, lbws were 12.33% (323 lbws out of a total of 2620 dismissals). Bradman was in his prime but the new lbw law was conceived only in the late 1930s. Muralitharan, Warne and Akram between them secured 407 lbw dismissals – that's 84 more lbws than all bowlers from the 1930s.

- In the period 1940-49, lbws were 12.66% (166 lbws out of a total of 1311 dismissals). Bradman played only 15 Tests in this period; the first decade in cricket history to 'feel' the new lbw law. Kumble alone secured 156 lbws – that's just 10 lbws less than the tally of all bowlers from the 1940s.

Over the next few decades lbws kept climbing and men like Sobers and Viv Richards faced a far greater challenge than their predecessors. Finally, in the period 1990-99, lbws were 16.60% (1754 lbws out of a total of 10,564 dismissals). Sachin was in his prime and faced the greatest challenge!

In the 21st century, things only got worse. In the period 2000-06, lbws were 17.08% (1578 lbws out of a total of 9241 dismissals). Sachin stayed on top of the game, battling lbw odds like never before.

Look at the manifold increase in bowler, fielder and umpire finger-raising on account of the batsman's leg being 'before the wicket'. It offers a flavour of how radically the playing environment had altered, against batsmen. Unlike Bradman, Sachin performed his high-wire acts without a net and with close-up cameras following his every move.

Like Bradman, his batting peers too benefited from lenient lbw laws:

- Of 57 dismissals, McCabe was lbw on only 5 occasions (9% of the time)

- Of 50 dismissals, Woodfull was lbw only twice (4% of the time)

- Of 74 dismissals E H Hendren was lbw on 3 occasions (4% of the time)

- Of 44 dismissals, Ponsford was lbw only... wait a minute, he was never declared lbw!

Unlike Bradman, Sachin and his batting peers suffered from the 'new accuracy' of technology and tighter lbw legislation:

- Of 170 Test dismissals Hayden was lbw 26 times (15% of the time)

- Of 226 Test dismissals Lara was lbw on 37 occasions (16% of the time)

- Of 208 Test dismissals Kallis has been lbw 33 times (16% of the time)

- Of 231 Test dismissals Ponting has been lbw 41 times (18% of the time)

Note: as of 6 January 2011.

It is fair to compare Bradman with his peers (who faced about the same 'lbw odds' he did). But for Bradman's sake, it is safer not to compare him with batsmen from the 1950s and since; they were 3-5 times more likely to be lbw than he was. Some were dismissed when they were 1 run short of 50 runs or 1 short of a ton or 1 short of a double ton, but they all had to go. They could not just stay on – as Bradman could – and score the next run and the next... the next ton and the next. For a fifth of his Test career, Sachin has had to go because he was declared lbw.

A footnote on lbw: Bradman proved his greatness by rising above the petty considerations of a batsman (his own position). Sachin and every other cricketer must sit humbly at Bradman's feet to imbibe that spirit. Writing in Wisden in 1939, he argued, inexplicably to some, **in favour** of the new lbw law. In his essay, Bradman wrote that according to the liberal lbw legislation at the time, the part of a batsman's body hit by a delivery had to be between wicket and wicket. He agreed that it offered batsmen 'too much latitude'.[26]Yes, he was only a few matches short of retirement, but Bradman was honestly admitting that he and his peers had enjoyed 'too much latitude' for most of their careers.

Wisden's Match Report for the 'Fourth Test Match, Australia v South Africa, January 1932' is faithful to Bradman's prowess but it is also faithful to the context in which he scored his unbeaten 299 in Adelaide: '...During one particular hour... he survived several appeals for leg-before and catches at the wicket.'

Caught

Did the ball hit wrist or forearm before it was caught? Or did it hit the glove... or the bat? Did the ball land and stay in the fielder's palm? Or did it touch the grass first anyway?

Of Bradman's 70 dismissals, the majority – 39 dismissals – were catches.

In the absence of high technology scrutiny, 56% of the time Bradman was dismissed, he was caught. He was caught most often, in spite of his tendency to play safe and keep the ball low – on or near the ground. One wonders if Bradman's dismissals would have more than trebled had all the wicket-keepers, close-in, mid and out-fielders of his era been aided by TV replays, pitch microphones and murderous appealing.

Wisden's Match Report of the M.C.C. team in Australia and New Zealand in 1946-47 quoted Australian critic, Ray Robinson, lamenting in *The Cricketer* the crucial impact of debatable umpiring. Robinson believed umpires were wrong not to have dismissed Bradman (caught for 28 in the First Test), Edrich (lbw for 89 in the Third Test), and Washbrook (caught behind for 39 in the Fourth Test). He was convinced that these were turning points and wrote that Australia would actually have been on the backfoot in the second innings, had Bradman been declared out 'four hours earlier'. He argued that it would have changed the outcome of the First Test 'incalculably' had Bradman been dismissed for 159 fewer runs.

Sachin was rarely let off the hook. Of Sachin's 258 dismissals in Test cricket he has been declared caught on 152 occasions or 59% of the time and in ODIs he has been declared caught 63% of the time (244 caught dismissals out of a total of 390 dismissals).

---

[26] *Cricket at the crossroads*; Donald Bradman; Wisden Cricketers' Almanack, 1939.

Dismissals through catches in Tests: Bradman (56%), Sachin (59%).

In the overwhelmingly intrusive environment of high-tech cricket, after having played over three times the Tests that Bradman did and having played consistently attacking and aggressive cricket, Sachin's record is incredible.

What happened in the Bradman era? A report dated 13 March 1929 in *The Canberra Times* tells us. The report titled *Colts in Action, Bradman and Fairfax in form* tells of how often Bradman got away with it. Geary, for instance, first dropped Fairfax off Larwood and then dropped Bradman at mid-on. Then thanks to a fumble by Hobbs, Fairfax escaped a run-out. Unsurprisingly the day ended with Bradman at 109 and Fairfax at 50.

George Geary was a 36-year old in that match but was probably missing a couple of fielding sessions at the nets. Hobbs was a youthful 47-year old in that match and may be excused his 'fumble'. They and their mates did their bit to keep 'Bradman and Fairfax in form'!

Howzzat!

In the pre-War years, appealing (by bowlers, wicket-keepers and fielders) was at best wishful thinking and at worst... well, things never got that far – it was still a gentleman's game. The reverence that teams had, and showed the umpire, was above everything – the 'edge' that they clearly heard, the 'glance' that they clearly saw.

In modern cricket, players do not 'appeal', they 'demand.' Wicket-keepers, bowlers and fielders use every physical and psychological trick in the book to 'persuade' umpires to 'see the point'. Since the 1990s, many have succeeded.

The impact of modern-day appealing has had a disastrous impact on the careers of many modern-era batsmen. It is wicked to compare their records with those who batted in, shall we say, more civil climates. Bradman and his peers got away with it more often than they would care to admit.

When you are out in the middle, the slightest of 'nicks' is barely audible and almost never visible, particularly if the ball's trajectory on impact remains largely unchanged. Slip and wicket-keeper are none the wiser and the umpire can hardly be charged with not being blessed with super-hearing or super-vision.

A return throw is being executed by fielder, bowler or wicket-keeper; the ball is hurtling toward the stumps. The batsman twists mid-pitch and throws himself down. Out-stretched on the pitch, the edge of his bat kisses the crease. But bowlers, fielders, wicket-keepers and umpires can't tell with any degree of accuracy where that edge lay at the moment the ball smashed into the bails. In the heat and sweat of ground action, their eyes cannot be impeccably frozen on crease and bails – at the same millisecond. Especially if they are, for the most part blinking, walking, bending, twisting, running, leaping.

Technology, like a Grim Reaper, swung its scythe in a great big arc right across the cricket field, slicing both bat and ball to size – and with it the 'greatness' of the greats. It cut away at achievement, making 'achievers' look more mortal with each swipe. Since the 1990s, batsmen have found it impossible to escape run-out, lbw, caught-behind or caught-at-slip decisions on account of human error. The 'benefit of doubt' was fast becoming an endangered species.

In late 1992, the ICC had approved third-umpire involvement in decision making. With improved decisions, on-field disagreements fell, finger-spinners thrived, bat-pad catches were more easily nailed and lbw dismissals went up smartly. This is dangerously close to admitting that the history books need to be reviewed if not entirely re-written.

The field umpire in Bradman's era did not consult god (the third umpire) – the field umpire was god!

The field umpire in Sachin's era has been happy for 'god' to prevail because 'god' sees all, hears all and knows all.

Bradman had hung up his pads long before 'god' arrived.

CHAPTER 9

The Devil is in the Detail – Part 2

UNBEATEN, BOWLED, BOUNDARIES, BATTING AVERAGE AND
STRIKE-RATE

Unbeaten

SACHIN REACHED AT LEAST SIX of his Test hundreds, not with a single, two or four but with a six. He holds the world record for... wait a second, getting out in the nineties. He has been dismissed at least 26 times (18 in ODIs and 8 in Tests) on scores of 90 to 99. In Tests, on two occasions his score has been between 190 and 199. Once he was lbw (against England in 2002) and on another occasion he remained unbeaten (against Pakistan in 2004). On all occasions these scores have been against strong teams including Australia, England, Pakistan, Sri Lanka, South Africa and the West Indies. Critics agree that at least a couple of these 'nineties' dismissals involved dodgy umpiring, whether it was the occasional 'catch' off a no-ball or off an arm-guard (instead of a glove).

If he had been bull-headed he may have converted many of those 26 scores into centuries as well and he would already be well past 125 centuries in international cricket. But he has almost always held the team interest above his own and often lost his wicket trying to intimidate the bowling or coping with disappearing partners. On occasion he has been nervous when approaching a personal milestone. But for the most part his focus has been elsewhere: push up the Indian run-rate, put rival fielders on the defensive and set an example of aggression to jittery partners about to take strike alongside him. If he has played safe in the nineties, it was more out of fear of letting the team down, by 'gifting' a prized wicket and risking a further tumble of wickets, rather than out of fear of missing a private milestone. Again, there may have been exceptions where a personal landmark has weighed more heavily on his mind, but these have been just that – exceptions.

While on the subject of nineties: Sachin's record of getting out in the nineties is often perversely held against him to suggest that he has been unable to handle pressure as well as some others. Hardened Sachin fans will tell you, 'to get out the most in the nineties you have to get there the most!' And if he's ended up with the most hundreds, he's dealt with the nervous nineties better than any other batsman.

Of course Sachin was dismissed more easily – he did not seem to care too much whether he hit along the ground or not. One shudders to imagine what his record would have been had he played in the pre-War years – hitting all over the park, but escaping all the lbw, caught, caught-behind, caught-at-slips, run-out decisions that went against him. Thanks to the playing environment of his time, Sachin almost never got away with it – and rightly so.

This is not to suggest that Sachin was not-out on instances when the records say otherwise (some argue that he was a victim of unfair or inaccurate decision-making in at least 30 Tests). On the contrary, Sachin's is a far more honest record of what happened on the field. If there were exceptions where he has been unfairly judged by umpires, they again remain just that – exceptions. In Bradman's case it was probably the reverse. He was probably out on many occasions when he was declared not-out at innings-close. Or he was probably declared out only much later on in the innings when he had already piled on a mass of runs. Undoubtedly, he exploited what 'breaks' he got, more tenaciously than others of his era. That does not make the picture any less distinct.

Bradman was not to blame. He was a sportsman to the core – the likes of which we seldom see in modern cricket. He 'walked' every time he was declared out. But if he wasn't 'declared' out, he didn't walk. Like his peers, he got away with it on many occasions.

In Headingley in 1930, Larwood believed that Bradman was out even before he had scored. Later, he told his biographer Duncan Hamilton as much.[27]

Even if you take *any* Larwood statement on Bradman with a truckload of salt, what do you think happened on the field?

Bradman went on to score a 50 when he was probably lbw at 7. He pounded through a hundred, when he was probably caught-behind at 52. He powered to 150 when he was probably caught at slip at 103. He blazed through to a 200 when he was probably run-out at 151. He notched up a 250 when he was probably lbw and run-out and caught-behind and caught-at-slip several times during a single innings. Only something short of the Roman Goddess of beauty scampering onto the pitch with nothing on but the drinks cart could get him out.

Six of Bradman's Test tons were not-out occasions. Over his entire career, he was declared not-out 12.5% of the time (10 out of 80 Test innings). Naturally, he stayed on to maintain his rather unreal batting average. He stayed on day after day, as fielders, bowlers, umpires and spectators – so used to seeing him settle down – were numbed into a kind of stupor by his dominance of the opposition. They too were not to blame.

With all that Sachin had going against him (when compared to Bradman's era) he was not-out 11% of the time in Test cricket (32 unbeaten innings out of 290 innings). In ODIs where the ground keeps moving beneath a batsman's feet every few overs, Sachin has been not-out 9% of the time (41 not-out occasions in 442 matches).

Given how untested Bradman's batting mates were, one would have expected him to have borne a far greater team burden compared to Sachin, whose batting mates were experienced Test hands.

Not-out record in Tests: Bradman (12.5%), Sachin (11%)

Look carefully at the comparison above. It is an extraordinary testament to Sachin's Herculean batting prowess. Having played three times as many Test innings and over twice as many rivals as Bradman did, in an era in which pitch-action scrutiny, effective bowling and aggressive fielding peaked, Sachin's not-out record is a stunning expression of his genius. The justly admired Lara, having played 226 Test innings (compared to Sachin's 290 innings) was unbeaten only 3% of the time (6 unbeaten innings out of 226). Lara's batting mates were not in the calibre of Sachin's more accomplished batting mates, yet Sachin has carried the greater team burden.

---

[27] *Harold Larwood* (*The Little Bastard*; Page 122, Chapter 5); Duncan Hamilton; Quercus, Paperback Edition 2010 (published 2009).

Bowled

His record of being dismissed bowled is another measure of a batsman's greatness because it tells you where he has been 'beaten' by the bowler and where he has not – in flight *or* length *or* line *or* pace *or* spin... *or* in some of the above. But – and this is most important – this particular mark of greatness is necessarily linked to ease of scoring – a healthy strike-rate and relative comfort in hitting sixes. It is so much more than merely ensuring you are never – or rarely – bowled. A lot depends on what you are doing while not being bowled – scoring easily and dominating the bowling. This mark of greatness is also necessarily linked to success in a wide range of Tests, 'away' Tests, against a range of bowlers, fielders and in a range of grounds and pitches.

In Bradman's era, even the better batsmen had an unflattering record.

- Bradman: 33% (23 'bowled' dismissals out of 70 dismissals)

- Hammond: 31% (38 'bowled' dismissals out of 124)

- Woodfull: 32% (16 'bowled' dismissals out of 50)

- Ponsford: miserably high at 43% (19 'bowled' dismissals out of 44)

In this respect Hammond is the best by far because his record was across 124 dismissals – he had been tested the most.

In Sachin's era, the better batsmen were... extraordinary. They dwarfed Bradman and his peers because they had played three times as many matches against twice that many rival teams and in around 50 grounds around the world, in a far tighter lbw environment and with far greater mid-pitch scrutiny. But here again, Sachin stands on the tallest mountain (*See Table 15 in the Appendix, for an understanding of Sachin's superiority among contemporary batsman when it comes to 'bowled' dismissals*).

Now, look a little closer at Bradman.

Of his 70 dismissals, he was bowled on 23 occasions (or 33% of the time). If, just to put an image to it, Bradman was dismissed six times in a single 6-ball over, as many as 1.98 deliveries (or 33% of 6 deliveries) would find his stumps. Just to be clear, this is pure fantasy – no batsman is dismissed more than once in an over. But the idea, the image can be very real. Therefore, *imagine* Bradman is dismissed first ball, then takes guard again and is dismissed, takes guard again and is dismissed... and so on until the last ball of the over. *If* there were such a scenario, the bowler would find

Bradman's stumps in as many as two deliveries (assuming we round-off 1.98 to 2).

Look at Sachin's record. In Test cricket, he was bowled only 18% of the time (46 out of 258 dismissals). If, just to put an image to it, Sachin was dismissed six times in a 6-ball over, only 1.08 deliveries (or 18% of 6 deliveries) would find his stumps. The bowler would find his stumps in just one delivery (assuming we round-off 1.08 to 1). As if to top this, Sachin's record in this respect remains almost unaffected whether that 'over' is bowled to him in the leisurely environment of Test cricket or the riotously charged atmosphere of ODI cricket. If anything, Sachin has been even more stoic in ODI cricket, intuitively and Atlas-like, spreading his shoulders wider to bear the team on his back. In ODI cricket, he was bowled only 16% of the time (65 out of 390 dismissals).

But wait, there's more...

In spite of the relatively limited amount of cricket he played (an average of 5 Tests a 'playing' year) and an abundantly cautious approach, Bradman was 'bowled' every year he played (barring 1929 when he played only 2 Tests anyway).

In spite of the fierce competition he has been up against, the sheer volume of Test cricket he has played each year (an average of 8-10 Tests a year), and in spite of his predominantly aggressive style, Sachin has **not** been 'bowled' in the years 1992 (he played 8 Tests), 1993 (he played 8 Tests), 2000 (he played 6 Tests) and 2005 (he played 6 Tests).

Additionally, Sachin has been bowled only once in the years 1990 (he played 7 Tests), 1991 (but he played only 2 Tests), 1995 (but he played only 3 Tests), 1998 (he played 5 Tests), 2001 (he played 10 Tests) and 2003 (he played 5 Tests). With his obviously slowing reflexes, he has been bowled once too often since 2012 but for the bulk of his career, his record has been exceptional.

His low record of being 'bowled' is an exceptionally odd statistic for Sachin. He is known to dance out of the crease to intimidate the bowling when he feels his team needs a bit of combative display. He is also known to play the most astonishing array of shots in the book – hooks, swings, lofted shots, delayed edges, delicate glances, upper cuts, unorthodox shots including the inelegant but often annoyingly effective reverse sweep. He has also been forced to make wild gear-shifts in terms of the way he paces his innings because of the trembling bosom of India's middle order.

However, this is an ominous statistic for Bradman.

Why?

Boundaries

'Bradman never hit in the air.' – *A miracle has been moved from among us, 1949: Sir Donald Bradman by R C Robertson-Glasgow, Wisden Almanack Online archive 1949*

Bradman was caution personified; in his entire Test career he hit just 681 fours. He also hit only 6 sixes (5 against England and 1 against India). Only 2,760 of his runs came from boundaries, or roughly only 39% of all his Test runs. If Bradman faced a 6-ball over and he scored off each ball, 2.34 deliveries (39% of 6 deliveries) would end up as boundaries; he would run for the others. Of those 2 'boundaries' (assuming we round-off 2.34 to 2), he would be aiming for fours, not a six. Still, the handful of quality bowlers of his era found Bradman's fiercely guarded stumps – frequently! Remember, he was bowled 33% of the time compared to Sachin's record of being bowled only 18% of the time.

Sachin's demeanour may have been cautious. Inside, he was all aggression. In Tests, he has hit 64 sixes and 1,892 fours; 7,952 runs from boundaries alone (54% of all his Test runs). Sachin's 7,952-run **boundary** tally is higher than the combined 7,170 **run** tally of Bradman's mates McCabe, Woodfull and Ponsford. If Sachin faced a 6-ball over and he scored off each ball, 3.24 deliveries (54% of 6 deliveries) would end up as boundaries. He scored boundaries off half the over (assuming we round-off 3.24 to 3 deliveries). Still, the army of quality bowlers of his era could not find his stumps as easily.

In March 1998, in a Test against Australia, Sachin hammered 14 fours and 4 sixes in a single innings; half his score of 155 came off boundaries.

Sachin: "Ran for" vs. Boundaries (only Tests)

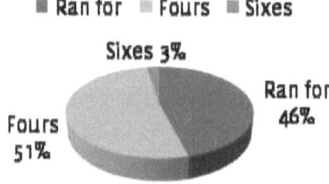

■ Ran for ▪ Fours ■ Sixes

Sixes 3%

Ran for 46%

Fours 51%

Bradman: "Ran for" vs. Boundaries

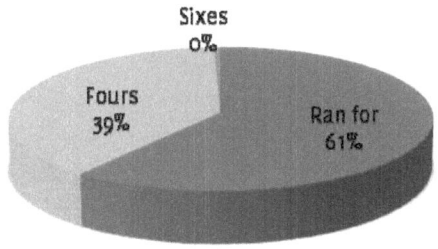

Chart 11: 'Ran for' vs. 'Boundaries': Bradman vs. Sachin – a comparison

From the charts above, it is safe to say that one of these gentlemen 'ran' an awful lot.

In ODIs it has been no different. Sachin has hit 185 sixes and 1,927 fours which translates to 8,818 runs from boundaries alone (*half* of all his ODI runs). If Sachin faced a 6-ball ODI over and he scored off each ball, three deliveries (or half of the over) would end up as boundaries; only for the other three deliveries would he be aiming to run. Either way, Sachin was not aiming to keep the ball low; all he ever wanted was a chance to go out and batter the bowling.

In April 1998 in an ODI against Australia, Sachin faced just 89 deliveries but hit 7 sixes and 5 fours; 62% of his 100 runs came off boundaries.

On 13 November 1998 in Sharjah, India were playing Zimbabwe in the Coca Cola Champions Trophy ODI final. Zimbabwe put up 196 runs. Sachin opened with Ganguly. Both men were on the field for exactly 140 minutes. Both men faced about the same number of deliveries – Ganguly 90, Sachin 92. The similarities end there.

Sachin exploded on that noisy desert ground hitting 6 sixes and 12 fours. By the time he finished unbeaten he had scored 124 runs at a strike-rate of 135. India won by 10 wickets with 120 balls to spare. He had scored over 60% of the team runs. Roughly 68% of all his runs had come from boundaries alone. That night Sachin was declared Player of the Match, then Player of the Series. Ganguly, for his part, scored a healthy 63.

Only a few days before this match, on 8 November 1998 Sachin's unbeaten 118 in an ODI against Zimbabwe in Sharjah helped India win by 7 wickets.

He had scored 60% of the team runs. Around 58% of his runs came off boundaries and he was Player of the Match.

In January 2007 in an ODI in Vadodara, India were playing West Indies. Uthappa fell when the score was 47. Ganguly fell when the score was 148. Dravid fell when the score was 266. Sachin stayed right through the Indian innings. When he walked off unbeaten he had scored a 100 runs, off 76 balls at a strike-rate of 132. Around 46% of his runs had come from boundaries alone and he had scored about 30% of the team total of 341. India won the match by 160 runs. Sachin was declared Player of the Match and Player of the Series.

 In spite of an impossibly vast contrast in styles, Bradman's caution ended with him being bowled 33% of the time and Sachin's aggression ended with him being bowled only 18% of the time. Bradman's record being over a fleeting 50 Tests, Sachin's over an unbelievable 177 Tests.

Frankly, Bradman era bowlers had to rely more on 'bowling' the batsman out. Fielding would take many decades to mature anyway. An lbw was like manna from heaven and every bowler at the time knew that manna almost never fell in England or Australia – Bradman's batting venues. A bowler would probably just have to stand helpless, hands on hips, watching as Bradman was rapped full on the pads but calmly scurried across for two runs. The bowler may as well have chewed on his lips, praying for the batsman to trip on his shoe-laces. But with Bradman, never was a lace out of place. Later, manna did fall but Bradman was long gone.

Larwood's biographer Duncan Hamilton, writing about the Bradman era confirmed that batsmen could afford to laughingly amass runs because, for good batsmen, pitches were like an 'as-much-as-you-can-eat' buffet. Bowlers like Larwood had to toil to keep batsmen in check. Hamilton was convinced that that sort of 'gorging on runs' would be inconceivable in the modern era.[28]

Buffet? Gorging on runs? We might as well imagine the rhapsodic stupor of a mosquito in a morgue!

What does all this mean?

---

[28] *Harold Larwood* (*Beer, Fags and a Cheese Sandwich*; Page 102, Chapter 4); Duncan Hamilton; Quercus, Paperback Edition 2010 (published 2009).

Rudolph Lambert Fernandez

If Bradman is *twice* as likely (in modern cricket) to be run-out and lbw and caught by a fielder and caught-and-bowled and 'appealed off the pitch' and bowled (as he would have been in the early 20th century) it is perhaps fair to suggest that his record of runs, tons, double tons, triple tons would be far less impressive than it would be had modern era conditions existed. Bradman's Test run pile, Test century haul and batting average would probably be far more modest than the extra-large figures currently embossed against his name.

Sunil Gavaskar, in his book *Straight Drive*, argued that with increased competitiveness and careers in the balance, it made sense to use electronic help and not allow mistakes that could change match and series fortunes. In a chapter titled *Third Eye is a Boon*, he recalled how Jonty Rhodes once escaped a not-out appeal that was put to the reputed Steve Bucknor. In spite of being in the wrong place on the field to judge correctly, Bucknor chose not to ask for the third umpire's view. Action replays saw Rhodes out of his crease but he stayed on and changed the course of that series.[29] The brief reprieve that Rhodes enjoyed (in a career otherwise kept 'honest' by technology) was Bradman's experience right through his career – one joyful reprieve after another.

Sachin hit the cricketing world like a thunder-storm when the cricketing world was being hit by a hurricane. At every level of the game, the bar had gone up, and not just by a few inches. Lbw, run-out, stumped, caught, caught-behind – every element of the game that seemed so familiar to players before him, now seemed so distant, so removed from the field. Giant eyes now glowered from above, watching every move, influencing decisions, tearing down old images and building new ones. Reputations built over decades, were now ripped apart in a matter of minutes.

What happened to cricket in the 1990s was not evolution; it was more like an explosion. It suspended all parameters in operation and threw in radically new ones. It changed the way spectators (in the stadium and in the drawing room), umpires, cricket writers, commentators and historians viewed the players. Achievements that until then were celebrated were no longer enough. Players had to jump far higher, hit a lot harder and run much faster than ever before. Centuries, double-centuries and triple-centuries were no longer enough; the journey was now more important than the destination.

Over-rate, Run-rate and Power-play walked the field like new tyrants,

---

[29] *Straight Drive (Third eye is a boon;* Page 65); Sunil Gavaskar; Rupa & Co; Paperback 2011 (published 2009).

bullying players into doing things they would otherwise never do. Action replays were not just academic discussions in the commentary box. They were transmitted on mammoth screens before thousands in the stadium and to millions of homes far from the field. Spectators could cheer and curse in real-time as they watched movements on the pitch that until then remained hidden from view. The emotions on a batsman's face, the fear in his eyes, the tension on his brow, the tautness of his jaw, his disappointment at a shot hit straight to a fielder, his frustration at granting a maiden over, his fury at failing to read the ball in flight.

Every cover-drive dissected a dozen times over. Every leg-glance analysed for art and artistry.

What did the modern era player make of all this?

Run accumulation is for the mediocre. Refinement and more is expected; tact, now as essential as tactics.

The impact on players was cataclysmic. It was as if the star that was cricket and had been there until a moment ago, had suddenly collapsed under the sheer force of its own gravity. In its place was... nothing, or almost nothing: a black hole in the cricket universe. A player in the 1990s could not be blamed for feeling like some giant hand had picked him by the scruff of his neck and hurled him into the depths of a black hole. Standards honoured until then, were suddenly cast aside like they never existed. Monuments painstakingly built until the 1980s lay like so much rubble, scattered across a landscape of forgotten pitches.

The sacred had suddenly become profane.

Following an era where mammoth pyramids were erected to celebrate a career of 50 Tests, came one where even a career of 150 Tests received nothing more than a footnote. Following an era where a haul of 150 Test wickets was considered superhuman, emerged one where a haul of 300 Test wickets was considered standard. From an era where 29 Test tons were the achievement of a century, players were thrust into an era where even 39 Test tons were the norm. From an era where prefixes such as 'great, greatest, fast, fastest' rolled off both pen and tongue with equal alacrity, players were flung into an era where good was simply not good enough, fast was simply not fast enough and great was simply not great enough. A victim of its own pace, this new era of cricket had neither the time nor the space for the prefix 'greatest'.

Bradman's figures, when compared to those of modern-era batsmen,

Rudolph Lambert Fernandez

suggest more than they should and hide more than they reveal. They hide the reality of his relatively modest challenge, particularly where it had to do with the impact of decision-making. In the modern era, the margin of error in umpiring had not disappeared but it was hurtling in that direction. It was now much harder to remain unbeaten. It was now more difficult to survive hostile appealing. Run-outs, lbw dismissals and catches were now commonplace and their growing inevitability touched all players, pedestrian and prolific alike. Field umpires were no longer from just a handful of nationalities but from across the world. Like an irreverent physio-chemical process, technology was ruthlessly stripping marvellous works of their glory – the patches in the painting were now showing, the asymmetry in the sculpture was now more obvious, the discord in the concerto was now painfully audible.

Umpire Tony Hill is reported to have said that he preferred to have (not refuse) the benefit of good judgement, even if it came from a gadget, because it helped take errors 'out of the game'.[30]

Naturally, in Bradman's era these 'mistakes' stayed put - in the game!

Moral of the story?

- Our visual record of Bradman's achievements, relative to that of modern-day cricketers, remains 'incomplete'.

- Our 'omniscience' (and therefore our 'justice') is recent.

- 'Error', so marginal today, was ubiquitous in the pre-War era.

- The reality of Bradman's achievement remained 'unseen, unknown' until modern-day wonders showed us what we have been missing.

Batting average and strike-rate

What about batting average and strike-rate as measures of enduring greatness? Both are jolly measures all right as long as they are not considered in isolation but against the backdrop of playing environment.

Bradman's average of 99.94 is the best known statistic in cricket. Sachin's, at about 55 (as in 2011), is less well-known. But batting average flatters to deceive – especially in a brief batting career.

If a salesman is given a target of a daily average of $100 sale of his product and the 5-day week goes by thus – $10, $10, $10, $50, $600 – is he reliable?

---

[30] *NZ cricket umpire believes technology helps*; www.stuff.co.nz, 21 July 2011.

Is he worth rewarding? Has he succeeded? Perhaps not quite in the way the manager intended although his daily average is indeed $136 and well above the target. The manager simply cannot rely on a lucky Friday every week. He has to have a salesman who delivers more consistently, even if he hovers only just above the target. So he may well look for someone who can deliver $80, $110, $100, $95 and $120 and has a more 'honest' average of $101 than sit back happy with his man Friday. On paper, the Friday freak has a far higher average. In the real world, the other guy is the better (greater?) salesman.

Bradman had scores of '250 and above' in only 5 innings but – this is important – because of his brief career, these 5 innings disproportionately and irrevocably skewed his batting average to a zone (99.94) inaccessible to other batsmen. Some 21% of his runs (1,461 out of Bradman's 6,996 runs) came from just 5 innings – 254, 334, 299, 304 and 270.

Now, these 5 high-score innings were turning points. All were before 1937. His last 'high' was the 270 runs against England in Melbourne on 1 January 1937; he was never again able to exceed 250 runs.

Let's take a closer look.

Wisden's Match Report of the 'Second Test Match, England v Australia, June 1930' is accurate about Bradman's superb batsmanship but equally accurate about the context in which he scored his 254 at Lord's. The report called Bradman's opposition 'indifferent', singling out English bowler Allen for being 'innocuous and expensive'. It also acknowledged that Bradman's mates, Ponsford and Woodfull, who went before him, thoroughly weakened the bowling – it was ripe for him to exploit, when he eventually came on.

Wisden's Match Report of the 'Third Test Match, England v Australia, July 1930' is honest about Bradman's exploitation of the conditions but equally honest about what those conditions were when he scored his 334 runs in Leeds. The report confirmed that none of the English bowlers were effective or intimidating – not Tyldesley, not Geary, not Larwood.

Then referring to the 'life' that Bradman had – and by implication, the heavy price that England paid for poor fielding as well, the report went on to say that had the fielding been sharper, Bradman would have been out on more than a couple of occasions.

But the fielders weren't sharp... and Bradman went on to his 334.

Wisden's Match Report of the 'Fourth Test Match, Australia v South Africa, January 1932' is faithful to Bradman's prowess but also faithful to

Rudolph Lambert Fernandez

the context in which he scored his unbeaten 299 in Adelaide. It confirmed that Bradman survived 'several appeals' for lbws and catches.

Wisden's Match Report of the 'Fourth Test Match, England v Australia, July 1934' is candid about Bradman's spectacular innings but equally candid about the playing environment that enabled his 304 in Leeds. The report confirmed how England made it all too easy for Australia with fielders dropping sitters all over the ground and bowlers looking harmless.

This was pretty much the story until 1937. Then a couple of things happened. Reform started on the lbw law and batsmen were compelled to become more cautious, bowlers and fielders more aggressive... not just in their bowling and fielding but also in their appealing. Umpires were also, gradually, becoming more receptive to these appeals; half of Bradman's lbw dismissals came *after* that last high (of 270 runs in Melbourne, January 1937).

Of the 20 Tests that followed, Bradman saw the best bowler of the new era in 10 Tests – Alec Bedser, whose Test career haul rivals that of Darren Gough and Andrew Flintoff. Naturally, his high-scores fell away and he was never able to repeat the scores he had gotten used to.

Bradman's 99.94 had a context. It gives him his rightly deserved place at the top of the table in that era. But it is a grave injustice to place it against the batting averages of generations that succeeded him.

In this respect, a batsman's strike-rate (runs scored per 100 balls faced) is a far more reliable, more accurate tool than batting average (runs scored per innings) to assess enduring greatness. But it's seldom spoken about when referring to Bradman. For nearly half his exceedingly short career of 80 innings, Bradman had scores of less than 40. Some 22 out of Bradman's 80-innings career – about a fourth of his career - saw him score 18 or fewer runs.

What was Bradman's strike-rate? How many runs was he capable of scoring per 100 balls bowled?

Bradman's strike-rate was 58.61. This too had a context.

First, Bradman's opposition was, always, inferior. The West Indies were debutants. The South Africans were losers – 83% of the time. England were irretrievably inferior to Australia, yet he saw them in successive Tests for half his playing span. And India were... well, just re-read that bit in Chapter 3!

Second, Bradman's opportunity to actually face as many as 100 balls was several times higher than batsmen who emerged after the 1940s, let alone Sachin who emerged several decades later. Thanks to the placid bowling environment he enjoyed, Bradman was far less likely to be caught, caught-behind, caught-and-bowled, run-out, lbw, bowled or stumped than those who came after him. Besides, he played in a handful of grounds, the majority at 'home'.

Finally, Bradman was virginally cautious and therefore more likely to see a full 100 deliveries. His dismissals generally fell into the 'indisputable' category. He was bowled or caught most often, rarely declared lbw and almost never run-out. A sign, if one was needed, of the cataractic umpiring of his age.

What has been Sachin's strike-rate? How many runs has he been capable of scoring per 100 balls bowled?

Sachin's strike-rate, when compared to Bradman's, has been an incredible 55 (as of 2011).

Why incredible?

Sachin played in a highly competitive, highly intrusive environment where he was far more likely to get caught, caught-behind, run-out, lbw, bowled, stumped and caught-and-bowled. Besides, he saw over twice the number of rival teams and played in over five times as many Test grounds around the world. Additionally, he has been several times more aggressive than Bradman and at far greater risk of dismissal well before he faced even 40 balls, let alone 50, 70, 80 or 100 balls.

Strike-rate in Tests: Bradman 58.6, Sachin 55 (as in 2011)

At first glance that looks like an admission of Bradman's superiority but the devil, as we have seen, is in the detail: Sachin's strike-rate is across over three times Bradman's ephemeral play-span of 80 innings. It's time historians looked at this afresh and corrected the injustice not just to Sachin but to batting generations from the 1950s, 60s, 70s and 80s.

Compared to the challenge that Sachin – and indeed other modern batsmen – faced, Bradman's challenge was, to put it mildly, a walk in the park.

CHAPTER 10

The Razor's Edge - Reflections On Risk

'It is always the adventurous who accomplish great things.'

– Charles de Montesquieu

DR. SIMON PRIEST, CEO AND President of virtual TEAMWORKS. com is considered an authority on behaviour in adventure or outdoor sport. Priest worked with several researchers (G Carpenter, P Martin, R Baillie, K Klint and others). His research touched a range of sporting activities, particularly those that involve risk and he proposed a model of risk-taking behaviour that explained the strong link with personal competence.

Priest said that sportsmen will be encouraged to select risks that suit their level of perceived competence in the belief that they can positively influence the uncertainty to a final outcome in their favour. His Adventure Experience Paradigm was founded on two factors – personal skill and situational challenge.

A debutant rock climber for instance assumes a reasonable level of success or personal competence if he completes his first climb with few rests and no bruises. Particularly true if he is convinced that his skill is entirely his and has nothing to do with external factors. The applause, the positive feeling of accomplishment will invariably lead to higher motivation, greater self-confidence and a hunger to take on a more challenging climb; climbing the same rock would probably kill with boredom.

Self-efficacy, Priest said, is more than self-confidence. It has three dimensions:

- Magnitude: degree of certainty associated with success as influenced by perceptions of risk and difficulty

- Strength: duration of expectations for success despite contradictory information

- Generality: potential for transfer of self-efficacy beliefs from one situation to another

These three elements decide whether a sportsman will avoid an activity he has tried and failed at, or whether he will work to the bone until he gets better at it. They also decide how long that effort will be sustained under stress. If the sportsman perceives success and a higher level of personal competence (from completing a tough climb) he will move on to greater things – a more 'difficult' rock. If he perceives failure or personal incompetence, he will probably give up the more arduous route, stick to the tried and tested, pick a lower level of risk or give up altogether. On rare occasions when levels of risk and competence are in sync, he will ride on 'the razor's edge' until he becomes fully astute.

This is of course a shoddy summary of theories formulated by the erudite Priest but it conveys the essence of a wisdom that has been used to study a range of 'risk-taking' outdoor sports. Priest was not alone. Others have explored risk behaviour and the link with anticipation-training, injury, ability and motivation.

Theories may have their critics. There may be more refined, more recent theories. But for our purposes, it is easy to see these on the cricket field, particularly in the way a batsman scores – a single, two, three, four or six. He is weighing perceived competence against perceived risk and accordingly, either stepping forward or holding back – in every sense. He weighs several things before playing a stroke: his performance in previous matches, in previous overs, against the bowlers running toward him (and those he has faced before). He weighs his previous success on the pitch he is standing on (and other pitches he has played on), his success against fielders spread out on the field (and those he has faced before). He is also considering the extent to which he can dominate the bowler – the one running in now or the fielder in the deep who is next in line. For his part, the bowler next in line, often varies his own line, length, pace and body-language based on what he has seen the batsman do to the bowler just before him.

A good batsman uses the full vocabulary of shots at his disposal to 'talk' to these bowlers. The greatest batsmen possess the greatest vocabulary, not as an exception but as a rule. They wield it with ease compared to lesser batsmen who are compelled to choose a lower level of risk when 'talking' to bowlers or fielders. They wield it with ease compared to other batsmen who could not be bothered with 'talking' to anyone at all – who just want more runs on the board.

Imagine the weight of expectation on Sachin's shoulders, each time he goes out to bat. Millions of hyper-ventilating fans, all expecting him to hammer every ball, regardless of the pitch condition, the light, the ferocity of bowling, the aggression of fielders or the bundle of nerves at the non-striker's. Every shot he plays is cheered. Every run he takes is applauded. Imagine the pressure of not playing a shot, not reading the ball, not running, being out for a duck, being caught, bowled or run-out, being out at 49, being out at 91, at 93... Imagine the pressure of not scoring a 100 international hundreds. Is it possible to 'pressure' someone just short of such a momentous landmark?

This is a sort of insane pressure that has never been felt by any sportsman. You'd need a tungsten-steel spinal cord to simply survive from day to day with your head still screwed on right. You'd need inexhaustible reserves of energy and enthusiasm to show up at the nets each morning, to swing 'this' way every time you swung 'that', to rise every time you fell.

In spite of this pressure, Sachin seems to have had an intuitive understanding of where the fielders are and has used it to plan his fours and sixes. It suggests economy of movement not the mindless slog of a pinch-hitter. It suggests superior anticipation of where the ball is going to pitch and therefore where the bat needs to be at point of impact. It suggests a near-immaculate sense of timing. He has been 'middling' more (and better) than the best batsmen in the world; more often than not it has hit his bat in the 'sweet spot' and gone precisely where he has wanted it to go.

If fours demonstrate a batsman's control, sixes are a more exquisite articulation of that control. If fours demonstrate a batsman's ability to dictate terms to the bowling, sixes demonstrate his command over it. The amateur driver appears excited with his ability to control the wheel at 80mph until he sees the professional doing it at 180mph. The boy on the farm appears thrilled with his ability to race his pony at 5mph so his jaw drops as he sees a jockey race a thoroughbred at 55mph.

The freedom with which Sachin has hit sixes suggests that he knows what he is doing. It suggests a confidence in his ability to a) 'middle' b) consistently elude fielders and c) comfortably clear the ropes. As a batsman grows in confidence during an innings he tends to hit boundaries more fluently. A boundary is a barometer – if ever there was one in the middle – that faithfully indicates the measure of a batsman's confidence. If spectators cheer a square cut rushing away for a four, they roar their appreciation at a straight drive hit over the bowler's head for a six. They instantly recognise a batsman's growing confidence, his mastery... and are prepared to reward it, in real-time.

Now, a brief but necessary diversion before we return to the theme of scoring style: Sachin's 100 international hundreds.

Critics are champing at the bit to prove that this newly invented 'century of centuries' is utter drivel. They are keen to correct retarded fans. They are at pains to remind us that this whole business of 100 international hundreds is excessive.

Ayaz Memon has referred to the idea of Sachin's 100 tons as 'contrived, a mix of apples and oranges'.[31]

Mukul Kesavan has derided the 100 tons as a 'meaningless statistic', because he felt that it put two distinctive grades of performance on par with each other, artificially creating a single grade.[32]

Now, is the concept of an 'international hundred' credible?

The critics mean well but their anguish is misplaced.

Those who trash Sachin's feat of a 100 international tons as 'contrived' or a creation of 'cricketing illiterates' seem to have missed the point. Actually, this whole business of 100 hundreds is far from idiotic; it is part of, if not central to, understanding Sachin's enduring greatness.

If Sachin had scored only 15 Test tons but as many as 85 ODI tons, they would be right in rubbishing the idea of 'a 100 international tons' as a non-statistic. But he has scored hundreds in both formats with equal ease. The six he hits in a turbo-charged ODI is no more a slog than the calculated lift he is able to generate in a sedate Test. He is essentially applying that same mastery over bowling and fielding in a wholly different context; it reflects an infinitely superior technique. He holds the world record for sixes while

---

[31] *There's something about Sachin*; Ayaz Memon; *Times of India*, 19 March 2012.

[32] *Why the 100th does not matter*; Mukul Kesavan; *ESPNcricinfo*, 3 December 2011.

Rudolph Lambert Fernandez

reaching a Test century – he has done it on six occasions.

An ODI opener is compelled to hit in the air in the early overs – no matter what the conditions, he simply cannot take his time. Lesser batsmen prefer to come in later to avoid the testosteronic new ball and fresh pacers. What did Sachin do? He fought to open India's ODI innings, when his captain and other seniors wanted to protect their most prized batsman. He *fought* to be in that position because of his confidence, his mastery.

ODIs have been around for nearly half a century and are an essential part of cricket history – protests from traditionalists notwithstanding. ODIs demand a unique set of batting skills in finding the gaps, in running between the wickets, in setting a target, in reaching one, in maintaining or upping the run-rate. These aren't skills for beach volleyball – they're cricketing skills.

A batsman at ease in *both* formats is surely more accomplished for the same reason that a tennis player is greater when he can cream the competition regardless of how they come to him – on grass or clay. It is not just the field that has changed but the way the ball moves across the court, the way he and his opponent move.

Batsmen who are accomplished in Tests, but barefacedly less so in ODIs, need to be more circumspect about the 'great' laurels thrust their way. Look at the table below:

Table J: Cricket's centurions – Test vs. ODIs [the Sachin edge]

Batsman	Test tons	ODI tons	Difference
Sachin	51	49	2 tons
Dravid	36	12	24
Ponting	41	30	11
Kallis	43	17	26
Lara	34	19	15
Steve Waugh	32	3	29

Note: as of July 2012.

Sachin has been scoring centuries with ease, whether he comes in at 4th position in a Test or in an ODI opening pair. In the case of every other batsman, it is indeed a fiction to simply add tons in one format to tons in another format and 'spin' an achievement where none exists. In Sachin's case, the arithmetic is no abracadabra. In his case the whole is indeed greater than the sum of its parts and reiterates why he is the greatest batsman in *cricket history.*

Sachin's feat deserves a trifle more than a pat on the back. And it is time that his adversaries and admirers respect it for what it is – a landmark to beat every other landmark in cricket, the summit of the cricketing mountain range.

That Sachin has been caught as many times as he has is a commentary as much on the burden he has been bearing on behalf of the team for a good part of his career as it is a commentary on the high quality of bowling, wicket-keeping and fielding he has faced. Particularly, the impact of the modern cricket fielder – running, jumping, flying, diving, skidding, rolling, flinging his way directly into the path of even the most domineering innings.

In March 1998, the Australians had an army – Mark Taylor, Ricky Ponting, Mark Waugh, Steve Waugh, Michael Bevan. The Indians had Sachin; but what he carried in his hand did not look like a bat, more like a mace. With it, he hammered 14 fours and 4 sixes and finished with an unbeaten 155. This was a *Test* match.

A few weeks later in an ODI against Australia, Sachin was at it again. The mace looked no less menacing: 5 fours and 7 sixes.

In the ICC World Cup in March 2003, Pakistan put up 273 runs in 50 overs and sent India in for the next 50 overs. Three tigers were bowling at both ends of the magnificent Centurion Park in South Africa - Akram, Akhtar and Younis. Sachin stood Thor-like, driving his bat like an iron hammer into the pitch. He stayed on as India's finest passed him by – Ganguly, Sehwag, Kaif, Dravid. He first put up 50 runs in 50 minutes off 37 deliveries. By the time he strode off the field, 55% of his 98 runs came off boundaries. He had scored off 75 balls at a strike rate of about 131. India won – by six wickets and the powers that be had no heated arguments when crowning the Player of the Match.

When you are out in the middle, even the humble single is a risk. So is a two and a three. So are glances and edges and delayed edges and late cuts; all risks. A four is also a risk: the ball can be stopped by a fielder if you do not hit with timing, at the right angle and with sufficient power. The ball can also be caught. A six is on top in a hierarchy of risks – the bungee jump of batting, as it were.

The greatest are those who are at ease scoring *across* the spectrum – singles, twos and threes, fours **and** sixes. After all, sixes are a part of cricket. They

　　　　　　　　　　　Rudolph Lambert Fernandez

are part of a legitimate armoury of strokes. They are part of a rightful set of tools to pile on runs, to set a target, to chase one, to put a rival on the defensive. They are part of a batsman's vocabulary and one that he uses to 'talk' to rival bowlers, fielders, wicket-keepers or 'stare down' a rival captain. They are also part of that spirit of sport; so impossible to define, yet so conspicuous by their absence.

Some say Bradman chose not to hit sixes because it was not customary in those days to hit in the air. It was not part of cricket culture at the time to hit hard and high.[33] It was not the 'done thing'. That is Bradman twice wronged. It is an insult to his greatness. It is also incorrect.

When you think about it there was little about Bradman's approach and style that was customary, from the way he gripped his bat to the way he ran between wickets or the way he plundered the bowling. Remember, Bradman was a rebel from the word go, one who unlike other mortals, did not 'believe in the law of averages'. He was a man in a hurry. He wanted to make runs as quickly as he could and he would make them in any way they came – elegantly or not, textbook shots or not. Bradman was all about effectiveness, not efficiency or style. He was obsessed with outcome and outcome alone. The journey (single, two, three, four) mattered less to him than the destination – a run, a ton, a double ton. The means – his array of shots – mattered less to him than the end.

Bradman was unlike the other batsmen of his era, who took their time to 'read' the pitch and the bowlers, before building an innings. He wanted to start piling on runs from the first minute he was out on the field. It is therefore extremely misleading to think that he was a conformist who essentially played his shots and scored runs the way everyone else did; only better, faster than they did. Bradman cared little for a bowler's reputation and if there was even the slightest hint that the bowler believed he was superior, Bradman wasted no time in putting him in place.

In 2001, *The Telegraph* in the UK had an obituary on Bradman. It quoted West Indian pacer Learie Constantine as saying that Bradman was unsparing toward weary or inconsistent bowlers and that, if he, Bradman, could make a bowler 'look foolish' he would go ahead and do just that.[34]

Bradman was a radical. It set him apart. Yet, for all his defiance of the

---

[33] *Sachin Tendulkar: A definitive biography (Tendulkar and Bradman: A comparison*; Page 395); Vaibhav Purandare; Roli Books, Fourth Revised Edition 2011 (published 2005).

[34] *Sir Donald Bradman, Obituary; The Telegraph*, 27 February 2001.

norm, he was probably reluctant to hit in the air for one very human reason – he feared losing his wicket. It was not out of deference to the batting culture of his time that he hit low and safe. When you cut to the chase, that's really all there is to it – he was prepared to risk hitting hard and quick but not beyond a point. He was perhaps unsure of his ability to control the ball in the air – even against the relatively placid bowling, wicket-keeping and fielding of his era.

Some 80% of the balls were bowled to him by English bowlers and nearly half of his career was a period of successive matches against England. He had all the time in the world to overpower them including mediocre ones from the West Indies, South Africa and India. Yet he appeared to find it impossible to conquer his anxiety about hitting in the air, to conquer the opponent within.

Bradman may have learned his lesson early, perhaps from the First Class matches he played in 1927; before his Test career. Perhaps he had watched others hitting hard and high and getting caught. Perhaps he had got caught himself in like manner and decided early on, that if it came to a choice between hitting high (and being caught) and hitting low and safe (and keeping his wicket) he would always choose the latter.

Bradman would occasionally 'unwind' in soft matches, such as when the Blackheath XI played Lithgow in November 1931. His 256 runs included 14 sixes and 29 fours, but it was off weaklings like Bill Black and Horrie Baker, both of whom gained their notoriety from being butchered by Bradman in that 'comfort' match rather than from excelling in Test cricket against England.

A closer look at the risk-taking behaviour of that era tells a different tale.

Table K: The 'habit' of sixes in the early 19th and 20th centuries

Batsman	Test career span	Sixes hit in a Test career	Test career runs	Runs from sixes (as % of Test career runs)
Don Bradman	1928-48	6	6996	36 (0.5%)
Keith Miller	1946-56	28	2958	168 (6%)
Wally Hammond	1927-47	27	7249	162 (2%)
Jimmy Sinclair	1896-1911	16	1069	96 (9%)
Frank Woolley	1909-34	15	3283	90 (3%)
Jock Cameron	1927-35	11	1239	66 (5%)
Clyde Walcott	1948-60	11	3798	66 (2%)

Rudolph Lambert Fernandez

| Frank Worrell | 1948-63 | 11 | 3860 | 66 (2%) |
| Arthur Morris | 1946-55 | 10 | 3533 | 60 (2%) |

Note: In the year 1910, six runs were granted for any hit 'over the boundary'; until then you had to hit 'out of the ground' to earn a six. Mr. Sinclair must have had good forearms.

If you wanted to make runs and dominate the bowling, you hit sixes. Everyone did, and repeatedly – in the 1890s, 1910s, 1920s, 1930s and 1940s. Englishmen Hendren and Edrich hit 9 sixes each, Jack Hobbs hit 8 sixes and so did Cyril Washbrook. Even Len Hutton hit 7 sixes. Wicket-keeper L E G Ames hit as many sixes as Bradman did. Apparently South Africa's Sinclair was merrily hitting sixes in the 19th century and carried on hitting them into the 20th century – 9% of his Test runs coming off sixes. The inimitable Wally Hammond once hit ten sixes in a single Test innings – as far back as 1933.

With a bit of effort it is easy to see where this is heading.

Hitting 'low and safe' was **not** the consensus, whether in the late 19th century or the early 20th century. If there was an unwritten code – to hit on or just above the ground – it appears that only Bradman followed it. But there wasn't any code.

Bradman loosened up in the odd soft match because he knew the stakes were far lower. If he did get out, there was no great loss – to the team or to his own international record. But that fear (of getting out) held him back in Tests, where he knew the stakes were higher. If it was not fear that held him back (but some internal code), then, knowing Bradman, he would never have broken it. That he did hit sixes (6 of them) in Tests suggests there was no such internal code; he was simply not confident enough to hit sixes more often and more consistently without losing his wicket.

For all his superiority over bowlers of his era, Bradman limited his dominance to the tried and tested groove – of hitting low and along the ground. He stayed cautious. Yet for all his caution as many as 56% of his Test dismissals were catches. For all his prudence, as many as 33% of his Test dismissals involved him being out bowled. Strange, when you realise that only 39% of his Test runs came off boundaries (fours and sixes).

In spite of his tendency to walk the razor's edge, the predominantly extra-terrestrial Sachin has been caught only 61% of the time in Test cricket and been bowled only 18% of the time. Strange when you see that as many as 54% of his Test runs have come off boundaries, including as many as 64 sixes.

Bradman was an attacking batsman all right, but he looked the part and played the part in the 1930s. The munitions men who came after him, took the word 'attack' to a higher plane, giving it an entirely new meaning – batsmen who tore through a bowling line-up, used experience to read a bowler's cues during run-up, used skill to spot the ball early out of the bowler's hands, set the tone for a delivery by stepping away from the wickets or out of the crease, deceived by staying still during run-up, then exploding at the last second.

They willed teams to victory by overcoming fear and doubt and failure. They simply challenged those same fears and doubts and failures. They relied not just on brute strength but on cunning and craft. Garry Sobers, Viv Richards, Clive Lloyd, Ian Botham, Gordon Greenidge, Javed Miandad, Adam Gilchrist, Brian Lara, Chris Cairns, Jacques Kallis, Virender Sehwag, Yuvraj Singh, Mathew Hayden, Ricky Ponting, Carl Hooper, Kapil Dev, Sanath Jayasuriya, Chris Gayle, Shahid Afridi, Wasim Akram, Inzamam-ul-Haq, Nathan Astle, M S Dhoni. They used their judgements of field placements and the distance of the ropes from the pitch, to time their shots so that more often than not, they got the better of bowlers and fielders.

Bradman hit 6 sixes from 50 Tests; Sidhu hit 38 sixes from 51 Tests.

Adam Gilchrist hit 100 sixes, from 96 Tests. Translate that into what he must have done in only 48 Tests (half of 96 Tests) and it works out to 50 sixes (as many Tests in Bradman's career). And batsmen who have cut their teeth in ODI and T20 cricket are taking six-hitting to a whole new level.

 'When a man has put a limit on what he will do, he has put a limit on what he can do.' – Charles M. Schwab

It seems that Bradman curtailed his ability to play the widest possible range of shots by limiting his willingness. He was apparently held back on all three counts – magnitude, strength and generality.

- Magnitude: Bradman's degree of certainty (or confidence) associated with success (if I hit in the air, I *can* control the ball, *I will* clear the ropes, *I will* clear the fielder in the deep) as influenced by perceptions of risk and difficulty, seemed low. Also low was the 'magnitude' of his self-efficacy belief.

- Strength: Seeing contradictory information (batsmen who hit in the air are usually caught) Bradman's duration of expectation for success (his expectation of consistently hitting in the air and not being caught)

Rudolph Lambert Fernandez

was drastically reduced. Also reduced was the 'strength' of his self-efficacy belief.

- Generality: Bradman's potential for transfer of self-efficacy beliefs from one situation to another was limited and so was the 'generality' of his self-efficacy belief. It appears that he simply could not transfer

'He that will not when he may,
He shall not when he will.'
– Robert Mannyng, *Handlyng Synne (1303)*

the confidence he showed in one situation (singles, twos, threes, fours) to another (sixes).

Somehow Sachin seemed certain of his ability to control the ball in the air – even against the best bowlers, fielders and wicket-keepers in cricket history. Sachin kept powering himself forward on all three counts. He had a far higher degree of certainty of success to give him the daring to tear apart bowling attacks with a quiet, calculated ferocity. After seeing other batsman hitting high and getting caught, he did not hold back – he just got better at it. He was also able to deploy the widest range of shots in Test and ODI cricket, in grounds around the world and against the widest range of quality bowling imaginable.

Sachin expanded his ability by widening his horizon. Like Bradman, he hated losing and was addicted to winning. Like Bradman, he loved to dominate. Unlike Bradman, he was never afraid of failing. He has never been afraid of getting his timing wrong, of not clearing the fielders or the ropes. He has never been afraid of misreading the ball in flight. If he did fail, he learned from his mistakes. If he did not play a shot well, he improved the next time around and trusted his instincts as they grew sharper with each match.

Sachin understood, better than anyone else, that winning is not always victory and losing is not always defeat. So match after match, series after series, he has risked his arm against the best bowlers and fielders in the world, hitting hard *and high*. To his delight he found that on his worst days he lost but there was no defeat and on his best days he won, even if there was no victory.

When an expert marathon runner suddenly slows down mid-race he is taking a risk – of not being able to catch up when the time is right. He takes that risk anyway, using his experience of how his body and mind feel, the dryness in his throat, the sweat on his neck, the tension in his limbs. He knows exactly when to slow down and when to speed up. The best in the world are able to peak at just the right moment. No wonder it is fascinating to watch: how effortless it seems when that one man on the track powers ahead of the others who until then have been steaming ahead, certain to 'breast' the ribbon.

When an ace footballer is a good distance from the rival goal he has several options as defenders close in on him. He can pass to another attacker, he can keep edging the ball closer to the goal until he can 'safely' score or he can chance his foot right where he is. Usually he is not looking for the perfect zone – he is prepared to kick 'right here, right now'. Naturally, amateurs see 'striking distance' a little differently from professionals. The best are able to fire even from the greatest distances. The greatest footballers exercise the full range of options with equal ease, never shying away from one or the other but choosing the option for the moment. When they do kick from such great distances, they apply the right degree of spin to send the ball soaring 'away', then to the shock of the keeper, suddenly, crashing 'toward' the goal.

This is true of nearly every sport. The sportsman is taking a risk not only with the tools of his sport – cricket bat, tennis racquet, golf club, hockey stick, horse, pole, sword – but also with the tools of his body and mind. In a great sportsman, these come together so he picks, as a master chef would, the right ingredients to come up with the most incredible finish. In the greatest sportsmen, this becomes a habit to the point where it seems natural, instinctive. It is anything but.

Imagine a boxer who can jab, duck, cross and parry but chooses not to hook or use an uppercut. It reflects a lack of some skill or confidence, manifest in an over-riding sense of caution. The tennis player who chooses never to spin the ball, the F1 driver who slows down too much at the turn, the jockey who never strains his mount, the pole-vaulter who never dares to bend the pole beyond a point. Sport is full of these men and women, which is why it is easy to pick the great from the good and the greatest from the great.

The 4-minute mile, the longest solo flight, the fastest 100m run, the highest pole vault, the longest long jump, the highest high jump – these remain landmarks until someone comes along and sets them aside. These milestones are set by those who push the limits. They dare what no else dares. It takes courage, determination, self-confidence, skill. It also takes experience from making mistakes - not from not making them!

Sachin's Test record against Bradman's:

- Out Bowled: Bradman (33%), Sachin (18%)
- Not-out: Bradman (12.5%), Sachin (11%)
- Out caught: Bradman (56%), Sachin (61%)
- Runs from Boundaries: Bradman (39%), Sachin (54%)

Lest we move on too hurriedly and miss the importance of the portrait above – Bradman's figures are from 50 Tests, Sachin's from an astonishing 177 Tests.

On their own, Sachin's exploits are sufficiently impressive to set him way ahead of Bradman because of the sheer challenge of his playing context – teams, grounds, bowling, fielding, wicket-keeping, hi-tech scrutiny, lbw legislation... the whole lot. But *when put together*, these figures become pure dynamite; particularly when you throw in his record of fours and sixes.

His habit of walking on the razor's edge, consistently and fluently using the full armoury of strokes, against the most dangerous bowlers and fielders, demonstrates Sachin's confidence. A confidence that comes not from bravado but sheer ability, built over years. A confidence that has seen him excel for over two decades in the most demanding regime of international cricket.

Sachin is like the ace jockey gently steering his mount through the huddle at the curve, the attacker nearing the goal but never hesitating to kick when the time is right, no matter how challenging the distance. He is like the Grand Slammer using just the right amount of spin to see the ball swirl back in the air, to score a point. He is like the Chess Grandmaster surprising even himself with a new lethal move on the board, just when his rival imagines he's got it all figured out.

In March 1994, India were playing New Zealand in an ODI at Eden Park in Auckland. Sachin's 82-run knock included just one single. One! Off a mere 49 balls, he hit 2 sixes, 15 fours and then ran for a three, 3 twos and one single. He had scored at a strike-rate of 167.34 and his score accounted for **57% of the team's runs.** He was Player of the Match and India won by 7 wickets with 160 balls to spare.

Bradman's 'never hit in the air' and 'why *fly* when you can *run*' philosophy greatly increased his chances of high scores, when compared to his more adventurous peers. It made him the run-machine he wanted to be but... he remains the poorer for it.

Sachin's calculated risks greatly reduced his chances of high scores, often choked him off in the nineties and scaled down his ability to get a double ton or triple ton. In spite of this 'handicap' he has scored a mountain of runs against every rival worth the name and… he remains the richer for it.

This isn't to say that if you hit 20 sixes you're greater than one who hits 19. Or that the man who has 15 sixes is greater than one who has hit 5. The point is not so much about the sixes as the spirit behind them.

In 1963, the Rt. Hon. Robert Menzies wrote that true artists were almost never conservative. They were always willing to mix things up a bit. This adventurous side to their personalities would inevitably reduce their 'tally' in the record books but they would prefer to stray just that little bit every now and then, for the 'fun of it'. Yes, there would be traditionalist well-wishers asking such artists to strip their repertoire of suicidal moves and to stick to the tried and tested groove. But, Menzies concluded, that if every batsman had stuck to this jaded script, fans and critics would have been denied the most delectable shots and cricket would have been the poorer for it - 'averages without spirit; performance without pleasure'. In Menzies' view the greatest batsmen were true artists, the ones who would try 'calculated (and sometimes uncalculated) risks'. These were the players who redeemed the game by lifting an innings, by transforming a match, from plain to pulsating.[35]

In the 21st century, some sports have acknowledged 'risk' as an element of enduring greatness by cheerfully arming judges with a new measure – Degree of Difficulty. It has been added to the traditional 20th century measure of 'Execution'.

Why? It is meant to better separate the middling from the mediocre. It is used to judge greatness in diving, figure-skating, gymnastics and a range of other sports.

What does it do? It rewards sportsmen and women skilled enough to consistently take on a higher level of risk. It recognises athletes who can more effectively connect a range of otherwise unconnected skills.

How? In diving, for instance, judges are looking for the number of somersaults, whether a dive involves a 'tuck' or a 'pike', the number of twists, the approach of the dive (backward or forward or armstand) and

---

[35] *Cricket - an enduring art*; Rt. Hon. Sir Robert Menzies, *Wisden Cricketers' Almanack*, 1963.

Rudolph Lambert Fernandez

the height of the platform from the water. They're also asking 'is there too much of a splash on impact?'

Australia's diving gold medallist Matthew Mitcham is convinced that the 4½ somersault, which until a few years ago was considered 'an impossible dream', is now in danger of becoming 'redundant' and being replaced by the new standard of the 5½ somersault. The increased speed and risk makes it a higher degree of difficulty dive.

Risk is a part of sport. One might argue that risk is at the heart of sport. Not senseless, ego-driven, fear-borne risk but intuitive risk, risk that comes from skill, from experience, from command over body and mind, from command of the sport and everything and everyone in it.

Poor performers avoid risk altogether or as much as they possibly can. Mediocre performers are *willing* to take risks but do not actually end up taking them. The good ones *take* risks but not as often as they might. The better ones take risks but are usually content with a lower level of risk. The best take a higher level of risk, as much risk as necessary, as often as necessary and come out on top... again and again and again. The greatest do what is 'necessary' but most of the time they live well above it – most of the time they *hit in the air!*

CHAPTER II

The Big Occasion – Last Man Standing

T HE ALBATROSS IS A GREAT wanderer. Sometimes it will fly up to 14,500km, covering 900km in a day at speeds of up to 80km an hour. But one of the greatest of sky wanderers is the Arctic tern. Those that nest in the Arctic fly to the Antarctic *and back* – each year. That's over 40,000km. The albatross may fly across a continent or two; the tern across the world – from roof to roof, from end to end.

Sachin has been the cricketing world's flying mascot. His splendid journey has lasted over two decades and spanned continents. He's straddled all forms of the game. Yet considerable fuss is made over his 'match-winning' performances – the supposed *lack* of a sufficient number, that is!

Before we examine Sachin's record, let us briefly look at Bradman's Australia. England were a good team but never unbeatable. Australia were the better team.

Australia were winners with Bradman but they were winners without him as well, even if less spectacular winners. They could win without him; they rarely crumbled to a position where their fate depended on what he did or did not do. They held together. Somehow they batted *and* bowled *and* fielded *and...* won. A vital theme, but so poorly understood.

What was Australia's record **before** Bradman arrived?

Between 1876 and 1926 (50 years of cricket before Bradman) Australia played 37 Test series, primarily against England and 36 of them ended in a result – Australia won 18 of these. Over five decades of the pre-Bradman era, Australia won about half the time – the two teams appear evenly matched.

But this picture is deceptive. Take a closer look. By the turn of the century it is Australia that powered ahead... and stayed ahead. Between 1897 and 1926 (three decades of cricket before Bradman), Australia were by far the better team. They played 14 Test series against England, all ended in a result – Australia won nine. For close to three decades of the pre-Bradman era, Australia won 64% of the time.

Australia were in the habit of defeating England, *even before Bradman came along* – they played England most of the time anyway. Indeed before Bradman came along, it seemed that the only thing the Australians were any good at was hammering England.

Now take an even closer look:

- 1897-98: Australia win the Ashes

- Australia win the Ashes again in 1899

- and again in 1901-02

- and again in 1902

- In 1902-03 Australia take a break from hammering England and hammer South Africa instead, winning the series against them.

- England briefly hit back, winning two series (1903-04 and 1905) but are on the mat again with Australia winning in 1907-08 and again in 1909.

- In 1910-11 Australia take a break from hammering England and have a go at South Africa again, winning the series against them.

- England experience a brief revival of sorts winning in 1911-12 and twice in 1912 but it is more 'brief' than 'revival'. Soon Australia are at it again and monotony sets in.

- December 1920, Australia win by 377 runs

- December 1920/Jan 1921, Australia win by an innings

- January 1921, Australia win by 119 runs

- February 1921, Australia win by eight wickets

- Feb/March 1921, Australia win by nine wickets

- May 1921, Australia win by ten wickets

With a bit of effort, it is possible to see what's happening here.

- June 1921, Australia win by eight wickets

- 2-5 July 1921, Australia win by 219 runs

- Over July and August 1921, they play two matches and England is unable to win either of them – both are drawn

- ...then another match against England in December 1924, Australia win again, by 193 runs

- ...then four matches against England in 1925, Australia win three.

One wonders why no one thought up the idea of *The Invincibles* before Bradman came along.

After Bradman arrived, Australia carried on this tradition of gleefully grinding England into the ground. Between 1928 and 1948 (the Bradman years) Australia played 13 Test Series in all (not just against England); 12 ended in a result – Australia won 10 (or 83% of the time). Not that Australia suddenly had a more hulking batting line up in the form of Bradman. At the time – barring Bradman – if opposing batsmen were lined up shoulder to shoulder, England had as good or better batsmen.

Australia had the best batsmen and bowlers of that era. Most importantly, however, Australia remained the better *team*. It was more fun with Bradman around but their victory record improved dramatically after their eyes fell on far weaker teams – a little more of South Africa (than they had seen in the pre-Bradman years) and, for the first time, sinfully juicy 'full tosses' in the form of the West Indies and India.

Bradman's arrival on the scene could not have been timed better for Australia, and worse, for everyone else. Of course Bradman's arrival had a bit to do with Australia's victory margins but we must be careful not to overstate that case. Nearly half his innings saw him score fewer than 40 runs and about a fourth of his innings saw him score fewer than 18 runs. Australia's dramatic improvement in fortunes had much more to do with the new, relatively crippled opposition they faced.

Australia were not a fickle side. They knew how to win a match, how to win a series, how to set a target, how to chase one, how to enforce a follow-on.

Rudolph Lambert Fernandez

Bradman gave them a brief leg-up, but they were a capable team on their own. Even with Bradman gone, England were still losing to Australia – they lost the Ashes in 1950-51; out of five matches played they lost four.

But the critics who exaggerate Bradman's importance to the Australian team of his era are often the ones who rant about Sachin having failed his team on big occasions, and having been inconsistent: a crude, grossly simplistic and unfair assessment. He is the batsman with the highest runs in

- World Cups

- multi-team tournament finals

- a single World Cup

So much for the big occasions; they do not get bigger than these.

But Test cricket first...

In Old Trafford in 1990, Sachin's Test hundred came amidst a feeble performance by his fellow batsmen. Even as a 17-year old he helped save the side from defeat.

In August 2002 at the Headingley Test in Leeds, two Indian batsmen scored centuries in a single innings – Ganguly (128), Dravid (148). There was a third. Sachin towered above them with 193 in that same innings. India won. Who was the 'match-winner'? Was it Ganguly? Was it Dravid? Or was it Sachin? Or was it Kumble who took 3 wickets in England's first innings and 4 in their second? Or was it Sehwag who took 3 catches in England's first innings and another 3 in their second?

Vijay Santhanam and Shyam Balasubramanian have tackled this issue superbly in their book *If Cricket is Religion, Sachin is God*. They point out how daft it is to ascribe to an individual the result of a Test – win or lose or draw. Cricket is a team game, more so than other games because there are *eleven to a side* – not three, not six, not nine. The burden of team success rests more lightly on the shoulders of a Test cricketer than it does on the shoulders of a tennis ace in a doubles match or a runner in a 4-man relay team. As the authors suggest, the fuss about 'match-winning' Test performances is made usually by those who have not taken the trouble to, or do not have the capacity to understand the game.

Yet, critics have gotten so used to carping about Sachin's allegedly poor record of 'match-winning' that it is now accepted fact.

Consider this. Across the three centuries of Test cricket history, on only 47 occasions have teams pulled off whitewashes (winning every Test in a series of three or more matches). India shares the lowest place with South Africa but the only times (in 1992-93 against England and in 1993-94 against Sri Lanka) they succeeded in a whitewash was when they had Sachin on board.

Table L: Whitewashes in Test cricket history

Team	No: of whitewashes in Test cricket history
Australia	19 Test series – only one involved Bradman and it was the one against one of the weakest teams of that era (South Africa)
England	13
Pakistan	5
West Indies	3
Sri Lanka	3
South Africa	2
India	2 Test series – both involved Sachin and they were against established teams (England and Sri Lanka)
Total	47

Note: as of 2011.

Bradman enjoyed the comfort of being in the most effective Test team in cricket history – the batsmen were about average, the bowlers were the best in the world but they were dynamite 'as a team'.

Sachin has shone in spite of being in one of the most inconsistent Test teams ever – the bowlers and batsmen were good in Tests, both were temperamental in ODIs and 'as a team', they were incurably inconsistent in both formats.

On the one hand you've got some commentators, like Javagal Srinath, admitting that Sachin's individual Test effort has often been responsible for team success. But on the other hand you've got others, like Mukul Kesavan, quibbling that Sachin's innings while tributes to his greatness as an individual have not exactly been milestones in Indian Test cricket history.[36]

---

[36] *Men in White: A Book of Cricket* (*The Indian Game*; Page 259); Mukul Kesavan; Penguin Books; 2010 (published 2007).

Rudolph Lambert Fernandez

That sounds right. It even feels right. Is it?

Nirmal Shekar, writing in *The Sportstar* (11-17 August 2001), succinctly tackled just this sort of issue when he said that a genius must not be punished merely because he is surrounded by mediocrity.

In 1998 at Chennai, in the Test against Australia, Sachin felt he had failed India in the first innings, having scored just 4 before being caught. In the second innings, four Indian batsmen came before him: Mongia fell at 18. Sidhu fell at 64 after seeing off 127 deliveries. Not to be outdone Dravid fell at 56 after seeing off 149 deliveries! Under extraordinary pressure, Sachin came good for India. His 155 put India in a commanding position. In spite of having to steady the innings each time a partner left the field, he scored at a strike-rate of 81; eighty of his runs came off boundaries. He had scored 37% of the team's runs. It was a Test all right, but Sachin had decided early on that he had to be aggressive to put the Australians on the back foot. India won by 179 runs.

Table 5 in the Appendix has a list of Sachin's record of being *unbeaten* in an Indian 2nd innings. Table 6 has a list of Sachin's record of centuries in an Indian 2nd innings. These lists demonstrate how crucial Sachin has been to Indian Test cricket not just in a match or series and not just over five years or ten.

It is correct to say that Sachin's innings are tributes to his greatness as an individual. But is it right to go on and say that they have not exactly been milestones in Indian Test cricket?

Let us test this.

A modest measure of a batsman's greatness is the number and range of partnerships he has to build across both innings of a Test. Not just with fellow batting greats, but with bowlers, fielders and wicket-keeper. When padded-up they are all 'batting mates' and a great batsman cannot choose who will stay with him and for how long. He can only try his best to score and inspire his partner to do the same – put bowlers on the backfoot, put pressure on the fielders.

Bradman built 180 Test partnerships with other Australian batsmen, often a couple of partnerships in each innings he played. Sachin has built over 800 Test partnerships with other Indian batsmen, often a couple in each innings he has played.

Of all Bradman's partnerships with other Australian Test cricketers, half of these were with six men – Woodfull, Ponsford, Morris, Brown, Hassett and

McCabe. Sachin's Test partnerships with Indians have been built with over sixty men – from Vengsarkar, now over 56 years old, to Raina, just over 25 years old. Yet Bradman is still considered the landmark in Australian cricket while Sachin is credited merely with feathering his own nest!

Bradman had the benefit of building a long-term understanding with a few with whom he built the vast majority of his partnerships. It freed him up as he tackled the bowling, set a rhythm of running between wickets, adapted to field-placement changes, dealt with a fall of wickets and the range of other challenges that a leading batsman faces on the field.

Sachin has had the benefit of building this long-term understanding with a few, but only a handful of them have stayed the distance. Every few years, he has had to evolve a rapport with a new range of partners. For a decade, many were older than him, more experienced. For another decade many were younger than him, less experienced. For his sake and for the team's, he has had to either coax them into his batting rhythm or transform his pace to ensure that he's able to get the best of 'the new man in' – more often it has been the latter.

Let us take a closer look at Test partnerships.

Only once had Bradman started a partnership when Australia were *7 down with less than 200 on the board* – in December 1932, he started a partnership with T W Wall when Australia were 7 down for 156 runs against England in Melbourne. On eight occasions, Sachin has had to start a partnership with India 7 down with less than 200 on the board.

1. In July 1990, against England at Lord's, he had to start a partnership with Kiran More when India were 7 down for just 158.

2. In February 1992, against Australia in Perth, he had to start a partnership with Manoj Prabhakar; India were 7 down for just 159.

3. In November 1992, against South Africa in Johannesburg, he had to start a partnership with More; India were 7 down for just 155.

4. In June 1996, against England in Birmingham, he had to start a partnership with Javagal Srinath; India were 7 down for just 185.

5. In December 1999, against Australia in Melbourne, he had to start a partnership with Javagal Srinath; India were 7 down for just 167.

6. In February 2000, against South Africa in Mumbai, he had to start a partnership with Ajit Agarkar; India were 7 down for just 167.

7. In December 2002, against New Zealand in Wellington, he had to start a partnership with Harbhajan Singh; India were 7 down for 88.

8. In January 2010, against Bangladesh in Chittagong, he had to start a partnership with Zaheer Khan; India were 7 down for 182.

Sachin may not have built solid partnerships on every occasion but his perch has been no less precarious.

Only once had Bradman started a partnership when Australia were *8 down with less than 200 on the board* (in 1932, against England in Melbourne). On five occasions, Sachin has had to start a partnership when India were 8 down with less than 200 on the board:

1. In February 1992, against Australia in Perth, he had to start a partnership with Kiran More; India were 8 down for 159.

2. In November 1992, against South Africa in Johannesburg, he had to start a partnership with Kumble; India were 8 down for 174.

3. In June 1996, against England in Birmingham, he had to start a partnership with Paras Mhambrey; India were 8 down for 193.

4. In December 1999, against Australia in Melbourne, he had to start a partnership with Kumble; India were 8 down for 169.

5. In December 2002, against New Zealand in Wellington, he had to start a partnership with Zaheer Khan; India were 8 down for just 96.

Again, Sachin may not have built successful partnerships every time but his predicament has been no less forlorn.

On only two occasions had Bradman started a partnership when Australia were *9 wickets down* (first in 1932 against England, when Australia were 9 down for an uncomfortable 186; then again in 1932 against South Africa, but Australia were 9 down for a comfortable 499). Sachin has had to attempt partnerships when India were *9 down* on nine occasions. In December 2002, for instance, against New Zealand in Wellington; India were 9 down for a laughable 121.

Table M: Test Partnerships - Sachin has faced far greater odds

Team Situation in Test cricket	Number of times Bradman has had to start Test partnerships	Number of times Sachin has had to start Test partnerships
3 wickets down but team score 35 or below	1	14
4 wickets down but team score 40 or below	1	7
5 wickets down but team score below 100	2	12
6 wickets down but team score below 200	2	12
7 wickets down but team score below 170	1	6
8 wickets down but team score below 200	1	5
9 wickets down but team score below 400	1	5

Note: Sachin's statistics as of 6 January 2011.

Look carefully at the above snapshot and consider that Sachin came in at No: 4 for most of his career, while Bradman came in at No: 3 for most of his – in the few crises he did face, it is Bradman who had the greater chance of setting things right for his team. Bradman had more batsmen coming after him, more time to settle in, greater scope to shape the team's innings and with the team being only 'one down' was under less pressure. Sachin had fewer batsmen after him, less time to settle in and less scope to shape the team's innings and with the team being 'two down' was under more pressure. Besides, Sachin had to be far more wary of being lbw, caught, run-out, bowled, stumped. He has had to consolidate or accelerate when the pressure on him – as 'Sachin' – and at No:4, has been far, far greater.

Sachin has been through an immeasurably more tortuous journey and although he has not come out looking spectacular in every partnership or innings, he has come good for India on several occasions. His most inspiring innings have not been glamorous centuries or double-centuries.

In June 2001, India were playing Zimbabwe in a Test at Bulawayo. Zimbabwe had put up a rather unimpressive 173 in their first innings. But when India

Rudolph Lambert Fernandez

went in to bat, wickets fell in quick succession and suddenly India were 5 down for 98. Sachin set the tone for the rest; 48 of his 74 runs came off boundaries in that first innings. Others took the cue and came good in the second innings; Sachin stayed unbeaten to guide India to victory, by 8 wickets.

In October 2010, India were playing Australia in the Border-Gavaskar Trophy Test in Mohali, Australia had put up 428 in the first innings. In India's first innings, Gambhir, Sehwag, Sharma and Dravid fell before Sachin. He had come in when the score was 151, then put in a gritty performance; 52 of his 98 runs coming off boundaries. Eventually India managed 405 runs. India's second innings was worrying at one stage with them being 5 down for 76. Sachin then set the tone; 20 of his 38 runs came off boundaries. His contribution, relatively meagre in runs, was key to India's victory: it emboldened the Indians to take on the Australians.

Look at India's Test record:

- India have been playing international cricket since 1932. For two decades, they had not registered a series victory – they lost all the time (winning first only as late as 1952).

- Between 1952 and 1988-89, *before* Sachin arrived on the scene, out of 56 Test Series that India had played, 43 ended with a result; the remaining 13 were drawn. India won only 37% of the time (16 wins out of 43 Series with a result). Finally, victories were flowing in but as a trickle.

- Between 1989-90 and 2011-12, *after* Sachin started playing, out of 74 Test Series that India played, 57 ended with a result; the remaining 17 were drawn. India won 60% of the time (34 wins out of 57 Series with a result). With Sachin being the only constant (batsman or bowler or fielder) over two decades, Indian Test victories came thick and fast.

- Some 94% of his not-out performances have been in Indian victories or draws (30 out of 32 not-outs have been victories or draws; only 2 not-outs have come in losses). Half his not-outs (16 out of 32 not-outs) have been in Indian victories.

Note: as of 6 January 2011.

Ganguly, Dravid and Laxman showed up only in 1996 and Sehwag only in 2001 – Sachin has been playing since 1989. Yes, there have been other leading lights in India's Test horizon but none as constant, as consistent, as crucial as Sachin. His innings over two decades have been *central* to India's success in Tests.

To suggest that Sachin has not come good for India on big occasions and not consistently come up with match-winning performances, is to miss the point. To allow a more accurate judgement of Sachin's contribution, look at his team record above in tandem with his individual record below.

Most (5 awards) Player of the *Series* awards for an Indian in Tests; a tally shared with Sehwag.

Most (14 awards) Player of the *Match* awards for an Indian in Tests; a distinction he shares with no other Indian.

Naturally, such honours are not given to batsmen because they look good on camera or sing the national anthem without going off-key. They are handed to batsmen who, by virtue of their *individual* performance, have lifted the *entire team's* performance. They are given to batsmen who, often *almost single*-handedly, have either brought their team to within a whisker of victory or have helped assure victory when defeat seemed a more decided outcome.

In the December 1989 Test against Pakistan at Sialkot, Sachin came in when India were **4 down for 38** runs. This was only a few days after he had started his international career and he ended up scoring nearly 25% of the team runs. As a 16-year old he batted alongside Sidhu and put on a 101-run partnership against a belligerent Pakistan attack that included the great Imran Khan, Waqar Younis and Wasim Akram.

India's Test record had been rather average until Sachin came along. Given that he's outlasted and outplayed his mates since 1989 and scored more runs than any other Indian and in the most challenging circumstances, it is strange to hear complaints about his Test innings not 'being landmarks in Indian Test cricket'. If anything, Sachin is **the** landmark in Indian Test cricket. A hundred years from now, cricketers – not just Indian cricketers – will be remembered by those who came before Sachin, those who played alongside him and those who succeeded him.

Sachin's Test contributions may not have been as outstanding as his ODI performances but they pale only in comparison; on their own, they have quietly and surely helped steady India when the team needed steadying the most. He has had to take guard in one crisis after another and has done it gracefully and courageously year after year.

Thankfully, there is decidedly less bickering about how crucial Sachin has been to Indian ODI success. His record (of having to start partnerships when the team was 5 down with May Day team scores) is incredible given that Sachin has come so early in the batting order for much of his ODI career.

- December 1990: an ODI against Sri Lanka in Margao; he had to start a partnership with Manoj Prabhakar when India were **5 down for 93 runs.**

- January 1992: an ODI against the West Indies in Brisbane; he had to start a partnership with Prabhakar when India were **5 down for 62 runs.**

- February 2003: an ODI against Australia at the Centurion; he had to start a partnership with Mongia when India were **5 down for 50 runs.**

- September 2006: an ODI against the West Indies in KL; he had to start a partnership with Harbhajan - India were **6 down for 78 runs.**

- October 2007: an ODI against Australia in Vadodara; he had to start a partnership with Irfan Pathan when India were **5 down for 43 runs.**

In February 1996, India were playing Australia at the Wankhede in the Wills World Cup. Australia had put up 258. Sachin went out with one intention – to attack. What was the Indian batting order doing beside him? Ajay Jadeja fell scoring 1. Kambli fell for a duck. Azharuddin after seeing off 40 deliveries scored 10. Things were looking irrevocably bleak for India when Sachin horsewhipped McGrath, Warne and the others. As the Indian batting line-up crumbled around him he was compelled to lie low, but it was not long before he was back up again to 90 from 84 balls. Around 70% of his runs had come off boundaries. He accounted for 37% of the team's runs at a strike-rate of 107. Was Sachin responsible for the loss?

In the Wills World Cup in New Delhi in March 1996, India were playing Sri Lanka. India had to set Sri Lanka a stiff target but Manoj Prabhakar fell for 7 and Manjrekar for 32. Sachin's run-a-ball 137, with five sixes and eight fours against cunning bowlers like Vaas, Muralitharan and Jayasuriya brought India close to a victory. That the team just could not pull it together and India lost by six wickets is true, but Sachin's score was over *half* of the team score. Was Sachin responsible for the loss?

- In ODIs, he has the most (15 awards) Player of the *Series* awards for any cricketer *in the world*. That's twice the tally of the next Indian in line (Ganguly has 7 such awards). Globally, the next batsman in line is Jayasuriya with 11 such awards.

- In ODIs, he has the most (62 awards) Player of the *Match* awards for any *cricketer in the world.* That's twice the tally of the next Indian in line (Ganguly has 31 such awards). Globally, the next batsman in line is Jayasuriya with 48 such awards.

- Sachin's hand in India's ODI fortunes is telling (as of 6 January 2011):

- Sachin has been unbeaten in 41 matches: 34 of these performances have been Indian wins, two in losses and the rest in 'no-result' matches. Some 83% of his unbeaten performances have led to victories.

- Of these 34 Sachin 'winning' not-out performances, 19 have included his scores of *80 and above*: 56% of his 'winning' unbeaten performances have been with high scores, crucial to an ODI win. They included centuries and of course that glorious double ton, the first by any man in an ODI.

- Of his remaining 7 not-out performances, only two have resulted in a loss. In 1993, India lost even after he had scored an unbeaten 82 in Jaipur against England. In 2006, India lost even after he had scored an unbeaten 141 against the West Indies in Kuala Lumpur.

- 61% of his ODI runs (10,737 of all his 17,598 ODI runs) have come in winning matches.

- In the winning matches his strike rate has been 91; leaving little doubt about the 'cause and effect' when it comes to his performance and India's fortunes. An extraordinary strike-rate over two decades and 442 matches, given the tendency of the Indian middle order to simply fold under the slightest pressure.

- Around 72% of his ODI tons (33 out of 46 tons) and 60% of his fifties (56 out of 93 fifties) have led to Indian victories.

- Around 63% of his fours (1,215 out of 1,927 fours) and 62% of his sixes (114 out of 185 sixes) have led to Indian victories.

(See Table 9 in the Appendix for Sachin's spectacular ODI saga.)

When Sachin stayed on, almost always, India won. If he was dismissed early, they usually lost. For a good deal of his career, India simply depended on him to get the run-rate going, to intimidate the bowling, to put rivals on the defensive. Were it not for India's fickle batting line-up and his having to change gears every few minutes his ODI record would have been even more staggering. Given that he has batted in 2nd position for most of his ODI career, his not-out record in winning matches suggests that for the majority of these performances he has seen the entire Indian batting order come on to the pitch and go back.

Sachin's 18,000 runs have been *pivotal* to India's ODI record. He has been the one holding up the innings on most occasions and on most occasions he has been the one running out of partners. He has been the one shifting gear up or down, as partners of varying calibre came on to the pitch – and left in quick succession. It is bizarre for someone who has contributed so crucially over two decades, to be blamed for not coming up with 'match-winning performances' or for not coming good on 'big occasions'.

Essentially, Sachin has provided the emotional, physical, mental and dare we say it, spiritual foundation, for the Indian team to build an innings. His presence in the team has inspired them, as a group and as individuals, to excel or at least to try much harder.

Javagal Srinath, India's lead bowler for many years, admitted that in his prime, when Sachin was dismissed, the team felt that the match was over. Srinath confessed that for the bulk of his career, Sachin's genius was in stark contrast to the 'diminishing value' of his team mates. If Sachin was declared out, rival bowlers and fielders suddenly bounced back, the attack looked more dangerous and the wicket suddenly sprouted all sorts of wickedness for Indian batsmen. That's how dependent India was, on Sachin.[37]

Whichever way you look at it, Sachin is under unspeakable pressure every time he steps on to the pitch because of the unprecedented scale of expectations. His die-hard fans expect a double ton or a ton, every time. His less demanding fans are... well, less demanding – they only expect him to unfailingly steer India to victory, no matter what India's bowlers, fielders and other batsmen are up to on the field, and no matter how overwhelming and professional the rival team.

With all the pressure that Bradman faced as a batsman in the early 20th century, Sachin's *existence* on and off the cricket field has no comparison with other sportsmen anywhere in the world, let alone other cricketers. For a better part of 20 years, the hopes and dreams of his fans have found their way to him, through internet and TV cables, through reams of newsprint, through possessive stares and admiring gazes, through excited shouts and screams, through claps and clinging hands and clawing fingers.

This mind-boggling pressure round the clock has throttled him when in

---

37 *Cricket's Colossus*; Javagal Srinath; *India Today* (Collector's Edition); September 2010.

full flow, arresting his stroke-play when he is about to cut loose, tempering his aggression when he is about to start belting the bowlers. The pressure has significantly cut down his strike-rate and batting average. For many years, under the glare of the media and critics, he had nearly given up his natural, instinctive style of playing. The ambient noise had cramped his art and for a good many years he kept flailing about struggling to regain his touch. That he has survived at all is a tribute to his extraordinary character. That he has put in one dignified performance after another is a tribute to his greatness.

In 1985, when the BBC showed the Australian TV mini-series *Bodyline*, it drew widespread anger from Bradman-worshippers and they directed that fury at an aged Larwood who had made Australia his home. Some callers thought that the actor playing Larwood (a man in his twenties) was indeed 81-year old Larwood.

When it comes to fanatics, 'deranged' does not quite capture it.

Sachin has faced the frenzy of the fanatic on a monumental scale that neither Larwood nor Bradman could have imagined. Unsurprisingly, he has failed with the bat on numerous occasions in both Tests and ODIs. Some of these failures are captured honestly and thoroughly in books by Gulu Ezekiel, Vaibhav Purandare, Gautam Bhattacharya and Vijay Santhanam and Shyam Balasubramanian.

Of course Sachin has fallen, but he has risen every time. Of course he has been beaten, but he has fought back every time. If anything his failures are a symbol of his fortitude, his courage and his resilience – the marks of greatness.

Those who accuse Sachin of not giving his best for his team need to think carefully about what the bookies and match-fixers reportedly whispered among themselves at the time they played their hand. A game was 'on' only after Sachin was out and it stayed 'off' as long as he was at the crease. Those who played to hidden odds and bets, retained their conviction in Sachin's innate ability to, almost single-handedly, turn a confrontation on its head: if he could, he most definitely would. Occasionally he would get out to clever bowling and fielding. In all other instances only injury, stress, a freak incident or 'determined' umpiring would get him out and they would have to wait for their chance, for lesser mortals to come on to the field so they could 'play' the odds again. A tribute from an unfortunate source, but an incredible one nevertheless, to Sachin's unquestionable commitment to winning, for his team.

Rudolph Lambert Fernandez

For decades, millions around the world have looked in awe at Bradman's batting average, thinking perhaps privately that it was too good to be true. They were right – it was. Bradman did not walk the minefield that Sachin did, for as long as he did. Yet having faced several times the odds (that Bradman did), Sachin is alone at the top. Given the sheer breadth and intensity of competition that he has straddled, his achievement is galactic.

Sachin is nowhere near the perfect batsman that he could be; he never has been close to that sort of perfection. He has always had his flaws, even when he first came out to bat as an aggressive young teenager. He lacks the staying power of some of his peers and predecessors, to habitually reach scores of 200. On more than a couple of occasions he has found it hard to translate 'form' at the nets into 'fulfilment' in the field. No one is as conscious of these flaws as he is.

One of Sachin's more obvious flaws on the field has been a tendency to 'gift' his wicket to rivals. In the first 15 years of his career, there were many occasions when he was sub-consciously trying to prove that he batted only for the team. So after having given the team a solid start, he would often 'throw' his wicket in some reckless display after having got to 50 or after having got to the 80s or 90s. Or he would do it soon after he reached a century. He seemed to be struggling to demonstrate that he was not obsessed with personal milestones. Perhaps somewhere down the line it occurred to him that if he – more than others – could get a century for the team *at will* then he ought to go ahead and do just that.

Sachin has always lacked Bradman's single-minded application at the crease – to scoring and scoring and scoring. He and the Indian team have suffered as a result. But it is also fair to say that Sachin had to contend with more distractions than Bradman did – on and off the field.

Following Bradman's departure from the game, cricket has seen superb batsmen.

- Few have intimidated entire teams by swaggering on to the pitch, then bludgeoning their way through a bowling attack, as the great Viv Richards has.

- Few have inspired millions of their countrymen to excel in cricket and beyond, through their courage and skill, as the great Sunil Gavaskar has.

- Few have swung the willow as gracefully as Gower, Viswanath, Azharuddin or Lara have or thrilled with their technical finesse as Laxman or Zaheer Abbas have.

- Few have turned a match on its head as Gilchrist, Afridi, Kapil Dev, Cairns, Graeme Pollock, Garry Sobers, Javed Miandad, Michael Bevan, Aravinda D'Silva or Steve Waugh have.

- Few have been as dogged as Dean Jones, Desmond Haynes or Dravid have been.

- Few have inspired their team to greater heights as Clive Lloyd, Border, Arjuna Ranatunga, Nathan Astle, Jacques Kallis, Kevin Pietersen, Flintoff, Martin Crowe, Saeed Anwar, Ponting, Martin Crowe, Greg Chappell or Gary Kirsten have.

- Few have battered the ball as brutally as Klusener, Botham, Jayasuriya, Mathew Hayden, Gilchrist, Gordon Greenidge or Virender Sehwag have.

Yet, with all his flaws, it is Sachin Ramesh Tendulkar who, with a combination of controlled aggression, prolific stroke-play, and exceptional technique, has emerged the most superior, resilient and versatile batsman the game has ever seen.

The world's most gifted batsmen often squint in disbelief when they watch the ultra-slow-motion replays of Sachin's upper cut. He arches his back to create a 'hole' for the good ball, the one that's solid on length and superb on line but pitched up, almost shoulder-high. Lesser batsmen instinctively know what to do with this sort of a delivery as it is too fast and too straight to 'pick'. They sensibly duck or step aside so that the ball lands safely in the gloves of the keeper. Not Sachin. His head still, his bat almost flat, pointing in the general direction of Third Man, he watches the ball as it hurtles toward his chin; then, at just the right moment, he lightly taps it up to see it soaring to the outfield. As one man, wicket-keeper and slip-cordon leap, their hands outstretched in vain as the ball flies to the boundary... for a six.

The astonished men on the field include the two field umpires and the non-striker. A close-up of the bowler's face is amusing as it is articulate. The commentators are competing for adjectives as they wrestle with slow-motion footage – the ball has flown off the *middle* of the bat.

They have gasped at his other shots as well – the square cut, the square drive, the cover drive, the off drive, the straight drive. They have stared in awe at his on drive, his pull, his hook, his leg glance. They have been short of breath each year as he stroked the ball in every direction, off every bowler.

'Doing easily what others find difficult is talent; doing what is impossible for talent is genius.' – *Henri-Frederic Amiel, Journal, December 17, 1856*

CHAPTER 12

The 99.94 Error – Part 1

WALL OF FAME, WISDEN, WALLY

'There is no crueller tyranny than that which is perpetuated under the shield of law and in the name of justice.'

– Charles de Montesquieu

COMPILATIONS OF CRICKET STATISTICS ARE laudable. No other game has such a diligent chronicle of field action – batting, bowling, fielding, wicket-keeping, captaincy, umpiring, winning, losing, the highest, the lowest, the most, the least. To archivists, nearly every breath inhaled and exhaled appears to be worthy of capturing in some form, worthy of recording for posterity. To them nearly every statistic is worth using: to compare, to celebrate, to critique. What appears useless now is simply archived anyway because '...you never know'. You never know when trick becomes trend, when freak becomes familiar.

Statistics go back more than a century, covering all possible games and tournaments. Every match, every series, every Test, every ODI, every World Cup, painstakingly catalogued – ball by ball, over by over, session by session, innings by innings, match by match, series by series. Tons, double tons, triple tons, ducks, extras, maidens, batting averages, strike-rates, economy rates, stumpings, lbw decisions, run-outs, singles, fours, sixes...

Why? What possible purpose could this mountain of minutiae serve?

Well, you never know.

You never know when extraordinary becomes everyday. You never know when rare becomes run-of-the-mill. An entire universe of activity, from the monumental to the mundane, documented so that future generations may gauge greatness and applaud achievement. No small feat. It speaks of a commitment, a passion that runs deep. It speaks of a respect for the game's history and a child-like hope for its future. It demonstrates to all custodians of cricket that those hours out in the middle were worth it because they have been captured irrevocably in statistics. They may have been stored in a historian's mind – he is now dead and his memory with him. They may have been caught on a still photograph – the print is now faded. They may have been recorded on a video film – the recording is now destroyed. The statistics endure. The best compilations in the cricketing world are, rightly, to be saluted by more ephemeral registers.

Wisden Cricketers' Almanack and ESPNcricinfo, for instance, are superb. Wisden, in particular – celebrating the game since the 1860s – is an awesome tribute to players of every nation, every level of talent from the classy to the colourless. They honour cricketing greats from all countries, regardless of race, age, colour or nationality. But in at least one respect they all appear to have got it wrong, consistently and for so many decades – the error that ranks Bradman above batsmen who played after him. It is the error that ranks him above those who were more accomplished, more proven as *enduring* performers than he was. An error that's alive to what was achieved but dead to the circumstances in which that achievement was possible. Dozens of batsmen have been wronged because their figures shine less brightly, appear less momentous.

We might call this the 99.94 error. An error of judgement that has failed to acknowledge the playing environment in which that magical figure – Bradman's batting average – emerged. This error draws on a power beyond Bradman and has an impact far wider than Bradman.

Intriguingly, the most respected cricket publications in the world stop short of naming Sachin as the greatest batsman ever. It is a theme worth exploring: why have editors, writers, historians, analysts, statisticians sought to deny him the credit that should have been his many years ago?

One tired theory has to do with 'match-winning' performances. As we have seen, Bradman's matches would not have been won, had not the Australian team of that day pulled together to make his contribution count. Australia saw an awful lot of England and were used to violating them, even before Bradman came along. When not facing England they faced teams who could be pounded into submission.

Sachin's performances have been heroic, but many of those matches would have been won had the Indian team of his day pulled together to make his contribution count.

In an ODI Sachin had steered India to 267 after 39 overs before he was caught while attempting a smash to the fence. With him gone India collapsed at 296 in the 49th over. We would be forgiven for imagining this scene of 'batting collapse' is from the 1990s or the early 2000s. Actually, it is more recent. It is an ODI 'grab' from Sachin's 99th international hundred, scored off just 92 deliveries (7 fours and 3 sixes) against South Africa on 12 March 2011. He was 38 years old and had been playing for over two decades, yet his younger team-mates managed *only 29 runs* in the 10 overs after his departure.

Below are headlines from *Sachin*: Tribute to a Legend by The Hindu Group [each headline describing different ODI and Test century knocks]

- Sri Lankans tame Indians despite Tendulkar's hundred
- Tendulkar's century in vain [5 April 1996 ODI against Pakistan in Singapore]
- Tendulkar stands firm among ruins; England poised for victory
- Tendulkar's century in vain [28 August 1996 ODI against Sri Lanka in Colombo]
- Tendulkar's brilliance just not enough
- Tendulkar stands tall among ruins
- Tendulkar's century goes in vain
- Tendulkar's mastery proves inadequate for India
- Tendulkar's effort goes waste
- Tendulkar's glorious innings in vain
- Despite Tendulkar India hurtles to big loss
- India fails to capitalise on Tendulkar's hundred

Note: The headlines sound wearily familiar but they are indeed about different ODI and Test innings.

Rudolph Lambert Fernandez

Many of the matches that India have lost lie on Sachin's table like so many dishonoured cheques, not because he had not signed the cheques, but because someone had been debiting his account even as he had been valiantly crediting it. The debits may not have been intentional and may not have been targeted specifically at him but their impact on him has been no less telling.

Happily for Bradman, his cheques were honoured by his team who rallied together, every time. Apart from his dream-run of successive matches against a single opponent, we have also seen that Bradman came in 3rd position against the backdrop of a relatively lack-lustre Australian batting line-up. With a weak lbw law and even weaker mid-pitch scrutiny, it is Bradman who had the greater chance, of reaching 20 deliveries, 50 deliveries, 100 deliveries, 150 deliveries. If anything, Bradman had the greater opportunity to *win* matches because there was little going on, to get him out.

Having said that, the idea of someone – anyone – almost single-handedly winning a match is more plausible, if at all, in ODI cricket. In 50 overs, the effort of an individual is potentially stark and decisive, even indispensable. In Test cricket it is far-fetched to expect any individual – Bradman and Sachin included – to *win* a match. A single bat cannot possibly carry the match, unless of course the other ten gentlemen have lapsed into coma, leaving the lone warrior to play pretty much everything to perfection.

The star performers – even the greatest – can cause injury, they can inflict potentially fatal wounds, but they cannot single-handedly throttle a rival to death. As with anything in cricket, there are exceptions and in the careers of the world's greatest batsmen, one can pick a few Tests where individual effort has made the difference between victory and defeat or defeat and a draw. But they remain just that, exceptions.

In January 1997 at Cape Town, three South Africans scored centuries in a single Test innings against India – Gary Kirsten, Brian McMillan and the mighty Lance Klusener. By the time these warriors dragged their bloody blades off that Newlands field, South Africa had put on 529 runs. The Indian team baulked at the idea of going in to bat against South Africa's bowlers – Allan Donald, Shaun Pollock, Cronje, Paul Adams and Klusener.

W V Raman saw 11 deliveries and after scoring five runs went back to the pavilion. Dravid saw 51 deliveries and after scoring two runs went back to the pavilion. Ganguly saw 38 deliveries and scored 23 runs. Venkatesh Prasad – bless him – went back without scoring at all, no doubt wondering why he was sent in with a bat and not a ball. V V S Laxman saw 23 deliveries and went back after scoring five runs.

Thankfully, Azharuddin stood beside Sachin as the two helped India put up a face-saving 359 runs. Sachin was compelled to play a deliberate innings but was stranded at 169 having run out of partners – Azharuddin left after scoring a heroic 115, but Mongia, Kumble and Srinath stayed true to form, departing after mercifully brief episodes. Sachin remained not-out with the hapless Dinesh and his valiant effort constituted the majority of India's response. It was not enough. The Indians never recovered from the first innings lashing and lost after an anaemic performance in the second innings. Was Sachin responsible for this loss?

In November 2001, in a Bloemfontein Test against South Africa, Sachin scored a magnificent 155 and Sehwag a gutsy 105 to start India off at 379 runs, yet India lost that match, by 9 wickets. Was Sachin responsible for this loss?

On both occasions, South Africa won because they were the better *team*. India lost not because Sachin failed India but because they were the poorer *team*. Tables 5 and 6 in the Appendix list Sachin's unbeaten scores and centuries in an Indian *second* innings. They demonstrate how crucial he has been to Indian Test cricket over two decades.

In ODI cricket – the microwave format – Sachin's greatness is more obvious. He has *almost* single-handedly won matches for India, at 'home', 'away', in daylight, at night, against the deadliest bowlers, the most athletic fielders, the most prolific wicket-keepers and the most astute captains. He did it in the 20th century and has been doing it in the 21st.

Then why has the title of the greatest batsman *in cricket history* eluded him?

The subversive theory suggests a conspiracy of some sort. Blatantly notorious umpiring decisions in South Africa and Australia have lent credence to this theory. But it needs to be fleshed out, to look harder at measures of greatness that were used in the early and mid-20th century. The idea of experts from the developed world sitting down together and consciously keeping Sachin out of the reckoning is too silly to be taken seriously by anyone. But we must scrutinise the methodologies being followed to honour or rate batsmen. The methodology of crowning appears suspect even when comparing Indian with Indian – no First World conspiracy after all.

Any way you look at it, it appears to be nothing more than a simple error of

Rudolph Lambert Fernandez

judgement. Importantly, it is nothing less either. A simple, but dangerous case of getting it wrong; a blunder so ubiquitous that it cannot be claimed by a single race or nationality. Almost all analysts are guilty – Indian, Australian, South African, English or Pakistani.

But Bradman has not been its only beneficiary and Sachin by no means its lone victim.

Wisden once asked Sir Neville Cardus to pick six *'Giants of the Wisden Century'*. He picked:

1. W G Grace

2. Donald Bradman

3. Sydney Barnes

4. Jack Hobbs

5. Tom Richardson

6. Victor Trumper

This list was published in 1963. We will never fully know how Sir Neville went about picking his six players but why didn't he pick **Wally Hammond**?

21st century readers might ask: 'Who was Hammond?'

Among batsmen with the most Test tons, Hammond's 22 tons place him ahead of David Boon, Aravinda de Silva, Gary Kirsten, Mark Waugh, Gordon Greenidge, Clive Lloyd, Desmond Haynes, David Gower and Jack Hobbs.

Of batsmen with the most Test runs, Hammond's 7,249 runs places him ahead of Bradman, Jack Hobbs, Ganguly, Greg Chappell, Jayasuriya, Hutton, Vengsarkar, Chris Gayle, Azharuddin, Viswanath, Compton, Zaheer Abbas, Ranatunga and Ian Chappell. Hammond is the fastest batsman in the world to get to 7,000 Test runs (off 131 innings); Sehwag comes second (off 134 innings).

Among 60 Test batsmen who had the most consecutive innings without a duck, Hammond shines with 67 consecutive innings (between 1929 and 1936) without a duck. Bradman does not figure in the list of 60 batsmen, but Sachin does – with 60 consecutive innings (between 2008 and 2011) without a duck. Hammond was way ahead of some on Sir Neville's Big Six but we shall examine another man symbolic of the 99.94 error – Jack Hobbs.

Apart from his outstanding record as a batsman (7,249 runs), Hammond's bowling (83 wickets) and fielding (110 catches) placed him leagues ahead of Jack Hobbs. Hammonds's 85-match career left his mark on some of the most defining moments in Test history in the early 20th century, since he was among those called to meet the Bradman challenge. He played 21 more matches, scored 1,839 more runs, bagged 82 more wickets and took 93 more catches than Hobbs did.

Like Viv Richards, Lara and Ponting in the late 20th century, Bradman had the most effective bowlers of his era, on his team. Like Sachin, Hammond was compelled to face the best bowlers of that era – they were Australian. Mysteriously, Hobbs made it to Sir Neville's list. Hammond didn't. We will never fully know how Sir Neville picked his Big Six, but Hammond more than challenges that reasoning.

Nearly half a century after that first list was published, Wisden published its *Five Cricketers of the Century*. Like Hammond, who was a victim of the 99.94 error in the 1963 list, Sachin became a victim of the same error when the next list was published in the year 2000... only that much more of a victim.

Voters were supposed to be guided by:

- Excellence at cricket during the 20th century that has made the greatest contribution to the game
- Leadership qualities
- Personality
- Character
- Impact on the public

At least that was the brief.

One would assume here, that 'excellence' refers more to excellence on the field than excellence off it and 'leadership' refers to leadership in any form on the field rather than just captaincy. One would also assume that 'contribution to the game' acknowledges contributions in any form – with the bat, with the ball, as a fielder. One would also include ODI contributions. ODIs, an integral part of international cricket, occupied the attention of the world's teams for three decades in the 20th century and are crucial when weighing a batsman's 'excellence', 'contribution' and 'impact'.

Fair assumptions when assessing 100 years of international cricket? As

Rudolph Lambert Fernandez

with all such ratings and rankings, one can never be sure; roles, qualities and achievements beyond the cricket field may have weighed on the voting panel more heavily than they should have. Perhaps ODIs did not figure as prominently as they should have in the imagination or memory of voters.

The 100-seat voting panel was divided among Test playing nations, rather loosely, on the strength of the number of Tests those nations had played: England was given 28 seats, Australia 20, South Africa 11, West Indies 11, India 10, New Zealand 8, Pakistan 8, Sri Lanka 3 and Zimbabwe 1 seat. Naturally, the bowl of experts that emerged at the *Wisden* table had more than a generous helping of Englishmen and Australians. The impact on the voting pattern was, shall we say, telling.

Perhaps considerable thought went into deciding panel composition but this is like loading a 100-seat panel (asked to name the *Five Greatest Chess Players*), with 50 Indians and 40 Iranians, merely because those nations have been playing chess for the last 1,500 years. Forget about Bobby Fischer's face; imagine the faces of Kasparov, Karpov and Kramnik as Indian after Indian was voted on the Big Five.

How did the voting play out? The five who were eventually named were:

1. Donald Bradman

2. Jack Hobbs

3. Garry Sobers

4. Viv Richards

5. Shane Warne

Bewilderingly, all 100 voted for Bradman – in spite of the fact that he played only 50 Tests and was not tested in ODIs. More outrageously, as many as 30 voted for Jack Hobbs. Sachin barely got a look in with 6 votes out of 100; about the same votes as R R Lindwall and Harold Larwood and way *behind* Botham, Hutton, Gavaskar, Hammond, Worrell and Compton.

We have already dealt with Bradman at sufficient length in this book. While he may have been an obvious choice in Sir Neville's list in 1963, should he really have been considered for the second list published in 2000?

Of the remaining three batsmen, we will leave Richards and Sobers alone. They have every right to be considered by voters looking at the greatest cricketers of the 20th century – they batted, bowled and fielded their way into the record books and into some of the most momentous periods in cricket, leading their teams to victory against the best in the world. Their figures dwarf those of Bradman and Hobbs anyway and they played in a far more competitive environment – Sobers in the 1950s, 60s and 70s and Richards in the 1970s and 80s. Richards is probably ahead of Sobers (who had not been tested by ODI cricket – one of the most revolutionary phases of 20th century cricket). It is another matter that both Richards and Sobers faced only five Test teams compared to the nine that Lara, Steve Waugh, Kallis and Ponting faced.

But Jack Hobbs?!

What do we make of his furtive re-appearance in the Wisden list of 2000 after his appearance in that first list in 1963?

In *Outlook* magazine's Special Commemorative Issue *Sir Sachin: Genius, Giant, Gentleman – a 51st century legend,* Ayaz Memon listed his All-time Test XI in his capacity as Issue Editor. Memon included Sachin Tendulkar, Viv Richards, Garry Sobers, Imran Khan (as captain), Adam Gilchrist (as wicket-keeper), Wasim Akram, Shane Warne, Muttiah Muralitharan. Then after declaring that 'comparing sportspersons across generations is sometimes perilous, often foolhardy... odious, silly or interminably vexing', Memon included both Bradman and Hobbs!

After Bradman, Hobbs is one of the most notorious illustrations of the 99.94 error. From time to time, others such as Compton, Cowdrey and Hutton glow far beyond their station, but none that demonstrate this error as Hobbs does.

CHAPTER 13

The 99.94 Error – Part 2

HOBBS, PERSPECTIVE AND THE EVOLUTION OF CRICKET

HOBBS PLAYED FROM 1908 TO 1914, then 1920-21 and finally 1924 to 1930. He played in the most placid era of 20th century cricket imaginable; a mere extension of the competitiveness faced by 19th century W G Grace: modern-day cricket in ultra-slow motion.

It is possible to pit each batsman in the Wisden list against Sachin, in turn and demonstrate his superiority over all of them. But we will focus on Hobbs. Like Bradman, he personifies the 99.94 error and the unpardonable damage it has wrought on the reputations of dozens of batsmen who excelled in the 20th century. We will focus on Sachin's career up until December 1999 so that comparison is limited to a study of 20th century achievement. But we are examining contribution to the game, so we will include facets beyond batting but limit analysis to contribution on the field, not off it.

Table N: Jack Hobbs and Sachin (i.e. Sachin in the 20th century alone)

Measure of greatness	Jack Hobbs	Sachin Tendulkar (career up to Dec 1999)
Test matches	61	73
Playing span	15 years	10 years
Dominant rivals	One (excluding South Africa and West Indies as they were nowhere near dominant); 67% of his matches were against Australia.	Seven (excluding Zimbabwe and Bangladesh as they were not dominant)
Test runs	5410; some 67% of his runs were against Australia.	5841; against 'the world'
Test centuries	15; some 80% of his tons were against Australia	23; against 'the world'
Tight lbw legislation	Non-existent; came into force only in 1937 and Hobbs had retired seven years before that - in 1930.	In full force
World-class bowling, fielding and wicket-keeping	A handful of quality bowlers in the one dominant rival team – Australia. The best bowlers, fielders and wicket-keepers of the 20th century were not yet born.	This era included the greatest bowlers, fielders and wicket-keepers. The most experienced, the most prolific, the most effective bowlers, fielders and wicket-keepers.
Position in batting order	Opener, almost always (the greatest possible chance to score runs, tons)	4th Position, almost always (far lower chance of scoring runs, tons)
TV replays, third umpire and on-pitch scrutiny	None; no impact on dismissals	In full force; full impact on dismissals
ODI matches	None	222 matches
ODI runs	None	8571
ODI centuries	None	23
Wickets taken as a bowler	One	91 (13 Tests + 78 ODIs)

Rudolph Lambert Fernandez

Catches taken as a fielder	17 catches over a 15-year span	125 catches over a 10-year span (50 in Tests + 75 in ODIs)
Volume, pace, intensity and competitiveness of cricket played.	Only one dominant rival, playing in a handful of grounds, matches spaced out over a leisurely calendar, only in the day, with a generous number of "rest" days.	The "world" playing cricket, Tests and ODIs, day and day-night matches, in the widest possible range of grounds.

Even if we exclude achievements in the 21st century, Sachin towers above Hobbs – on every score.

All this before we throw ODI cricket into the mix. Sachin's ODI achievements cannot be dismissed; they represent his contribution to cricket – not ice hockey! He scaled those ODI peaks in *the same* ten years as he was scaling peaks in Test cricket.

A careful look at the table above will show what an injustice it has been to even consider Hobbs in a list of this sort, let alone select him: a fine demonstration of the 99.94 error in action. The image of a flamboyant batsman from one age – Hobbs was all of that in the early 20th century – is simply 'frozen' in the mind and carried across decades to come 'alive', generations later. His playing environment and opposition do not 'travel' with him. The batsman alone is 'transposed' mind, body and soul to the new cricket playing era, with his skill, dominance and neatly pressed flannels intact. Even if he crash-lands in the middle of the most explosive era of cricket, looking terribly out of place.

Sachin used the widest array of shots in the world, controlled aggression, cunning and immensely superior skill to dominate the best teams. On balance, even if we are to discount Sachin's incredible achievements in the 21st century, he emerges one of the most influential cricketers of the 20th century who through his excellence at cricket has made one of the *greatest contributions to the game.*

Sachin has faced the greatest on-pitch scrutiny. His explosive performances left their imprint on all cricket – Test and ODI, in every cricketing continent. His *impact on the public* at a national and global level was unprecedented. His mark on the consciousness of batsmen, bowlers, fielders, captains, coaches, umpires, commentators and fans around the world was unique: he left that mark on the best – the fastest pacers, the most prodigious spinners, the most effective fielders and the most prolific wicket-keepers. He excelled on the fastest pitches, in front of the largest, most diverse crowds of spectators and under the greatest pressure imaginable.

Sachin may not have excelled as a captain. Many say that he was unable to cope with the lesser knowledge, skills, attitudes, passion, work ethic and team-spirit he found in a few of his mates. But he has always been a leader from the day he stepped on to the field as a 16-year old. He has led the batting fight and the bowling fight-back. He has stood shoulder-to-shoulder with captain after captain, reading the minds of rivals more easily than lesser players, translating that understanding into field placements, bowling tactics and powering the team forward with his array of shots and running between the wickets. He has always wanted to dominate but his character has meant that he has wanted to dominate through his cricket, rather than through power-play beyond the pitch.

Sledging, match-fixing, aggressive appealing, TV replays, the adulation of millions of fans and the scrutiny of hundreds of critics, the politics of domestic and international cricket, the phenomenon of ODI cricket. Aren't these more daunting tests – of character, of leadership, of personality – than the environment that existed in the 1910s and 20s? From a look at his on-field exploits, Sachin's 'excellence and contribution to the game, leadership, personality, character and impact on the public' are beyond the grasp of Hobbs.

The voting panel's analysis and judgement of batsmen who were eventually voted *Cricketers of the Century* remains unconvincing, to say the least. The votes that went to say Worrell (19), Compton (14) and Hutton (11) are inexcusable. Astoundingly, Sachin secured a mere 6 votes compared to the 30 that went in favour of Jack Hobbs, whose inclusion is untenable, no matter how you look at it.

'Some circumstantial evidence is very strong, as when you find a trout in the milk.' – Henry David Thoreau, Journal, November 1850

Jack Hobbs!

Like Bradman, Hobbs is a fine illustration of the 99.94 error: judgement about enduring greatness that is clouded by a frozen image. It is a way of looking as it were, a pair of spectacles through which one views all other realities – even newer, more immediate ones. Sachin and dozens of other batsmen have been victims. It explains their exclusions from the Top 10 of this or the Top 5 of that.

Hobbs was an exceptionally fine batsman and a gentleman who oozed charm and class, whether on the field or off it. Reportedly humble to a fault and gracious in recognising the less spectacular feats of his peers, Hobbs embodied all that was good and noble about cricket. Yet he unduly benefited from the 99.94 error and therefore unseated more deserving batsmen. Hobbs, in his disarmingly honest manner, would have been the first to point out the discrepancy.

Cricket has transformed so much since the 19th century that it is unfair to compare, across generations, particularly if these comparisons are poorly drawn. Ironically, it is one of Bradman's most eloquent admirers who, it seems, struggled to put things in perspective in his later years. Sir Neville Cardus, in a candid piece for Wisden Almanack 1968 titled – *The modern Golden Age, from 1948 until the present,* wrote that when comparing cricketers across epochs it was essential to consider the environment and the rules. He confessed that the Golden Age seemed somehow to always be 'in the past'; he implied that it needn't be. He also confessed that 'distance' from historical achievement tended to embellish our perception of such achievement. In a barely concealed confession about how writers like him had perhaps erroneously portrayed Bradman, he went on to say that during the Bradman era, a new ball came around only after 55 overs and Bradman and his peers 'exploited a defensive attack and field'.

Perhaps there is a strong enough case to judge players, whether bowlers or batsmen, by their playing environment? A bit like putting boxers in their broad weight categories to ensure a 'match', to ensure that spectators get their money's worth and that neither fighter is overwhelmed by the other? Imagine if weight categories were not respected and the super heavy-weight knocks out the little man in the first round; would the winner be called 'great'? Would the fight be called 'memorable'?

Here is a shot at possible phases that acknowledges the evolution of cricket and therefore the changing dynamics of the game:

Table 0: International cricket: an attempted snapshot of evolution to assess batting greatness

Evolution of cricket in Phases	Key developments, themes, batting personalities that set one phase apart from the next
Phase I 1890s to 1925-26	The only teams playing international cricket – South Africa, England and Australia. The most placid and uncompetitive environment possible. Jack Hobbs, who stopped playing Test cricket in 1930, belonged more to this era than the next one. Naturally, not much international cricket is played during the First World War 1914-18.

Evolution of cricket in Phases	Key developments, themes, batting personalities that set one phase apart from the next
Phase II **1926 to 1946**	New Zealand, the West Indies and India join the fray and mix things up a bit, but not by much. This was *before* crucial new lbw rules and televised cricket came into their own. There was no 'world-class' because there was no cricket 'world' yet. With relatively less competition abroad or at home, in rival teams or in home teams, it was far easier to shine. Perhaps the best time-capsule for Bradman to be judged against batsmen of his era where he was, without a shred of doubt, the Emperor. But batsmen like Hammond were also dominant and saw a more superior rival in Australia than Bradman did in facing England. Naturally, no international cricket is played during the Second World War 1939-45.
Phase III **1946-1970**	This was after a far-reaching revision in the laws of international cricket. A markedly more competitive era. But it was *before* TV replays were allowed to decide on outcomes on the field and *before* the first ODI. The West Indies, England, South Africa and Australia were the dominant teams. Cowdrey, although he retired in 1975 belonged more to this era than the next one. Others included Hutton, Barrington, Kanhai, Neil Harvey, Compton, Garry Sobers. Pakistan join international cricket in 1952.
Phase IV **1970-1992**	When competitiveness in Test cricket was taken to the next level. It was also when ODI matches evolved alongside the notion of multi-nation, multi-tournament World Cups. The West Indies were the undisputed kings for much of this era but Pakistan and India were asserting themselves. Sri Lanka enter Test cricket in 1982. Miandad, Gower, Greenidge, Ian Chappell, Viswanath, Vengsarkar, Greg Chappell, Desmond Haynes, Clive Lloyd, Gavaskar, Border were among the leading lights with star all-rounders like Botham, Richards and Kapil. India won some big tournaments but were yet to become world-class. With relatively greater competition abroad and at home, in rival teams or in home teams it was getting more difficult to shine. But South Africa are missing in action on account of their 'exile' from international cricket, returning only as late as 1991.

Rudolph Lambert Fernandez

Evolution of cricket in Phases	Key developments, themes, batting personalities that set one phase apart from the next
Phase V **1992 to the present day** **The 'world' at cricket**	Cricket is greatest when an innings, match or series is at its most competitive, when it draws innovation and improvisation from batsmen and bowlers alike. Tests in the 1990s was transformed – by ODI cricket – to a more result-oriented form: a kind of Test cricket that had never been played before. Captains were pressing for a win, not a draw. Batsmen were not allowed the luxury of simply sunning themselves... and others. Bowlers trained in the heat of the faster-paced version were using those same tools in Test cricket. Rest days, common until the 1980s, were no longer a regular feature. Neutral umpiring started in the late 1980s but came into its own only in the 1990s. Some of the better batsmen of this era include Azharuddin, Aravinda de Silva, Jayasuriya, Ganguly, Gary Kirsten, Sehwag, Mark Waugh, Steve Waugh, Sangakkara, Matthew Hayden, Haq, Kallis, Lara, Dravid, Ponting, Mahela Jayawardene, Chanderpaul, Kevin Pietersen, Gilchrist. This is also the era that saw South Africa return to international cricket after nearly quarter of a century in exile. They bring to the party some of the craftiest bowlers, wicket-keepers, fielders and batsmen in Test and ODI history. Floodlit cricket comes into its own. The most competitive cricket era; the 'world' at cricket – the fastest pitches, the fastest pacers, the greatest spinners, the most prolific wicket-keepers, the most intrusive on-pitch scrutiny (whether by umpires, TV referees, commentators or spectators). This is when the highest number of world-class teams in Test and ODI cricket emerged, with cricket being played in grounds across the world including the Middle East, Singapore and Canada. The era when less established teams of the 1970s and 80s came into their own. With the greatest competition abroad and at home, in rival teams or in home teams it was most difficult to 'shine'. This happens to be the era in which Sachin emerged... and excelled. About the only era where a 'greatest in the world' is not an exaggeration.

This is by no means an exhaustive list of batting greats.

But while there was less talent to go around in Phase I and II there was plenty of it in Phase IV and V. The tiny stream had become a river. A couple of batting greats naturally do not fit as neatly into a single slot and more work needs to be done to more accurately 'place' them. Perhaps historians will do a more elegant job.

Yes, once in a century someone like Sachin comes along and demolishes these time-barriers by beating everything, everyone, everywhere, almost every time in almost every way. Once in 200 years someone like Sachin can truthfully be described as the greatest batsman *in history*: the best and the toughest have had a shot at him for the longest possible time and he has come out on top. But overall, comparisons drawn *within* phases will be more honest and honourable than *across* phases. The future may allow for further refinement – to account for T20 cricket and the entry of even more invasive 'decision-making'.

In the late 21st century, it may no longer be the usual suspects but Netherlands, Ireland, Scotland, Namibia, Canada, the US and the UAE who are counted among established teams. Who knows, we might even have converts from the football world with teams from Brazil, France, Argentina, Spain. Like the established teams of the early 20th century who were overthrown by newcomers, the established teams of the early 21st century may be taken by surprise, with the next great batsmen emerging from one of these countries. The next champion may be a Jean-Paul or a Gomez, a Louis or an Olanga.

These crowns should sit lightly on the heads of those who wear them – including Sachin – there's always the chance that someone new comes along, in the following century, to smash the roll of honour. However, for the most part, comparisons *within* phases like these would do justice to the gentlemen being compared.

We could fantasise all day about how Bradman might have fared against a world-class spin, pace or fielding attack. How Bradman might have performed against the real judgement of off-field referees, TV replays, pitch microphones. We could dream all year about what would have become of his average had he been declared run-out, lbw, caught-behind, caught-at-slip and stumped each time that he was actually dismissed. But he never did face these challenges. Sachin **has** faced all of these and more – in more matches, formats, grounds against more teams and across many more years.

In the modern cricketing world, you have to prove yourself – consistently *and* against the best *and* in the most diverse circumstances. It simply would not matter if you scored a huge number of centuries, double centuries and triple centuries. 'Good stuff' you will be told by the high priests of cricket, 'But, young man, we need to see you maintain your strike-rate over 100 Tests.' 'Congratulations, young chap,' you will be told by historians, 'but we need to see you do the same against a dangerous and diverse pace, spin and fielding attack.' 'Well done champ, but we need to see you succeed against at least seven or eight established teams.'

You would not be offered even grudging respect, unless you have worked your magic in far more than 50 matches, on many more grounds, in the most competitive environment. The prefix 'great' would take a long, long time. The prefix 'greatest' would simply take much longer.

CHAPTER 14

The High Priests of Cricket

O FTEN IT TAKES MORE THAN newspaper articles, photographs and statistics to bring home the truth. In, 'Sunny Days', his intimate account of cricket in the 1960s, 70s and 80s, Gavaskar recounts an incident when, following a medical procedure on an eye cyst, he was compelled to wear a patch on his right eye. He could not reach for a glass of water without missing it 'by a foot'. Gavaskar wrote of how his admiration for Pataudi and his handling of fast bowling grew with that brief enforced 'blindness' in one eye.[38]

Gavaskar was spelling out how greatness needs to be measured – by odds faced and defeated. But Gavaskar remains in a minority; the majority of experts don't appear to see greatness in perspective.

In the introductory chapter we briefly touched on the need to cast aside a kind of blindness before deciding on greatness. But there are times when all we need to 'see' the truth is a kind of blindness. Sometimes the only way to 'open' our eyes is to 'shut' them – happily for Gavaskar, he got there with just one eye shut.

Somehow, it seems more convenient to keep Bradman in the tabernacle, where everyone can pay him uninterrupted homage. By some invisible

---

38 *Sunny Days (On the Hop, Down Under*; Page 97, Chapter 11); Sunil Gavaskar; Rupa & Co; 20th Impression 2011 (published 1976).

consensus, everyone seems to have seized upon the one figure (his batting average) that, to all appearances, makes his position unassailable: a fetish that consumes everything including a closer look at the realities of his era. A mantra that holds even the most seasoned analysts in a kind of trance, compelling them to vote for him unquestioningly... every time.

The high priests are content for worshippers to have their own little ceremonies around the saints in the outer courtyards, as long as the chants do not get too noisy and disturb the Almighty in the tabernacle. They are relaxed about worshippers having favourites among the saints, preferring one over the other, choosing to seek the blessings of one saint, while feeling less need to prostrate before the other. What the priests – *and the saints* – will not stand for, is blasphemy. They will tolerate mood swings, not mutiny. No one, absolutely no one can challenge the throne. Even an attempt to suggest it is met with rebuke. Remember Matthew Engel's words as editor of the Wisden Almanack when he wondered whether everyone would indeed endorse Bradman while voting on the greatest cricketers of the century?

In December 2011, newspapers reported that Dr. Nicholas Rohde from Griffith University had used economic theory to compare batsmen from different epochs and concluded that Sachin is the greatest batsman *in cricket history* and ahead of Bradman. While this was greeted with much celebration by Sachin fans and fanatics, it was not long before irate high priests slammed their fists down on the altar denouncing the very thought as sacrilegious.[39]

But there appears to be no conspiracy, no racism, no cultural hegemony, no grand design; it is good old error of judgement. The high priests are more victims than villains; they need counsel not criticism.

Fortunately, in the debate about Bradman, the issue is not about race or colour or nationality or age. The error is an error of 'generation' and of 'perspective'. An error where an unwritten code – an incredible batting average, for example – is thoughtlessly repeated, until it becomes law; one that rudely, recklessly claims to transcend every playing generation. One that refuses to recognise the peculiar circumstances in which that law emerged. An error that refuses to acknowledge that the new order does not stand alongside the old but above it, does not replace the old but renews it, does not destroy the old but helps us see it in a new light. The new order

---

39 *Bradman will always be The Don;* Nirmal Shekar; *The Hindu,* 23 December 2011.

does not demolish the achievements that came before it but helps future generations place them in perspective and honour them for what they are – *not for what they are not*.

The conspiracy of consent around Bradman is unique. The pontiffs who write about cricket are supposedly steeped in the roots but they have misunderstood the roots. The high priests have mistaken the idol to be the real thing.

The roots of cricket are fun, fortitude and fair play. The roots are competitiveness, camaraderie and cheering the under-dog. The roots are humour, honour, honesty. The spirit of the game respects and rewards the greatest player, regardless of his race, age, colour, nationality... or generation. The spirit of the game ought to respect a man's achievement against the backdrop of 'gravity', not in a 'vacuum'. Was he jumping on earth, battling the inexorable pull of gravity? Or was he jumping on the moon with no gravity worth worrying about? The distance a jumper has covered, the height he has scaled, have to be assessed in those terms.

A batsman's figures are much like an exquisitely crafted violin – glorious neck and body and impeccably tuned strings. It takes a bow in the virtuoso's hands to bring out the music. A bow run over with barely any pressure sounds more like a screech. Played with the right amount of pressure, it can sound angelic. Ultimately, it is the intensity, quality and consistency of a batsman's *challenge* that defines whether the 'music' within him rings true and clear. It is a batsman's playing environment – the odds he has faced – that makes his statistics come alive. Until then, his figures – like all designer violins – remain frightfully impressive, but hardly endow him with *enduring* greatness.

"It is a great advantage for a system of philosophy to be substantially true" – Santayana, The Unknowable

The error of 'generation' is necessarily also one of 'perspective'. It can therefore affect the credibility of comparisons even within a generation.

The spirit of the game ought to encourage custodians of cricket to look much harder for the truth. They owe it to themselves and the many great batsmen who have come after Bradman. Sadly, there is nothing fair or honest about the 99.94 error. It remains an unwritten commandment, all codified and complete.

What next?

The solution is not to replace the existing chroniclers and analysts with

Rudolph Lambert Fernandez

new ones. There is nothing worse than replacing an old kind of blindness with a new kind. The solution is for those same editors, historians and writers to introspect. What gives them their mandate? The spirit of cricket, of course! They should – they must – be guided by that spirit and realise that they write, they record not for one race, one country, one class, one generation, but for all. Cricket belongs to everyone. The day some of us claim it for ourselves – particularly in our repeated errors of judgement - that day we forfeit it.

The solution is not to overthrow the Temple but to renew it, to help the Temple renew itself. The solution is not to disband the college of high priests but to help them see anew. The high priests we speak of include cricket statisticians, historians, writers, editors, commentators, analysts. We are also speaking here of players from generations past, who are still alive and can influence the way the history of the game is documented. We are speaking of bowlers who have given up bowling, of batsmen who have hung up their pads, wicket-keepers who have hung up their gloves and captains who have hung up their caps. If only they were to see anew.

One of the greatest Test batsmen, Sunil Gavaskar, is reported to have stuck his neck out and said that for all Bradman's achievements, when it came to technique and temperament, Sachin was the closest to batting perfection that he had seen. Gavaskar may belong to a minority all right – one hopes that this minority will, in time, grow to become an overwhelming majority.

The reform, if we can call it that, must start with an acceptance of a *possible* error. Then it may not be long before people more fully accept the shamefully destructive impact on the reputations of many great batsmen in the late 20th century. An impact that has put in the shade the true stature of batsmen who were in Bradman's mould but far greater because they saw far greater odds and excelled for far longer than he did. Sachin's achievements speak for him and his unmatched greatness. They also speak for others who came before him and it is time these cricketers stepped up and claimed their rightful place in history. Let no further injustice be done to such batsmen. Let no further blood be spilled on the field. By all means let us rate them and rank them, but let us also be fair.

Even the greatest of ships is no more than a worthless piece of scrap when it is rusting on a beach. It is the mighty ocean and its mountainous waves that define greatness in a ship – the storms she has braved. It is the face of a clock and those features that tell us how accurate the hands are – otherwise it might as well be a block of wood. Always and everywhere, it is the 'playing environment' that defines good or better, complete or perfect.

History is faithful when recording achievement but fastidious when recognising greatness, especially enduring greatness. 'What' is something, which is why she gives it a second look, but when, how, where, why and who – that's everything else. Yes, she wants to know 'what' was achieved, but time and place are everything else. Yes, she is anxious to know 'what' took place, but remains unmoved until she hears of circumstance and climate.

Statistics are fine, but the moment they become an end in themselves they lose their power, their meaning. Figures are welcome, but if perceived out of context they defile the spirit of cricket and lose their sanctity. Figures are *something*, but context... why, that's everything else!

Rudolph Lambert Fernandez

CHAPTER 15

The General Sherman And The Legacy Of Longevity

'Greatness be nothing unless it be lasting' – Napoleon Bonaparte

IN SEPTEMBER 2010, WHEN INDIA Today put together their Collector's Edition *Sachin Tendulkar*: Cricket's Colossus, several veterans put down their thoughts about Sachin. One was an Australian. Ian Chappell in his essay *Older Bolder*, put Sachin's achievement in perspective. He said that in 1930, Bradman's scoring rate was 3.70 runs per over but 18 years later (in 1948) this had fallen to 2.77 runs per over. Chappell argued that despite the perception that Sachin had gotten 'slower' as he had aged his run rate remained about the same for the first and second half of his career with an overall rate of 3.27 per over and in his later years actually increased to 3.43 per over.

The General Sherman, actually a giant Sequoia in a California park, is the tallest tree in the world. About 275 feet high, 102 feet wide at the base and weighing roughly 2,000 tons, it is close to 3,000 years old. One of the most awesome living things, it has survived disasters that destroyed lesser species – hurricanes that heaved giants from the ground and twisted other trees out of shape, typhoons that tore weaker plants from their roots and droughts that ravaged entire forests. The sun rose a thousand times and the Sherman kept soaring. The sun set ten thousand times and the Sherman kept soaring. The Sherman kept soaring until it needed to soar no longer; it towered above every living creature, the only ones soaring higher were birds.

There is something breathtakingly majestic about a tree that outlasts everything in sight, something sovereign about bark and branch outliving, outgrowing everything else. The Sherman inspires awe not just because of its longevity, but because of what that longevity implies.

It is October 2010 and Sachin is with his mates in Bangalore taking on the Australians in the second Test of the Border-Gavaskar Trophy Test Series. The Australians set up a mammoth 478 in the first innings and India go in to bat.

One may be forgiven for thinking that with 20 years of cricket behind him Sachin is riding easy in the team with a justifiable sense of entitlement, letting the others do the work, while he steps lightly, letting the youngsters do the pushing as he puts his hand gently – almost symbolically – to the plough. But India's first innings unravels quickly. Sehwag falls when the score is at 37, Dravid at 38. Youngster M Vijay manfully stands alongside Sachin as India's Iron Man goes about building the innings, then Vijay falls, at 346. Pujara follows but falls when the score is 350. He is followed by Raina who goes when the score is at 411.

The tiny Sachin takes on the other end: the 186cm Ben Hilfenhaus, the 189cm Mitchell Johnson and the 203cm Peter George. He reaches his hundred, not with a single or a two but with two huge sixes. He has scored 43% of the team's runs and has helped India provide the semblance of an answer to Australia with a score of 495.

Australia come back with a relatively meek 223 in their second innings but it is far from over for India and a familiar scene plays out. Sehwag falls when the score is 17, Vijay falls at 89 and Pujara at 146. Sachin stays through the innings steering India to a victory, by seven wickets. His unbeaten 53 may not find prominence in India's Test record but he has – again – risen above fatigue and injury to craft his innings, speeding up and slowing down as more energetic partners hopped on to the pitch and off it.

Four people have been watching him closely. Umpires B F Bowden from New Zealand, I J Gould from England, TV Umpire Amiesh Saheba from India and Match Referee B C Broad from England. They have been watching closely to see if he is run-out, stumped, caught-behind, caught-at-slips or lbw. They have been scrutinising his every move. He has come through, brilliantly for himself and his team. The powers that be declare him Player of the Match and Player of the Series.

The Great Pyramids, the Taj Mahal, the Cathedral of Notre-Dame de Paris and the Sistine Chapel – they are great not just because of their incredible symmetry, their awe-inspiring grandeur but also because they have outlasted and outclassed the pretenders. They have weathered the ravages of time. They have been quiet, if disapproving, witnesses to war. They have watched empires rise and fall. They have survived the worst and come through, looking more glorious, more magnificent with every passing century.

Sachin's longevity, at the highest level of the game, when it has been at its most competitive, has long been brushed aside. But the longer you are 'out there', the longer the critics can fault you, the longer your rivals have to pick chinks in your armour and attack them. The longer you are out there the longer your skills, your knowledge, your instincts are tested. The longer you are out there, the greater the chance of your being found out, of being exposed. The longer you are out there, the greater the risk of your becoming a victim of pride, of pettiness and of self-destruction.

Arnold Schwarzenegger became Mr. Europe in his teens. He then became the youngest Mr. Olympia, a title he won seven times. He was also Mr. Universe five times. He started competing in body-building competitions in 1965 and officially retired in 1980. He stayed on and survived for fifteen years in a sport where burn-out is the norm and a world-beating victory, the exception. He proved his superiority at the highest level, year after year, in competition after competition, in the widest range of formats and against the best, from around the world. No wonder he is considered one of the greatest icons in body-building history.

Players who started their career with Sachin in 1989 include Nasser Hussain, Alec Stewart, Saeed Anwar, Chris Cairns, Mike Atherton and Mark Taylor. They applaud Sachin today not because he played long after they quit but because he played the best cricket possible, at the highest level, all over the world, against the toughest, youngest, most aggressive players the game has ever seen.

Sachin holds no monopoly over longevity. In Test cricket, others have lasted a long time: Steve Waugh (20 years), Sobers (19 years). Sachin has lasted longer but what he has achieved in that time and the odds he has defeated, in both Test and ODI cricket, are astonishing. This bird was soaring across not just countries or continents but across the world – from roof to roof, from end to end.

'Great works are performed not by strength but by perseverance' – *Samuel Johnson*

A career of 50 matches over ten years does not, in fairness, give a world-class cricketer the opportunity to persevere. A career of 650 matches over two decades, gives him, shall we say, more than a fair chance.

- The first ball Sachin faced in international cricket was bowled by Waqar Younis, now a father-figure to young Pakistani bowlers.

- Wasim Akram is the first batsman that Sachin 'caught' in international cricket; Akram is now a sought-after commentator.

- The first six that Sachin hit in Test or ODI cricket was at Leeds off Eddie Hemmings in 1990; Eddie would now be in his late-sixties.

- Salil Ankola and Vivek Razdan debuted in ODI cricket with Sachin in 1989, against Pakistan in Gujranwala. A few years ago Ankola had to be admitted into rehab from alcohol abuse after a turbulent but indifferent career in films; he had started off as a promising fast bowler in the Indian ODI attack but played his last ODI in 1997. Razdan's Test and ODI career began in 1989 and ended in... well, it ended in 1990.

- As a bowler, Sachin's first Test victim was Merv Hughes, in Sydney in 1992. Hughes went on to become a selector in the Australian cricket firmament and is now over fifty years old.

Enduring greatness is a race of attrition. A process of distilling, a movement from a lower plane to a higher one, a process of refinement to isolate the greatest from the great, a process of sifting that becomes more honest with each sift.

The sands of time erode even the proudest peaks but it is this erosion that defines which peaks stand tall, how tall and for how long. Reinhold Messner wrote that the world's mountains are gradually crumbling and that in 10 million years, thanks to erosion, many ranges will be deserts. A mountain range that once stretched over 2,000 kilometres and rose five kilometres into the sky, is today the Gobi desert.[40]

It is a tribute to Sachin's greatness that the many milestones he has set seem likely to stand for a long time to come.

---

[40] *Seven Wonders*; Reinhold Messner; *The Economist*, 18-24 February 2012.

Rudolph Lambert Fernandez

CHAPTER 16

Epilogue
Unfair - To Whom?

I'M ALL FOR PASSIONATELY WRITTEN tributes, but in a piece in Wisden Cricketers' Almanack 1975, titled *The game's greatest box-office attraction*, Rowland Ryder wrote that Gilbert Laird Jessop was 'surely the most exciting cricketer of them all'.

We will never know why Jessop seemed to give this impression of an enduring icon when considering over 200 years of cricket history but we do know that the good Jessop played his first Test in 1899 and his last in 1912. Jessop may have got his kicks from clubbing the ball more cheerfully than his fellow-Englishmen but his Test career was all of 18 Tests and against only two rivals, Australia and South Africa. He may have been a lovable bloke all right but he ended with an almighty total of 569 Test runs.

Would you have been as sure as Ryder was that Jessop was 'surely the most exciting cricketer of them all'? I do not know but it is worth a thought.

Cricket writers need to think harder before they meekly accept folklore as fact, no matter how authoritative such 'first-hand accounts' sound. We owe the truth not just to players from the past but to those from the present and future as well. There's a flip-side to this coin.

You may have *seen* a flamboyant batsman at an impressionable age or when hormones were kicking in. That does not mean he's greater than those who have shone after or before him. Your having seen him does not make your judgement any truer than those who haven't. It is possible to study performance with a fair bit of objectivity even from a distance and without the expert lens, as long as a performer's figures are seen in perspective. Merely calling out batting averages and lining them up against the wall, is an inexcusably one-dimensional way of rating batsmen. It is also necessarily incorrect.

Australian Denise Annetts ended her career with an awesome batting average of 81.90. English cricketer Janette Brittin's batting average of 49.61 is nowhere close, but neither are the averages of other women cricketers. It takes a closer look to discover that Brittin perhaps faced and defeated greater odds than Annetts did.

Table P: Little women, big women and the 99.94 error

Parameter of playing context	Australia's Denise Annetts	England's Janette Brittin
Test Batting Average	81.90	49.61
Test playing span	4 years	9 years
ODI playing span	8 years	13 years
Test matches	10	27
Test Innings	13	44
Test runs	819	1,935
Unbeaten Test innings	3	5
Test centuries	6	5
Test 50s	6	11
Test rivals faced	3	4
ODI matches	43	63
ODI runs	1,126	2,121
ODI 100s	1	5
ODI rivals faced	6	11
ODI playing span	8 years	13 years

This is not an exhaustive comparison of the two who played in the same era, but there's enough here to suggest that we do not use Annetts' daunting Test batting average alone to blindly anoint her the greatest batswoman in history. It also demonstrates, in an unforgivably limited way, why such an infinitely vast difference exists between the two men we've been discussing.

It is July 1993. 20-year old Sachin is in Colombo playing in a Test against Sri Lanka. His unbeaten 104 helps India win the match. He is batting alongside men who have played well over 100 Tests each. Already, he's seen a lot of international cricket. He's played close to 30 Tests (each in different grounds, the first 20 or so 'away') and around 50 ODIs against established teams. Already, his Test achievements include an unbeaten 119 at Manchester, an unbeaten 148 at Sydney, a 114 at Perth, a 111 at Johannesburg and a 165 at Chennai.

Cut to November 1928. 20-year old Bradman is taking guard for the first time in international cricket; he's in Australia (where he will play 62% of his 50 Tests) and facing England (a team he will play for 72% of his career). Over the next two years he will see no other team; he will then play no other team in successive matches over a further five years later on in his career.

Fast-forward to August 1948. 40-year old Bradman is in England (where he has played 79% of all his 80 innings) playing his last Test, as it happens – against England (against whom he has scored 72% of all his runs). Over half his playing span, he's seen no other team. After 6,996 runs and 29 centuries from 50 international matches played in nine grounds against one worthy rival, he's heralded as the greatest batsman in history.

Now cut back to the 21st century. The 39-year old Sachin is still playing at the highest level of the game. After 33,000 runs and 100 centuries from 650 international matches played on 59 Test grounds and 95 ODI grounds against 'the world' he's being called the greatest batsman... *after Bradman*.

Comparisons are unfair. But that's a verdict half-pronounced. In Sachin's case, the comparison with Bradman has always been unfair... to Sachin.

When Europe was the world, perhaps there was a time when, to some, the Rhine was the greatest river. It stretched over 1,320 km, releasing water at the rate of 77,000 cu feet a second. To them, the Rhine may have stayed the greatest, until someone discovered the Danube, stretching over 2,850km, releasing water at 200,000 cu. ft. a second. Then someone saw the Volga stretching over 3,688km, releasing water at 300,000 cu. ft. a second. And, that was that. The Volga was the greatest of them all. And one night an explorer spied the mighty Amazon, stretching over 6,500km, discharging water at 6 million cu. ft. a second. The world turned upside down – the awesome Rhine, now no more than a puddle!

The Rhine hasn't changed. It's still a great river. But with the grand Amazon now before us, we tend to see the Rhine a little... well, a little differently.

Earlier on in this book I referred to Mukul Kesavan's fury at Manjrekar's inclusion of Barry Richards in a list of batting greats that had Sachin, Viv Richards and Graeme Pollock. Kesavan suggests that, among other things, what may have persuaded Manjrekar to think of Barry was because Barry figured in Bradman's All-Time XI.

Kesavan (again unwittingly, I'm afraid) points the spotlight at Bradman. Almost everyone is happy to put the 'unseen, mythic' figure of Bradman above the very visible, very real achievements of those who followed him. Kesavan, rightly, argues in favour of first-hand experience. But, as we have seen, there is a little more to it.

While *first-hand* experience helps, it is not – should never be – the sole arbiter of truth. And to this experiential method of judging greatness we can boldly add our antidote to the 99.94 error – perspective!

In 1928, the same year that Bradman was taking guard in his first Test at Brisbane, Johnny Weissmuller set a world Olympics record of 58 seconds in the men's 100m freestyle swimming championships. In 2009, someone took about 52 seconds to cover that same distance in the freestyle swimming championships; Britta Steffen's was a world record among women. Today, men are covering that distance in around 46 seconds.

Sachin has re-defined the word 'miracle' in cricket. He has set the bar higher than ever. Not just for Indians but for sportsmen around the world. Sachin's ODI double-hundred is a classic example of all that he stands for – focus, passion, skill, work ethic, team-spirit, perseverance, genius.

The Gwalior ground is tense on the 24th of February 2010, for India's battle against South Africa. Sachin hammers 50 off 37 deliveries, including 9 fours. The South Africans are in awe of his skill – is he 38 years old or 16? He gets his hundred off 90 deliveries, having scored 13 fours. The umpires begin to wonder at his resilience – has he actually got a joint-breaking 600 or so international matches behind him or is he just starting out? He reaches 150 off 118 deliveries, having hit 22 fours and a six. The commentators marvel at his aggression – has he actually played and beaten all international teams or is this his first outing? He reaches 200 off just 147 balls, having hit 25 fours and 3 sixes.

Young guns like Sehwag, Karthik and Pathan are dismissed, while Sachin remains not-out with Dhoni to ensure that India is in a position to eventually win the match, by 153 runs. He's scored 118 off boundaries alone. He has hit with the abandon of a teenager who cares not about records or reputation. His strike-rate of 136 leaves the youngsters in awe. In what has become a ritual, he's accounted for half of the team's runs and is declared Player of the Match. Yes, statisticians are right to do their statistics, but they must never be the only ones deciding on enduring greatness in sport. After all, they are technicians, who provide the cables and plugs. Their aggregates and averages provide the microphones, the bulbs. Their tallies and totals provide the stage, the setting, the curtain, the musical ensemble. They must proceed thus far and no further. Enduring greatness must be decided by the painters, writers, musicians and sculptors who see beyond the canvas and the colour, who hear beyond the sounds, the silences. Enduring greatness must be decided by those who can 'lift the veil', those who can stand in the middle and 'find the gaps'.

The musician needs his technician and the expertise he provides, but it is he – the artist – who has the final say. It is not about discarding what the technician offers. Every artist needs his material in just the right proportion, at just the right time, in just the right sequence. But it is he who wields that material to 'create' a harmony. It is he who 'finds' a truth that was hidden in the material all along. Great sport, like great art, is so much more than the 'sum of its parts'.

It is time the great artists of cricket (cricketers or not) looked inward and reflected on the way greatness in cricket is recorded, ranked and rewarded. Batsmen, bowlers, fielders, wicket-keepers, captains, umpires, coaches, writers – it is time they reflected on the way they have celebrated greatness in cricket, particularly in the cruelly dishonourable way they have treated the greatest batsman in cricket history.

Sachin is one piece of coal that has indeed become a diamond – from extreme and sustained heat and pressure. Albatross and Arctic tern all rolled into one, he has flown the distance. Marvellous Pyramid and awesome Cathedral at the same time, he towers above the greats – the cricket world's own General Sherman.

Bradman will always be the greatest batsman *of his time*: nothing and no one can take that away from him. After Grace, it was Bradman who set a benchmark in cricket. Sachin does not tread his own path but follows in their footsteps. He owes them a debt because they were the first to demonstrate that there were no limits on the field, except those you set in your mind and for yourself. Without Grace, there would be no Bradman. Without Bradman, there would be no Sachin. And we celebrate Bradman each time we celebrate anything that's good about cricket.

While the point of this book has been to demonstrate the vast differences between these two great players and Sachin's infinite superiority, it would be a pity if this were to be read as scorning the similarities between them – their desire to dominate, their eagerness to excel, their genius. Thankfully, these have been celebrated no end by other writers.

Let no further injustice be done to the many batsmen who came after Bradman who were greater because they faced more daunting odds. Cricket players, commentators, spectators and writers pride themselves on cricket being a game of fair-play. They celebrate it, write about it, talk about it. If they wish to cherish that spirit when recording all that's great about cricket and its players, it is time they corrected a grave error. The comparisons so far have been ridiculously one-sided; more than fair to Bradman and grossly unfair to Sachin.

For half a century, Bradman has been on a pedestal. He belonged there in the early 20th century but did he belong there even in the modern era? With his incisive cricketing mind it is unfortunate that he did not challenge the prevailing wisdom and speak up – even if privately he knew the truth all along.

Chroniclers of cricket history must now set the record straight. Coaches who wish to teach youngsters the nuance of the game must now tell their wards: the greatest batsman of the *pre-War era* was a man named Donald Bradman, but the greatest batsman *in history* started playing in the late 20th century and carried on at the highest level into the 21st century.

As far as measuring and recognising greatness in cricket is concerned, the covers now need to come off, the bails need to be re-set, the crease needs to be re-drawn and an entirely new field needs to be spread out. It is not a matter of tinkering with what's been written – that would be worse than leaving it all as before. It is a matter of writing anew, drawing afresh, starting from scratch. It is not a matter of coming around the wicket, instead of over it – we need a new ball, a new scoreboard, a new scorer, a new sight-screen, a new groundsman, a new ground.

It is unlikely that we will ever be able to dismiss statistics and simply savour glorious cover-drives for their glory and not for their impact on individual or team fortunes. But we can certainly look above and beyond the mere statistic to assess a shot, a series of shots, an innings, a career, in perspective. A great batsman is so much more than his batting average. The greatest batsman *in cricket history* needs to be measured by much more than that.

Over the years, sportsmen and women have defined and re-defined greatness through their excellence on the track, in the field, in the pool.

Rudolph Lambert Fernandez

But they've all bowed graciously to those who came after them, the ones who re-defined greatness. They've all saluted superior achievement in the spirit of all sport.

Spitz won seven golds in the 1972 Olympics. Then Phelps won eight golds in the 2008 Olympics. By 2012, Phelps was the most decorated Olympian ever, with 22 medals (18 of them golds). And he'd done it all: 100m, 200m, freestyle, butterfly, relay, individual medley. Naturally, people wonder if there will ever be another swimmer like him. There probably will be. Right now, Phelps seems all by himself.

Somewhere in the 21st century or beyond there's probably a boy (a girl?) waiting to step on to the pitch and make history: one who may break all of Sachin's records and put him in the shade. We await that moment with the hope and eagerness that celebrates distinction in the great game of cricket. Until then, Sachin Ramesh Tendulkar will have to stay on his summit, in solitary magnificence.

Sachin's presence on the field has a baffling beauty that tells us that he was born to play cricket and do little else. Hundreds of those who have known him intimately have come to that conclusion. He is most fulfilled when he is playing cricket. He is happiest with a bat, but stays happy even when handed the ball or when sent out to the deep. He is thrilled with a ton, but is not disgusted with a two. He sees no enemy, only another batsman. He sees no villain, just another bowler. He sees no battle, just another ball-game. His celebration does not start with the champagne, it starts from the first boundary he hits, the first ball he bowls, the first run he saves, the first wicket he takes. His departure from the game (not just from the field) is a tragedy. But because of his unrivalled love for cricket, it is far more tragic for him than it will ever be for us.

May every aspiring bowler, fielder, wicket-keeper and batsman yearn to have his child-like love for the game, his respect for skill regardless of the colour, attitude or age it comes clothed in, his gratitude for lessons taught. May every aspiring sportsman learn to be like him – modest in the face of certain victory, majestic in the face of assured defeat.

Rudolph Lambert Fernandez
Chennai, India, January 2014.

Rudolph Lambert Fernandez

APPENDIX

Table 1: Bradman and the Greatest Batsman in cricket history – a snapshot

The challenge?	BRADMAN	SACHIN [Note: as of 6 January 2011]
Age at start of international career	20	16
International matches	50 Tests played (72% against a single team). A total of 80 Test innings.	619 matches played (177 Tests and 442 ODIs). A total of 290 Test innings.
International runs	6,996 (from Tests alone) – 72% against a single team	32,290 (14,692 in Tests and 17,598 in ODIs), against the world's best.
International centuries	29 (in Tests) – 66% against just one team	97 (51 in Tests and 46 in ODIs); against 'the world'
International fifties	13 fifties in Tests	152 fifties (59 in Tests and 93 in ODIs)
Boundary (fours)	681 fours in Tests (approx 2,724 runs)	1,892 fours in Tests (7,568 runs) 1,927 fours in ODIs (7,708 runs)
Boundary (sixes)	6 sixes in Tests (36 runs)	64 sixes in Tests (384 runs) 185 sixes in ODIs (1,110 runs)
International Playing career	10 years (only Tests)	23years (Tests and ODIs); day matches and day-night matches

World-class rivals	One (England) Over 75 of every 100 balls faced, bowled by Englishmen. *22 successive* matches *over five years* against England alone. First nine matches were against England. By his 33rd Test he had played England alone in 22 matches. Note: West Indies, South Africa and India were nowhere near world-class	Eight Test playing nations (Australia, England, Pakistan, South Africa, Sri Lanka, New Zealand, West Indies, Zimbabwe) ALL the world's ODI teams. By his 33rd Test he had played eight nations. In 2010 alone he played five nations – one more than Bradman played in his entire career. Note: Bangladesh were nowhere near world-class.
Dismissed caught	39 (56% but over only 70 dismissals)	152 times 'caught' in Tests (59% out of 258 dismissals) 244 times 'caught' in ODIs (63% out of 390 dismissals)
Dismissed run-out	1 out of 70 dismissals (1%); an unsurprising record given the fielding and umpiring context. The ideal environment to score tons, double-tons. Almost no impact on batting average.	7 out of 258 Test dismissals (3%) 32 out of 390 ODI dismissals (8%) The fielding and umpiring context had a telling impact on tons, double-tons.

Rudolph Lambert Fernandez

Hostile playing environment	64% of Tests played at "home" in Australia. As much as 62% of Test tons and 62% of all his Test runs were at "home". 63% of his 22 successive matches against England, over five years, were all at "home".	Only 45% of Tests played at "home" in India. Only 45% of Test runs and only 43% of Test tons at "home".
Hostile bowling	Mercifully brief exposure during the Bodyline series	Baptism by fire in 1989 against a deadly Pakistan attack and no let-up since then – bowling aggression and grave injury commonplace in the 1980s, 90s and 2000s.
International cricket grounds	9 Test grounds in all. First four matches at "home" in Australia. A fifth of his entire career was played in Melbourne.	56 Test grounds Sachin's first 32 Tests in 32 different grounds around the world. Barring the Test in Chandigarh in 1990, his first 20 Tests were "away".
Batting position in Tests	3rd (70% of the time); greater luxury of building an innings, tons, double tons, triple tons, Test records.	4th (82% of the time); less luxury to build an innings, tons, double tons, Test records.
Dismissed lbw	6 lbw dismissals (9% out of 70 dismissals). Lenient legislation ensured that lbws had almost no impact on batting average and ability to score high.	52 lbw dismissals in Tests (20% out of 258 dismissals). Stiff lbw legislation ensured a decisive impact on batting average and ability to score high. 37 lbw dismissals in ODIs (9% out of 390 dismissals); **the same** % as Bradman *in Tests* ...in the 1920s and 30s in spite of the furious appealing and intrusive umpiring in Sachin's era.

| World-class bowling | Bowlers with over 300 Test wickets – none.

Bowlers with 10 or more "caught-and-bowled" dismissals – none.

Bowlers with 60 or more "bowled" dismissals – one.

Bowlers with career averages (runs conceded per wicket taken) of less than 26 – four.

Only 1-2 quality bowlers at a time; usually Englishmen.

Not a single bowler had experience of over 40 matches.

Rival bowlers (English) had career bowling averages that were tame in comparison to Australian bowlers in Bradman's team.

Bradman was dismissed 'caught and bowled' 4 times (from 70 dismissals) | Bowlers with over 300 Test wickets – sixteen.

Bowlers with 10 or more "caught-and-bowled" dismissals – six.

Bowlers with 60 or more "out bowled" dismissals – over a dozen.

Bowlers with career averages (runs conceded per wicket taken) of less than 26 – at least seventeen.

Well over three dozen of the world's most effective, prolific, consistent bowlers; many at the same time in each series he has played.

Has faced the greatest left-arm, right-arm, pace and spin bowlers. Almost all bowlers had experience of bowling in over 50 matches; some well over 100 matches.

Rival bowlers with the lowest career bowling averages in Test history.

Sachin was dismissed 'caught and bowled' 5 times (from 258 dismissals). |

Rudolph Lambert Fernandez

Rival fielders, wicket-keepers	Rival fielders with 70 or more Test catches – one fielder. Wicket-keepers with relatively meagre Test experience	Rival fielders with 70 or more Test catches –21 fielders [10 fielders with 125 or more catches] The world's greatest, most prolific, most experienced wicket-keepers.
On-pitch scrutiny	TV coverage began as late as 10 years into career. No impact on dismissals – declared run-out only once	First 'victim' in the world; on-pitch scrutiny unparalleled. Full impact on dismissals. Suffocatingly intrusive playing environment
Appealing by rival teams	Timid, virtually non-existent... little/no impact on umpire's decision	Aggressive, sustained, intimidatory... and often 'successful'; crucial impact on umpire's decision
Dismissed 'bowled'	23 times bowled in Tests (33% out of 70 dismissals). A surprising record because of his cautious style of batting and the lenient lbw environment.	46 times bowled in Tests (18% out of 258 dismissals). A surprising record because of his attacking style and the harsh lbw environment. 65 times bowled in ODIs (17% out of 390 dismissals)
Unbeaten record	10 not-outs (12.5% out of 80 Test innings across a 10-year playing span)	32 not-outs in Tests (11% out of 290 innings across a 21-year playing span) 41 not-outs in ODIs (9% out of 442 matches). An astounding result for Sachin in spite of the fierce competitiveness on the field, the pace of modern-day cricket, the intrusiveness of TV/third umpire decisions.

Playing style	Extreme caution – only 2,760 runs from boundaries (or only 39% of runs from boundaries). Only 6 sixes. In spite of his cautious playing style, he was dismissed 'caught' 56% of the time.	Attack through controlled aggression – 7,952 Test runs from boundaries (or as much as 54% of Test runs from boundaries). 64 sixes in Tests. Over half his Test runs came off boundaries, yet he was caught only 59% of the time.
Test Partnerships	180 partnerships; primarily with six Australian batting partners – in relatively relaxed situations. He was in the most powerful team in the world, the best bowlers were on his side.	Over 800 partnerships with over sixty Indian batting partners – in extremely challenging situations. He was in the weakest, most inconsistent Test team in the world and the best bowlers were almost always in rival teams.
Pace of cricket	Leisurely; often with a year or two between Tests.	Gruelling, often with barely any breathing space between Tests or ODIs and an overwhelmingly hectic travel, training and media schedule.

Rudolph Lambert Fernandez

Table 2: The Millennium Edition of Wisden Cricketers' Almanack published a list in the year 2000 of Five Cricketers of the Century.

- Bradman led with 100 votes, followed closely by Sobers with 90 votes and Hobbs third with 30. Warne and Viv Richards rounded off this Top 5 with 27 and 25 votes respectively.

- Sachin languished in 17th place (alongside Lindwall, Larwood) with all of 6 votes!

- Ranked *above* Sachin, from 6th place to 16th place, were a host of others including Compton, Hutton, Worrell, Gavaskar and Hammond.

Table 3: Test Grounds at "home"

Bradman (4)	Sachin (at least 14)
1. Sydney	1. Chandigarh
2. Melbourne	2. Kolkata
3. Adelaide	3. Chennai
4. Brisbane	4. Mumbai
	5. Delhi
	6. Lucknow
	7. Bangalore
	8. Ahmedabad
	9. Nagpur
	10. Mohali
	11. Cuttack
	12. Kanpur
	13. Mumbai (BS)
	14. Hyderabad (Deccan)

Table 4: Test Grounds "away"

*Note: if Sachin were to play in 8 more Test **away grounds** that number would equal the total **number of Tests** Bradman played in his entire career (at home or away).*

Bradman (5 grounds)	Sachin (at least 42 grounds)
1. Nottingham	1. Karachi
2. Leeds	2. Faisalabad
3. Lord's	3. Lahore
4. Manchester	4. Sialkot
5. The Oval	5. Christchurch
	6. Napier
	7. Auckland
	8. Lord's
	9. Manchester
	10. The Oval
	11. Brisbane
	12. Melbourne
	13. Sydney
	14. Adelaide
	15. Perth
	16. Harare
	17. Durban
	18. Johannesburg
	19. Port Elizabeth
	20. Cape Town
	21. Kandy
	22. Colombo (SSC)
	23. Colombo (PSS)
	24. Hamilton
	25. Birmingham
	26. Nottingham
	27. Kingston
	28. Port of Spain
	29. Bridgetown
	30. St. John's
	31. Georgetown
	32. Colombo (RPS)
	33. Wellington
	34. Dhaka
	35. Bulawayo
	36. Bloemfontein
	37. Leeds
	38. Multan
	39. Rawalpindi
	40. Chittagong
	41. Galle
	42. Centurion

Rudolph Lambert Fernandez

Table 5: Sachin's record of being unbeaten, in an Indian second innings:

Test Match	Rival and venue	Sachin's score (not-out)	Context
August 1990	England in Manchester	119	India's 2nd innings score was 343. Sachin's 119 was **35% of the team score**. He was Player of the Match. And, he'd come in after five Indian batsmen before him. The Match ended in a draw but Sachin did his best to secure a victory. He was 17 years old.
July 1993	Sri Lanka in Colombo	104	India's 2nd innings score was 359. Sachin's 104 was **29% of the team's score**. India won.
March 1998	Australia in Chennai	155	India's 2nd innings score was 418. Sachin's 155 was **37% of the team's score**. His fightback included 4 sixes and 14 fours. He was Player of the Match. India won by 179 runs.
February 1999	Sri Lanka in Colombo	124	India's 2nd innings score was 306. Sachin's 124 was **41% of the team's score**. The match was drawn but Sachin led the Indian shot at a victory.
October 1999	New Zealand in Mohali	126	India's 2nd innings score was 505. Sachin's 126 was **25% of the team's score**. The match was drawn but Sachin built a strong base for India.
December 2008	England in Chennai	103	India's 2nd innings score was 387. Sachin's 103 was **27% of the team's score**. Across both innings Sachin scored 140 to Sehwag's 92, yet it was Sehwag who was declared Player of the Match. India won by 6 wickets.
November 2009	Sri Lanka in Ahmedabad	100	India's 2nd innings score was 412. Sachin's 100 was **24% of the team's score**. The Test ended in a draw but Sachin led the Indian shot at a victory.

December 2010	South Africa at the Centurion	111	India's 2nd innings score was 459. Sachin's 111 was **24% of the team's score.** In spite of Sachin's valiant effort, India lost.

Note: Sachin has been incredibly consistent, over two decades. On many occasions he has seen India's entire batting line-up come and go.

Table 6: Sachin's Test record of centuries in an Indian second innings:

Test Match	Rival and venue	Sachin's score	Context
June 1996	England in Birmingham	122	India's 2nd innings score was 219. Sachin's 122 was **56% of the team's score and he reached his century with a six.** Still, India lost the match.
December 1998	New Zealand in Wellington	113	India's 2nd innings score was 356. Sachin's 113 was **32% of the team's score.** Still, New Zealand won the match.
January 1999	Pakistan in Chennai	136	India's 2nd innings score was 258. Sachin's 136 was **53% of the team's score and he was Player of the Match.** Still, Pakistan won… by 12 runs.
October 2002	West Indies in Kolkata	176	India's 2nd innings score was 471. Sachin's towering 176 was **37% of the team's score and he was Player of the Match.** The match was drawn.
February 2010	South Africa in Nagpur	100	India's 2nd innings score was 319. Sachin's 100 was **31% of the team's score.** Still, South Africa won.

Note: Look at how consistent Sachin has been over two decades and how crucial he has been to the team effort in the 2nd innings.

Rudolph Lambert Fernandez

Table 7: Sachin's tons, against the cricketing world

Test tons	ODI tons
■ 11 against Australia	■ 9 against Australia
■ 9 against Sri Lanka	■ 8 against Sri Lanka
■ 7 against South Africa	■ 5 against Pakistan
■ 7 against England	■ 5 against New Zealand
■ 5 against Bangladesh	■ 5 against South Africa
■ 4 against New Zealand	■ 5 against Zimbabwe
■ 3 against West Indies	■ 4 against West Indies
■ 3 against Zimbabwe	■ 4 against Kenya
■ 2 against Pakistan	■ 2 against England
	■ 1 against Bangladesh
	■ 1 against Namibia

*Note: 66% (19 out of 29) of Bradman's Test centuries were against England. Sachin is the only batsman in the world to score at least **two** centuries against all nine Test-playing nations. He holds the world record for the most ODI hundreds against a single nation (Australia); he also holds the world record for the second-highest number of ODI hundreds against a single nation (Sri Lanka).*

Table 8: Sachin's habit of centuries

Year	Centuries (Tests)	Centuries (ODIs)	Centuries (Total)
1990	1	0	1
1992	3	0	3
1993	2	0	2
1994	2	3	5
1995	0	1	1
1996	2	6	8
1997	4	2	6
1998	3	9	12
1999	5	3	8
2000	2	3	5
2001	3	4	7
2002	4	2	6
2003	3	0	3
2004	3	1	4

2005	1	1	2
2006	0	2	2
2007	2	1	3
2008	4	1	5
2009	2	3	5
2010	7	1	8
2011	1	2	3
2012	0	1	1
Total	51	49	100

Sachin has scored an average of over 4 centuries (Test and ODI) for each year he has played cricket. For five of these years (1996, 1998, 1999, 2001 and 2010) he has scored an average of over 8 centuries per year played.

Table 9: Sachin's spectacular ODI saga

- In 1996, with Sidhu in Sharjah, he went on to build a 231-run partnership against Pakistan. Sachin hit 118 (39% of team runs), with 44 runs coming off boundaries. India won by 28 runs and he was Player of the Match.

- Two years later in 1998 India were playing Australia in Dhaka in a Wills International Cup quarter-final. Ganguly fell when the score was 7; he had scored 1 after seeing off 6 deliveries. Azharuddin fell when the score was 8, having scored a duck after seeing off 3 deliveries. Sachin took stock, then picked up his 'axe' and went on the rampage. He scored 141 off just 128 deliveries at a strike-rate of 110, notching up as many as 70 runs from boundaries alone. India won by 44 runs and Sachin was *Player of the Match.*

- Three years later, in March 2001 at Indore, India's victory against Australia, by 118 runs, was built almost entirely on Sachin's century. Dravid fell for 15 runs. Ganguly fell for a duck. Badani fell for 23. Finally, it was Laxman who stood alongside Sachin as he whacked 19 deliveries for boundaries. He reached his century off just 94 deliveries and reached 139 off just 125 deliveries against bowlers like McGrath, Warne, Fleming, Symonds and Bevan. Sachin's score was nearly half the Indian total and he had scored at a strike-rate of 111. Again, in March 2001 at Bangalore, India's 60-run victory over Australia was built on Sachin's aggressive innings. He opened by scoring 35 off 26 balls (6 fours and a six) at a strike rate of 135. Other Indian batsmen came good but after losing Ganguly when the score stood at a miserable 16, they would probably have crumbled again had it not been for Sachin's defiant opening. The team carried the torch, but Sachin had lit the flame.

- Two years later in 2003, with VVS Laxman in Gwalior, he went on to build a 190-run partnership against Australia. Of his 100 runs, 42 came off boundaries. India won by 37 runs and he was Player of the Match. Sachin's 100 accounted for 35% of team runs.

- Four years later in 2007, with Gambhir in Mohali, he went on to build a 173-run partnership against Pakistan. Sachin got out at 99 (31% of team runs) but he had scored 62 runs off boundaries at a strike-rate of 109. Pakistan won that match but it was not from want of Sachin's effort or his contribution. Gambhir was an eight-year old child when Sachin started playing international cricket.

- Two years later, in November 2009 in an ODI in Hyderabad, Australia set a daunting 350-run target, having scored at 7 runs an over. Sachin came in and hammered 175 runs off 141 balls, yet Australia won... by three runs. He had scored half the team's runs, yet India lost. He had scored 50 off 47 balls, 100 off 81 balls and 150 off 122 balls. Somehow his critics will count that *Player of the Match* performance against him – as a 'century in a losing cause'.

Table 10: Tests played and Play span – the world's greatest batsmen

No: of Tests played by great Test batsmen		Playing span (years playing Test cricket) of great Test batsmen	
Sachin Tendulkar	188	Sachin Tendulkar 22 playing years	
Steve Waugh	168	*(he's played every one of those years.)*	
Rahul Dravid	164	Steve Waugh	20 playing years
Ricky Ponting	162	Garry Sobers	19 (did not play in 1964, 1970)
Allan Border	156	Jacques Kallis	18
Jacques Kallis	150	Ricky Ponting	18
V V S Laxman	134	Clive Lloyd	18 (did not play Tests in 1970)
Brian Lara	131	Greenidge	18
Sunil Gavaskar	125	Javed Miandad	18
Javed Miandad	124	Viv Richards	18
Viv Richards	21	Sunil Gavaskar	17
Donald Bradman	50	Desmond Haynes	17
		Allan Border	17
		Geoff Boycott	17 (did not play 1975 and 1976)
		Graham Gooch	17 (did not play 1976, 1977, 1983 and 1984)
		Rahul Dravid	17
		Brian Lara	16 (did not play in 1991)
		Donald Bradman	10 (over a 20-year span he played Tests for only 10 years)
Note: Some gentlemen have since played more Tests (figures as of January 2012)		*Note: Some gentlemen have since played more Tests (figures as of January 2012).*	

Rudolph Lambert Fernandez

Table 11: Bradman's successive Tests against a single team

First series of successive Tests against a single team – England (9 Tests). These represent 2 of his 10 playing years.	Second series of successive Tests against a single team – England (22 Tests). These represent 5 of his 10 playing years; half his career.
1. Brisbane, 30 November 1928	1. Melbourne, 30 December 1932
2. Melbourne, 29 December 1928	2. Adelaide, 13 January 1933
3. Adelaide, 1 February 1929	3. Brisbane, 10 February 1933
4. Melbourne, 8 March 1929	4. Sydney, 23 February 1933
5. Nottingham, 13 June 1930	5. Nottingham, 8 June 1934
6. Lord's, 27 June 1930	6. Lord's, 22 June 1934
7. Leeds, 11 July 1930	7. Manchester, 6 July 1934
8. Manchester, 25 July 1930	8. Leeds, 20 July 1934
9. The Oval, 16 August 1930	9. The Oval, 18 August 1934
	10. Brisbane, 4 December 1936
	11. Sydney, 18 December 1936
	12. Melbourne, 1 January 1937
	13. Adelaide, 29 January 1937
	14. Melbourne, 26 February 1937
	15. Nottingham, 10 June 1938
	16. Lord's, 24 June 1938
	17. Leeds, 22 July 1938
	18. Brisbane, 29 November 1946
	19. Sydney, 13 December 1946
	20. Melbourne, 1 January 1947
	21. Adelaide, 31 January 1947
	22. Sydney, 28 February 1947
	Note: He was absent in the match played against England in August 1938 at The Oval, or it would have meant 23 (not 22) successive matches against a single team.

Table 12: Bradman's record against rival teams (total of 6,996 runs from 50 Tests)

- 72% (5028 runs) against England from 36 matches

- 10% (715 runs) against India from 5 matches.

- 12% (806 runs) against South Africa from 4 matches.

- 6% (447 runs) against the West Indies from 5 matches.

Note: Of the 52 Tests against his name, Bradman was absent in the one against South Africa in February 1932 and in the one against England in August 1938; he played only 50 Tests.

Table 13: Sachin's Test runs against 'the world' (14,692 runs from 177 matches)

- 21% (3,151 runs) against Australia from 31 matches

- 15% (2,150 runs) against England, from 24 matches

- 14% (1,995 runs) against Sri Lanka, from 25 matches

- 12% (1,741 runs) against South Africa, from 25 matches

- 10% (1,532 runs) against New Zealand, from 22 matches

- About 9% (1,328 runs) against the West Indies, from 16 matches

- About 7% (1,057 runs) against Pakistan, from 18 matches

- Just over 6% (918 runs) against Zimbabwe, from nine matches

- The remaining 6% (820 runs) came against Bangladesh from seven matches.

Note: as of January 2011.

Table 14: Bradman was in the best bowling side of his era

Australia's Clarrie Grimmett took an incredible 216 wickets from just 37 matches with a career bowling average of 24.21. In comparison:

- England's Tate took a relatively paltry 155 wickets from 39 matches and ended with a career bowling average of 26.16

- England's much-respected Verity took a relatively meagre 144 from 40 matches and a career bowling average of 24.37

- England's Edrich took a ridiculously low 41 wickets from 39 matches and ended with an embarrassingly high career bowling average of 41.29

- England's Doug Wright took just 108 wickets from 34 matches and ended with a career bowling average of 39.11

- Australia's Bill O'Reilly took as many as 144 wickets from 27 matches with a career bowling average of 22.59.

- England's Voce took only 98 wickets from 27 matches with a career bowling average of 27.88.

- Australia's Arthur Mailey took as many as 99 wickets from 21 matches, while the much-feared Englishman Larwood took just 78 wickets from 21 matches.

- Australia's Keith Miller had a career bowling average of 22.97 over 55 matches; far superior to English bowlers who had played far fewer matches.

- Ray Lindwall had a career bowling average of 23.03 over as many 61 matches; far better than Englishman Bedser's of 24.89 over 51 matches.

- Bert Ironmonger had a bowling average of 17.97 across 14 matches; far superior to Englishman Bill Bowes's of 22.33 across 15 matches.

Table 15: Sachin and rival peers (% of 'bowled' Test dismissals)

Batsman	% of 'bowled' dismissals	Context
Kallis	22% (45 bowled out of 208 dismissals)	Kallis started out only in December 1995; he never got to face Kapil, Hadlee, Botham, Marshall, Imran, McDermott, Bruce Reid, Qadir, Merv Hughes, Roger Harper, Winston Benjamin and Patrick Patterson. He naturally escaped the South African attacks: Shaun Pollock, Ntini, Allan Donald and Dale Steyn. He played 32 fewer Tests (145, to Sachin's 177 Tests) **His 'away' Test exposure is 8% lower than Sachin's.**
Steve Waugh	18% (39 bowled out of 214 dismissals)	Waugh started in December 1985 and was done in January 2004. He naturally never got to face fellow-Australians Bruce Reid, Jason Gillespie, Stuart MacGill, Warne, McGrath, Brett Lee, McDermott or Merv Hughes. Neither did he see much of Dale Steyn and James Anderson. He played 9 fewer Tests (168, to Sachin's 177 Tests) **His 'away' Test exposure is 8% lower than Sachin's.**
Lara	16% (36 bowled out of 226 dismissals)	Lara started in December 1990 and was done in December 2006. He played **46 fewer Tests than Sachin did** (131, to Sachin's 177 Tests). Naturally, he never faced fearsomely effective fellow West Indians Walsh, Ambrose, Marshall, Bishop, Merv Dillon, Carl Hooper, Patrick Patterson, Kenny Benjamin, Winston Benjamin and Roger Harper. **His 'away' Test exposure was 5% lower than Sachin's.**

Ponting	14% (32 bowled out of 231 dismissals)	Ponting started out only in December 1995; he never faced Kapil Dev, Hadlee, Botham, Marshall, Imran, Qadir, Roger Harper, Winston Benjamin and Patrick Patterson.
		Naturally, he also never faced Bruce Reid, Warne, McGrath, Brett Lee, Merv Hughes and McDermott.
		He played 25 fewer Tests (152, to Sachin's 177 Tests)
		His 'away' Test exposure is 10% less than Sachin's.
Sachin	18% (46 bowled out of 258 dismissals)	His 'Test' exposure is 5-35% higher than others.
		His 'away' Test exposure is 5-10% higher.
		His 'away' Test ton performance is 4-11% higher.
		His 'away' Test fifties performance is 8-15% higher.
		He's been tested by the widest range of the most effective bowlers for the longest possible time and in the widest range of cricket grounds and borne a far greater 'team and national' burden than any batsman, from any nation.
		Yes, he may have never faced Kumble, Kapil or Harbhajan but he has faced all the others.

Note: dismissals as of 6 January 2011. The lower proportion of bowled dismissals of some other batsmen, in comparison to Sachin, only seems superior. It needs context – the column on the right. For details of 'away' exposure see Table B in book text. Sachin has been dismissed more frequently in 2012 and since than he has ever been, a sign of the fatigue that only he can feel. But for the bulk of his career, he has been head and shoulders above the rest.

Table 16: Why Sachin stands alone, on the highest summit of batting

In Test cricket history, Sachin is the

- Greatest run-getter; over 2,000 runs ahead of the next man.

- First and only batsman to reach 14,000 runs (in 279 innings); naturally he's also the first and only batsman to reach 15,000 runs.

- First and only batsman with 51 tons.

- Youngest batsman to score a 100 (a distinction shared with three others who were also aged 17 and scored a 100 at that age)

- First and only batsman with five Test hundreds before the age of 20.

- First and only batsman with at least 2 tons against all Test nations.

- First and only batsman to reach a Test ton with a sixer as many as six times

In ODI cricket history, Sachin is the

- Greatest run-getter; well over 4,000 runs ahead of the next man.

- First and only batsman with 49 tons; 19 tons ahead of the next man.

- First batsman with a double ton in an ODI

- First man unbeaten with a double hundred in an ODI.

- Batsman with the most ODI runs (1,894 runs in 1998) in a calendar year.

- Batsman with the most ODI 100s (9 tons in 1998) in a calendar year.

- Batsman with the most 4s in a single ODI innings (25 boundaries against South Africa in 2010). A tally shared with Sehwag but a feat achieved 20 years into his career, at a time when those who started out at the same time or after he did were busy doing voice exercises before joining the commentary box or polishing their writing before turning to sports writing!

- Batsman with the most runs in World Cups, multi-team tournament finals and the most runs in a single World Cup

- Batsman with the highest number of 50s in World Cups. He has scored 13 half centuries in World Cups; no other batsman in the world has scored more than 8 fifties in World Cups.

- Batsman with the highest number (15 awards) of Player of the Series awards and the highest number (62 awards) of Player of the Match awards for any cricketer in the world.

- Batsman with the highest number of ODI hundreds against a single country (Australia); he is also the batsman with the second-highest number of ODI hundreds against a single country (Sri Lanka).

- Batsman with the most ODI nineties (18); twice the tally of the next man

In Tests and ODIs Sachin is the

- First and only batsman with 100 centuries in international cricket

- First and only batsman with over 30,000 cricket runs

- Batsman with the most hundreds (combined Test and ODI) in a calendar year – eight tons in 1996, twelve tons in 1998, eight tons in 1999, seven tons in 2001, eight tons in 2010.

Author's Acknowledgements

There are, as ever, far too many to thank. I am compelled to begin with the thousands who first inspired me to write about Sachin – his critics. First, it was the comparison with Bradman that rankled. Later, comparisons with other batsmen inspired me to write. To this ever-growing army of critics, my humblest thanks – without you, I wouldn't have had a word to write on Sachin.

My brothers and I were coached by our father, Ignatius Fernandez. Schools taught us the alphabet. Our father taught us to write and keep writing until we felt we could get better at it. To this day, every time I write it is his verdict that I'm looking for. Our grandmother, Mary Angelo Fernandez, and our mother, Mabel Fernandez, taught us to read. We saw the pleasure with which they read and soon became addicts. Comics, paperbacks or hardbound – as long as the pages held fine writing, it didn't matter how they came to us. If I can string a sentence together, it is because of them. Alongside them are my brothers – Leo, Ivan and Konrad – fellow travellers in my journey as a person and a writer. Special thanks to Leo and Ivan who invested considerable time, effort and a lot more.

This book wouldn't have happened without my beloved wife, Lissy, and our children, Ramona and Augustus. Lissy stayed patient as my 'cricket' shelf grew from crammed to overflowing. She stayed pleasant as I obsessed with things Sachin and Bradman – often alone at my laptop for days on end. She offered solace – and gallons of coffee when I hit a blank wall. She rejoiced when a door, or window, opened a crack. I am grateful to her and our children. Their patience and cheerfulness allowed me the space to continue writing when I desperately needed to. Thanks also to my dear sisters, Teresa (Leo's wife), Marion (Ivan's wife), and Veronica (Konrad's wife) who, for some reason, kept seeing silver linings even when I saw none. All of them pored over the early manuscript and offered invaluable advice, whether to do with cricket or not.

My deepest thanks to Wisden, ESPNcricinfo, www.howstat.com, www. thatscricket.com, www.cricket-records.com and several other online and offline resources; without them cricket writers of the modern era might as well pack up and go home. I have relied on these and many more resources. Thanks to the many writers who have, over the years, written so eloquently and passionately on Sachin and Bradman – those books helped inform my understanding of both players but also helped me stay focused on unchartered territory.

Special thanks to Manu Joseph, Nirmala Lakshman, Suparna Sharma, Deepti Soni, Mainak De, John Thomas, Mike Flannery, T M Veeraraghav, James Alter, Arunabha Sengupta, Simu Thomas, Venu Palaparthi, N Ram, Basil Sylvester Pinto, Alex Britten, Mike Nithavrianakis, Dan Chugg, Marcus Winsley, Bharat Joshi, Vijay Santhanam, Shyam Balasubramanian, Suresh Menon, Gulu Ezekiel and also to the editors at SportsKeeda. To those I've mentioned, and to those I've not – ladies and gentlemen, I hope you all know how grateful I am for the role you played in this journey.

Thanks to all cricket fans. I'd love to hear from you.

Thanks to Bradman, the first to set unreal milestones in cricket.

Thanks finally to Sachin – the greatest batsman *in cricket history.*

Rudolph Lambert Fernandez
Chennai, India, January 2014.

Note on the Author

A S FAR BACK AS 2003, Rudolph Lambert Fernandez challenged the status quo – Bradman's undisputed rank as the greatest batsman in cricket history – by arguing that Sachin was in fact far greater. Ten years on, his book invites readers to a detailed comparison – the first of its kind.

Rudolph's writing on Sachin Tendulkar has appeared in The Hindu, Firstpost.com, The Asian Age, The Bengal Post, www.cricketcountry.com (an India-based cricket website) and www.sportskeeda.com (an India-based sports website). Rudolph's writing on cricket has appeared in The Statesman, www.dreamcricket.com (a US-based cricket website), www.alloutcricket.com (a UK-based cricket website), www.thecricketmagazine.com (a UK-based cricket website) and www.cricketnext.com (an India-based cricket website).

Rudolph invites readers to look beyond the mere obvious in cricket, especially in recording and rewarding batting greatness.

www.greaterthanbradman.com
Follow Rudolph @RudolphFernandz on Twitter
Email: greaterthanbradman@gmail.com
https://www.facebook.com/RudolphOnCricket

www.ingramcontent.com/pod-product-compliance
Lightning Source LLC
Chambersburg PA
CBHW020451130626
46549CB00001B/382